Incas and Other Men

by the same author

*

Biography

WILLIAM GODWIN (*Porcupine Press*)
THE INCOMPARABLE APHRA (*Boardman*)
THE ANARCHIST PRINCE
(In collaboration with Ivan Avakumovic) (*Boardman*)
PIERRE-JOSEPH PROUDHON (*Routledge & Kegan Paul*)

History

ANARCHISM (*Penguin Books*)

Criticism

THE PARADOX OF OSCAR WILDE (*Boardman*)
THE WRITER AND POLITICS (*Porcupine Press*)

Travel

FACES OF INDIA (*Faber*)
TO THE CITY OF THE DEAD (*Faber*)
RAVENS AND PROPHETS (*Wingate*)

Verse

THE WHITE ISLAND (*Fortune Press*)
THE CENTRE CANNOT HOLD (*Routledge & Kegan Paul*)
IMAGINE THE SOUTH (*Untide Press*)

Letters

THE LETTERS OF CHARLES LAMB (*Grey Walls*)

Anthology

HUNDRED YEARS OF REVOLUTION: 1848 AND AFTER
(*Porcupine Press*)

INCAS AND OTHER MEN

Travels in the Andes

by

GEORGE WOODCOCK

FABER AND FABER

24 Russell Square

London

First published in mcmlix
by Faber and Faber Limited
24 Russell Square London W.C.1
First published in this edition mcmlxv
Printed in Great Britain by
Latimer Trend & Co Ltd Whitstable
All rights reserved

© *George Woodcock 1959*

Contents

Illustrations

Acknowledgments

The journey I describe in the following pages was greatly enriched by the kindness of the many people, Peruvians and foreign residents alike, whom we met on our way. In my narrative I have mentioned by name or pseudonym the individuals to whom we were principally indebted; they appear of necessity as characters in the story, but here I would at least like to make my gratitude to them clear. Also, in a more general way, I wish to acknowledge my indebtedness to the staffs of the Canadian Embassy, the Canadian Pacific Airlines and the British Council in Lima, all of whom, by giving their advice freely and sometimes in more material ways, were most helpful to us.

I owe also a particular debt in connection with the illustrations I have used. Neither my wife nor I can claim to be an expert photographer, and while we were in Peru we suffered also an exasperating series of camera breakdowns which robbed us of many potentially interesting photographs. Fortunately, however, my colleague at the University of British Columbia, Professor A. W. Wainman, and a photographer of the Canadian Pacific Airlines had both—independently—visited during the previous year many of the places to which we travelled. Since, for the most part, their photographs were so much better than our own, I decided to avail myself freely of the kindness with which both Professor Wainman and the Canadian Pacific Airlines placed their prints at my disposal.

G.W.

Prologue

It was early July, the winter of the southern hemisphere. The dusk of the previous evening had fallen on familiar territory, on a green hog's back of the Sierra Madre shaking clear of its enveloping mist and on the sharp image, seen through an unexpected break in the clouds, of a yellow Mexican beach silvered by the Pacific waves. Now it was the second night of flying since my wife and I had boarded in Vancouver the Canadian Pacific plane which flies in a long arc around the coasts linking Hong Kong with Lima and Buenos Aires. I awoke to see the lights on the wings flashing with rhythmic fuzziness into the grey vapours through which we were descending; I remembered that we were due to stop in Ecuador for refuelling, and a few moments later the lights became sharp and clear as they pierced down to the shining runway at Guayaquil.

This was only a minor stop, an hour at a small airport on our way to Peru, but even such a slight introduction to a new continent seemed full of possibilities as we walked down into the lake of brilliance that had been created around the plane in the almost palpable density of the tropical night. Up from the invisible sea the wind moaned and brushed our faces with its tepid dampness, rustling the shining palm fronds behind the hangars, and bringing with it the thick, unidentifiable sweetness of tropical flowers. Just beyond the lights, in a great echoing circle, the tree frogs chirped in chorus and the insects whirred and grated in a creaking harmony whose insistence almost drowned the noises made by the men and the machines working around the plane.

Beside the path of broken shells up which we walked to the airport building, pale night-moths fluttered around the lolling hibiscus flowers, and a notice in English read: 'Welcome to Guayaquil, 132 miles south of the Equator.' But inside, behind a long, worn counter, the yellow-faced mestizo clerk stared in-

15

differently at us and our fellow passengers: at the bland and bear-like Canadian business man whom the pilots treated with so much deference, at the strident squabbling of the American engineer and his wife who were bound for a copper mine in the Andes, at the austere-faced Japanese woman whose shimmering grey kimono and golden obi gave the scene its one touch of incongruous grace. And the three diminutive Indian guards in creased brown uniforms looked out into the night with such withdrawn languor that one felt nothing would have been easier than to walk among the palm trees and disappear into the forests of Ecuador without troubling about a single formality. The feeling of laxity may have been illusory. Even so, it was a relief from the preceding afternoon in Mexico City, when the immigration guards had officiously impounded our passports for the three or four hours we had waited.

There was something disturbingly familiar about the atmosphere of the Guayaquil airport. The sounds and smells of the tropical night, the melancholy soldiers, the tall, skeletal Negro who peddled panama hats among the passengers, the dingy bar lined with rum bottles and rusting tins of English food, the general air of shabby lassitude, as if the land and its people were afflicted by some insidious wasting sickness—one had looked at the scene too often already in the mirror of literature. A fragment of Conrad, a slice of Greene—the comparisons came to one's mind with a feeling that the parody had not quite come off, that art had been more convincing than life.

Besides, one does not leave home in search of the familiar, and as we returned to the plane after our hour in Ecuador we wondered uneasily how much more of our journey would draw so near to our expectations. But it was almost as if the spirit of the continent were celebrating our arrival with some gentle trick of hospitality, deferring to our preconceptions by presenting a brief curtain raiser of South-America-as-Others-See-It before we began to discover the reality for ourselves. For never, during the remainder of our journey, were we to experience quite the same approximation between expectation and actuality. Often, in Peru, the places we reached were to be exciting beyond our expectations, and just as often they were to be disappointing beyond our fears. But always, in some way or another, there was to be that continual remaking of one's mental picture which is the reward and the penalty of travelling.

Leaving Guayaquil, our plane flew on down the Pacific coast. The night was clear, with strange southern constellations forming above us, and the lights of tiny ports occasionally marking the edges of the land below. Already we were over Peru, and in three or four hours we would land. We did not know what kind of situation would await us in Lima. During the weeks immediately before our departure, Peru had been passing through a political crisis. President Manuel Odria, after ruling as a military dictator for eight years, had granted free elections, and his nominee had been defeated. In the streets of Lima and Callao, bus-burning riots had followed the elections, and Odria, still in office until the new President could be installed at the end of July, had suspended constitutional guarantees. This, it was feared, might be the prelude to his resuming power by another military coup like that by which he had gained it in 1948. The foreign press talked freely of 'a state of high political tension'.

As we drew near to Lima the dawn began softly to indicate the massive outlines of the Andes against the bluish suffusion of the eastern sky. Then a layer of mist floated beneath us, clinging low over the land, and we saw nothing of Lima until, at daybreak, the plane broke through the grey ceiling over the desert to the south of the city.

Lima lies in the tropics, nearer to the Equator than such swelter-ing cities as Aden, but the morning into which we stepped was as bleakly untropical as a Glasgow dawn. A cold drizzle settled on our faces and pearled our clothes, and in the airport building the grey-uniformed police were muffled in greatcoats, and the hotel porters blew into their hands as they waited for customers beside the immigration desk. The only break in the chilly atmosphere of that first morning was the moment, unique in my experience of crossing frontiers, when the immigration officer asked my profes-sion, shouted the word 'Escritero!' with apparent delight, and stamped my passport with an enthusiasm which suggested that

Peru was suffering from an insatiable longing for the arrival of foreign writers. There was no excessive formality and nothing that yet suggested to us the atmosphere of a country in crisis.

A few moments later we stood on the raised driveway outside the airport and looked out over the sandy waste towards Lima. The flat housetops, stretching northward to the minaret outlines of campaniles and skyscrapers, produced an almost oriental effect; at that first view across its treeless outskirts Lima had something of the look of a Crusaders' city under a lowering northern sky.

The town was barely awakening as we travelled towards it in the hotel station wagon. In the suburb of San Isidro, where olive trees planted by the Spaniards grew among the modern villas, only the squat Indian servant girls were about, hurrying to market with their long black plaits swinging behind them. And among the fanciful Moresque pavilions of the Avenida Wilson the gardeners were watering green lawns and beds of tropical lilies in the shade of eucalyptus trees and blood-red poinsianas.

But the freshness of these peripheral streets was almost lost in our first impression of central Lima at seven in the morning. The pavements were dusty and unswept; the shops were barred with shutters of dull grey steel; the few people who hurried to work, under the grey sky and the drizzle, wore drab clothes and morose expressions. In the best of moods it would have seemed a place without colour or character. But I am sure our immediate feeling of revulsion was due mostly to the fact that, after two nights with little sleep, we had reached the stage of exhaustion when discouragement is easy. At some time on his journey every traveller comes upon the moment when he asks himself how he could have imagined that the place to which his travels have brought him would be worth the trouble of getting there. For us, in Peru, that moment came as we looked out from the balcony of our enormous, musty hotel room into the damp and colourless street below; over breakfast we discussed gloomily whether we should take the next plane back to Canada. Fortunately it did not leave for six days, and by that time we had become reconciled to Lima and had gone far beyond it.

Indeed, our reconciliation began on that first day, for, having slept long into the afternoon, we emerged—ourselves refreshed—into a city which resembled in little more than its actual buildings the place we had seen in the morning. Lima is one of those cities which, lacking a pronounced physical individuality, take their character from the life that goes on within them. Places of this kind can be as volatile as human beings, changing their moods from hour to hour, and Lima in the morning has the air of a person who wakes unwillingly and goes about her affairs in lassitude and disgust. She drags through the day, through the long siesta hours when the vultures sit like pigeons on the housetops, until the afternoon is almost ended and, then, as her inhabitants turn from work to leisure, her life is renewed. In Lima the brief period before the sharp and early tropical twilight is one of increasing liveliness as the bars and cafés and shops begin to fill, and the hours immediately after nightfall—which is always about six o'clock—are crowded with the strollers who drift up and down the narrow colonial streets between Pizarro's Plaza de Armas and the Plaza San Martin in the centre of the commercial quarter. At this time the life of the city is at its height, the dullness of the winter's day seems to evaporate in the lights of the open shops and wide arcades, and one senses a kind of contagious euphoria, which moved me on that first evening to note in my diary the change in mood 'from morning dejection to an evening feeling of delight'.

Of the political tension which foreign news reports had led us to expect we saw no more obvious signs than we had already seen at the airport; on this occasion at least History-in-the-Making seemed to wear a very placid aspect. Apart from the musical comedy guards in their plumed brass helmets and their dusty black uniforms outside the Presidential Palace, there were no troops to be seen in the city; the police—incongruously sun-helmeted under that winter sky—went laxly about their routine of directing traffic; and the Limans had none of the air of slightly hysterical preoccupation which one expects among people living on the edge of a political volcano. We concluded that either crises are so habitual in South America that ordinary life goes unaffected by them or the foreign journalists had greatly exaggerated the dangers of the situation. Afterwards we were to find that, in a less sensational way than we at first expected, the political change was very important. But this belongs to a later stage of my narrative.

Although, as I have said, our attitude towards Lima changed in a few hours from revulsion to pleasure, I was still unable to shed completely the lingering disappointment which occurs when a city or a person does not conform to the picture one has created in one's imagination. Always, when I had thought of Lima in the past, it had been the city which was once the political and cultural capital of South America; the city where a hundred marquises and counts lived in a semi-feudal splendour of gilded coaches and baroque mansions which travellers considered more magnificent even than golden Mexico; the city whose women were celebrated through the Spanish Empire for their beauty, their wit and the incomparable richness of their dress; the city which Alexander von Humboldt found to excel all others in the Americas in its 'zest for letters and for all that pleases an ardent and quick imagination'.

Out of these suggestions, which had lodged in my memory since childhood, I had built in my mind's eye a vision of sunlight and architectural splendour, of bright flowers and music and pale-skinned, beautiful women. But the Lima of the romantic fancy, in so far as it ever existed, has long disappeared. Earthquakes and revolutions, invaders and Philistine rebuilders, all have bitten away at the fabric of colonial Lima, and now a few baroque churches and an occasional eighteenth-century mansion with fanci-fully carved stonework and screened balconies in the Moorish manner are all that is left of the city of the Viceroys. Lima today strikes one as a modern city struggling out of a congested nine-teenth-century pattern of narrow streets and crowded plazas. Its architecture is subdued and undistinguished, its skies in winter—the only time we saw it—are clouded with a perpetual mist that gives a greyness of tone to the streets and buildings, and yet, des-pite these faults of background, Lima is still full of interest simply because it is a metropolis with an extraordinary variety of people. Since colonial days, in fact, it has become less Spanish only to become more cosmopolitan. To the original population of creoles—proud of their white skins and Spanish traditions—and of Negroes and half-breeds who over the centuries have created a Lima working-class culture of their own, each generation has added its new elements, and today Lima owes much of its character to these late-comers, to the Chinese restaurant-proprietors and the Japanese artisans, to the Italian shopkeepers and the American engineers, to the gaudy gypsies from the shacktowns on the hill of San Cristobal and the British traders, islanded in their nostalgic world of tennis and amateur theatricals and private schools.

Yet one of the essential facts about Lima is that it is not typical of Peru. Peruvians divide their country into the great geographical regions of the Coast, the Sierra (or the Andes) and the Montaña (or the Jungle), but they always think of Lima as a place apart.

Its apartness began with its very foundation, when Pizarro deliberately rejected the Inca metropolis of Cuzco and decided to build his own City of the Kings—as the capital was originally named—near to the sea so that his communications with Spain would not be endangered. Thus, from the start, Lima was a place that turned away from the Indian past and looked towards the greater world beyond the seas. It has not changed. Today it is an urban metropolis in a country two-thirds of whose people live on and by the land; an educated city, with a university older than Harvard, in a land where more than 40 per cent of the people are total illiterates; a cosmopolitan city within a few hours' journey of a great mountain area where half the population of Peru still lives within the orbit of an Indian culture whose roots in the Inca past are uncut and whose pattern of life lags two centuries behind the modern world. Lima, indeed, is as different from its hinterland as St. Petersburg was from the Russia of the boyar and the moujik.

And it was the hinterland, the Peru of the mountains and the jungle and the desert coasts, that we had come to see. On this first occasion we remained only three days in Lima, and the briefness of our stay was at least partly due to the fact that we found the city expensive beyond our expectations. Peru is nowhere a cheap country in the same sense as France in the Thirties or Mexico in the Forties, but it has degrees of expensiveness, and Lima, when we were there, was well on the way to competing with costly cities like Caracas. All the three reasonably good hotels charged the equivalent of ten or twelve dollars a night for a room alone, and between them and the cheaper establishments lay a great gulf in terms of comfort, cleanliness and repute. Once, when we suggested to a Peruvian that we might perhaps go to one of these less expensive hotels, he replied with haste and alarm: 'No, no, you cannot—only *bad* people go there.' We never learnt exactly what he meant by bad people, and we did not feel adventurous enough to find out by direct experience.

Instead, we hurried our preparations to travel into the mountains. But 'preparations to travel' is perhaps a rather pretentious phrase to describe what we actually did before leaving Lima. It evokes, in the minds of hardened travel-book readers like myself, thoughts of tents and mosquito nets, of trade beads and perhaps even an ornamented sword for the chief of the most potent tribe, whereas all we intended to do was to go wherever we could by the means available to ordinary Peruvians. As far as I can remember the only special things we bought in Lima, apart from maps, were a couple of pullovers for the mountain evenings, a phial of dysentery tablets, and a DDT bomb, all of which we were told would be necessary, and all of which in fact we used quite frequently.

Most of our time, indeed, was spent in gathering information that would help us to decide where we would go. Before departing from Canada our thoughts about Peru had crystallized around a number of places we wished specifically to visit—Cuzco, Lake Titicaca and Chan Chan in particular—but we had formed no very concrete idea as to how we would travel to or between them. This was due partly to a lack of specific information. In Vancouver we had been unable to buy even a moderately detailed map of the Andes, and, while I am sure that a little concentrated research by mail might have told us much about roads and railways, we are both inefficient travellers in matters of this kind. We usually set out with sketchy ideas of where we wish to go, and—as will become evident enough—we are inclined to change our minds and routes in response to the accidents and interests of the road. Any traveller in the old indomitable tradition would detect, I am sure, a reprehensible lack of purpose in our attitude. Yet, since we have always wished to observe the life of a country we visit rather than to attain what are usually known as objectives, I imagine that the apparently aimless wandering in which we often become involved may be just as effective for our purposes as the more disciplined methods of travel.

It was when we began in Lima to seek specific facts about the regions we intended to visit that we realized how much more the curious foreigner knows about Peru than the average Peruvian. We called at several government offices which in one way and another dealt with travel information, and came away with little more than a few badly printed and out-of-date leaflets which left us with the impression that the official tourist services were intended as a convenient source of sinecures rather than as a serious means of helping travellers.

On the other hand, I have rarely encountered people more able and inclined to be helpful to strangers who came, like ourselves, with very little to recommend them, than the foreign residents we met during our early days in Peru. The first of them was Norman Sanderson, the manager of the Canadian Pacific Airlines in Lima, on whom we called at his office on the busy street which Limans call La Colmena—The Beehive—during our first afternoon in the city. Through him we met the two other men who were most helpful at this stage in clarifying our ideas about what we should do and how we should travel in Peru. These were John Harriman of the British Council and Harry Horn, the Canadian Commercial Attaché.

All of these people will appear again; I introduce them now because it was on the basis of what they told us that we sketched out one evening, among the clatter of dice in the Crillon bar, three very provisional main journeys. One, we decided, would take us northward along the coast to the territory of the old Chimu and Moche cultures and into the great mountain valleys beneath the Cordillera Blanca. Another would go southward through the desert to the colonial city of Arequipa and then bend in a north-easterly arc to the altiplano around Lake Titicaca and afterwards to the Inca region of Cuzco and Machu Picchu. And the third would lead us directly from Lima into the Central

Sierra. It was with this last journey that we decided to begin. A day's railway travel would take us to the mountain town of Huancayo, and from Huancayo—at least according to our maps— there seemed to be so many possible routes—towards Cuzco, towards Cerro de Pasco, towards Huancavelica, towards the jungle valleys—that we decided to leave our plans of further travel in that region until we got there.

PART I

Journey to the Sierra

I

Journeys begin early in Peru, often before and never long after sunrise, for no Peruvian likes to reach his destination after dark. This preference originated when travel in the Andes was by mule-back over narrow paths, but it retains a good deal of relevance in a country where the roads run, often precariously, through some of the steepest mountains in the world. And it remains so deeply rooted that even the trains on the few Peruvian railways start with at least the intention of reaching the end of the day's journey by sunset.

So it was in the darkness before dawn that we left our hotel and drove to the station near the river, from which the trains leave for the Sierra. With their flower-beds and blossoming oleanders and green palings, the platforms had already a rural look, and most of the passengers who crowded them were obviously country people. In the ease of long habit they had arranged themselves according to status, and it was where the second-class carriages would draw in that the confusion was greatest.

There the Indian and half-breed peasants were jostling for position, a garish, untidy, inexplicably good-humoured crowd in which the women outshone the men by the vigour of their actions as well as the brilliance of their bell-shaped skirts. Slinging their children in brightly striped cloths upon their backs, they pushed staunchly, and used as battering rams or as protection from flank attacks the goods with which they were loaded—baskets, cardboard boxes tied with string, bundles wrapped in brown ponchos and, above all, white cotton sugar bags stuffed like Christmas pillow cases. And, like Latin-American peasants everywhere, they took their livestock with them; on a train that went from the city to the country I had not expected to meet again those bedraggled chickens which had been the inevitable companions of our travels in rural Mexico three years before, but there they were, beady-eyed, scrawny, faintly protesting, like the small-part actors one sees in a hundred films and recognizes without ever having learnt their names.

We had decided to avoid the discomforts of travel until we came to places where they might become inevitable, and when the green carriages of the Train of the Sierra backed into the station we joined the sombrely dressed middle-class passengers in the Pullman coach, which was relatively uncrowded and, in South American terms, reasonably comfortable. That is to say, it was as good as an old English third-class carriage, while the second-class coaches, into which the Indians were still patiently packing themselves long after we had been seated, were barer and more wooden-seatedly Spartan than any I have seen in modern Europe.

The sun had risen when the train left Lima, whistling past the backs of high houses whose richly carved balconies suggested a respectable—even a prosperous—past in the days of the Viceroys. But a past it certainly was, for now the grey garments of the poor hung drying from the windows and beneath the dusty gracefulness of the rotting façades a long midden of garbage had been formed beside the railway lines.

On the other side, separating us from the scaling, stucco houses of the outlying slum called Below-the-Bridge, ran the Rimac, or rather its wide, untidy bed. When the summer rains of December fall high in the Andes, the river storms down the valley in a brown torrent, often breaking its dykes, and sometimes flooding the low-lying parts of Lima. But in winter only a reluctant brook winds languidly among the great gravel banks and at this season the dry bed becomes a kind of stony common land. Even early in the morning it was active and populated, presenting a curious panorama of the lower side of Lima life. Negro labourers were loading gravel into builders' trucks; other trucks were dumping piles of refuse to be washed away by the next floods; women were thumping clothes in the shrunken pools; men were tranquilly squatting among the stones, relieving the morning needs of nature and completely unconcerned that they were in full sight of the train; and over all this dismal terrain the scrawny dogs and ragged children wandered and the vultures congregated in small, industrious groups.

Lima is a small metropolis, and we soon emerged from among its shabby outskirts into the open farmland of the Rimac valley. This was a populous, well-cultivated countryside. The dark, reedy lanes of irrigation ditches quartered the meagre-looking sandy soil, and between them flourished lettuce-green vegetable fields and golden vineyards. The tall maize, softly yellowing, waved its tassels in the breeze that blew up from the Pacific; in the groves of bananas, winter was turning the leaves into ragged flaps of brown paper. Ox-carts dawdled along roads lined with yellow mud-block walls, and in many of the fields it was plough-ing season. The ground was being tilled partly by massive American tractors, partly by oxen slowly dragging those cumber-some wooden ploughs which the Spaniards brought four cen-turies ago; and in the cotton fields women bent over the rows of young plants, cultivating them with that back-breaking, short-handled hoe which has survived all over Peru from the earliest days of agriculture, changing its blade from stone to bronze, and later from bronze to iron, but never changing its essential form.

In Lima, except in the museums, one rarely experiences the sense of a life receding into an indefinite past which was aroused by this juxtaposition of modern and prehistoric methods of farming. But on the very edge of the city there was already an infinity of clues that led back into the unrecorded ages. A rubbly hillock would swell up from the floor of the valley, with a broken stone cross on its summit, and at a second glance one would recognize the mud bricks that had formed the platform of a pagan shrine whose influence Christianity sought to neutralize by imposing its own emblem. And in the middle distance, turning to the valley their blind and broken walls, the ruins of fortresses stood between the hills; their colour was the same as that of the ochreous slopes around them, but the sharp blue shadows they cast threw into relief their crumbling cubes and rectangles. The newest of them was at least five centuries old, but the rainless, frostless climate of the Peruvian desert had preserved these struc-tures of mud with astonishing completeness. The Peruvians call all such monuments by the name of *huaca*, and this suggestive word from the ancient Quechua language of the Incas means not only the shrine or fortress itself, but also the immanent mystery which the observer senses and acknowledges.

The hills among which the huacas were built closed steadily upon the valley as we travelled eastward. These first outposts of the Andes began in the suburbs of Lima as shadowy outlines distinguished only by a darker greyness from the mists that floated around their summits. But twenty miles up the valley the sky cleared as quickly as if a curtain had been withdrawn, the morning sun set the air quivering over the coloured fields, and the hills stood in sharp relief, defined by shadow and light, their steep sides rising to blunt and rounded tops over which the pylons marched like black skeletons from the power stations in the mountains. They were the most barren hills I had ever seen, more barren than Mexico, more barren than the burning deserts of Arizona, where one sees at least the scattered cacti that keep alive by storing the moisture of rare rainfalls. Here there were not even cacti. The slopes of shaly stone were unrelieved by the least shoot of green, and their extraordinary aridity emphasized the narrowness and vulnerability of the fertile lands beside the river. A few years' neglect of the irrigation ditches which the generations of Indian and Spanish farmers have used for a millennium, and the desert would return, as it has returned in other Peruvian valleys once cultivated by prehistoric peoples, lapping in its desiccating tide down to the very cane-brakes along the river banks.

In the long, thin oasis of the Rimac Valley the only town of any consequence was Chosica, about forty miles inland. Chosica is Peru's most important resort, a kind of Darjeeling of the Andean foothills; on the slopes overlooking it the villas of Lima business men glistened white and pink among dark orange trees, with a lightness of touch which seemed almost absurdly frivolous after the solemn buildings of Lima, a lightness emphasized by the carnival violence of the tropical creepers that flowed in red and purple over trees and walls and buildings. But the railway turned away from these gay architectural caprices and led us to Chosica's less presentable side, to that telltale other face which so often in Latin American countries reveals, as obviously as a Zola novel, the gulf between the pointlessly rich and the unnecessarily poor.

Peruvian custom decrees that manual work of any kind is a degradation for those who aspire to the slightest degree of social elevation; so extreme is this attitude that we would often see men walking through the streets followed by boys whom they employed to carry their briefcases, or even small paper parcels. Thus there is a constant demand for people to perform menial tasks at low wages, and wherever the rich happen to settle the poor congregate in large numbers.

At Chosica their flimsy huts of daub and cane were crowded along the railway banks. These huts, called chozas, one sees everywhere in the warmer parts of Peru. They keep out the wind and, since there is neither rain nor frost, they meet the elementary needs of their inhabitants; on the sea coast, by some fishing beach, they may even fit rather pleasantly into their setting, but those in Chosica were cheerless places, standing in patches of fetid-looking earth that had been trampled hard by bare feet and pecked clean by the chickens. It was only the Indian love of animals and birds that brought any feeling of life or colour. A few gamecocks strutted about, neat and cruel in their enamelled brilliance, and there were many small white dogs, woolly as children's toys, which belonged to a breed peculiar to the Andean region. Once, when the train stopped for a moment, we watched a young woman, dressed in something like a cotton nightdress drawn in at the waist by a red woven sash, quietly stalking across her yard a dark bird that looked like a moorhen. She caught it, held it in one hand while she stroked it, and then gave it to a little boy who had followed her out of the hut.

Beyond Chosica the hills grew together into the solid outworks of a mountain range. The first cacti appeared, then a winter pelt of grey bushes, and then the pines. The railway left the river-bank and began to clamber on the slopes of the valley, among apple orchards and thickets of wild figs. The desert was left behind, and we had passed into the temperate foothills.

By this time we had struck up a conversation with our table companion, a mining official from La Oroya beyond the mountains. Señor Merida had the ivory skin and the rather long face which one often meets among Peruvian creoles, melancholy in repose, unexpectedly gay in animation. He was, like most of his fellow countrymen, a sociable traveller, interested in strangers. He knew no English, but his courtesy rebelled against conducting a conversation with foreigners entirely in his own language, and so he would punctuate his Spanish with fragments of French dredged painfully from his receding schooldays. He named the trees we saw and explained the scenes that aroused our curiosity, asked tactful questions about ourselves and our homes, and talked of his children with the indulgent pride which Peruvians almost always take in their families. Now that a polite interval had passed since our conversation began, he asked us about our plans. What did we intend to do in Peru? Where would we go?

Our plans! We described the itinerary we had plotted out in Lima. There, over our pisco-sours in the Crillon bar, it had looked sound and complete enough, but against the background of the real mountains it began to appear amateurish and inadequate. We had not even yet decided where we would go after the end of our day's journey. Perhaps, we told Señor Merida, we would make a trans-mountain journey across the Sierra to Cuzco. Or perhaps we would go down one of the eastern valleys and take our first look at the Amazonian jungle.

Señor Merida looked melancholy. His politeness was clearly struggling against the conviction that we were irresponsible innocents wandering in a country of whose real nature we knew nothing, and in the end duty triumphed over courtesy. Señor Merida started with the jungle. 'There is only one way of going there,' he said. 'You must fly straight down to Iquitos, where there is a good hotel. Any other way will bring you endless trouble. At the very least you will waste a long time in travelling.'

It seemed pointless to remark that since we were in Peru for the express purpose of travelling, time spent in that occupation would not necessarily be wasted. Instead I pointed to the red lines of roads which—at least on our map—led down towards the jungle. 'Mais-quelles routes!' he sighed. 'They are fit only for mules, señor. Wait until you see them!'

As for our plan to travel from Huancayo to Cuzco, it seemed to him even more rash than the first. 'There is a road,' he admitted.

Arequipa: the Jesuit Cloister

Lima: working-class district on the edge of the city

Lima:
the church of
La Merced

An Andean Cemetery

The Highway through the Andes from Lima to Huancayo

Puno: the façade of the Cathedral

Lake Titicaca: the making of a boat of reeds

Lake Titicaca: Aymara musicians

Landscape near Cuzco

Cuzco:
Spanish buildings
on
Inca foundations

Cuzco:
The Gate of
Santa Clara

Cuzco: the fortress of Sacsahuaman

Inca architecture:
a trapezoid gateway in the
fortress of Sacsahuaman

Machu Picchu: the Palace of the Three Windows

The Inca fortress of Machu Picchu and the peak of Huayna Picchu

Arequipa: the city and the volcano Misti

Quechua Indians from the Cuzco region

uancayo:
Indian woman

Huancayo: the Sunday Market

The Potato Harvest in the Sierra

A Sierra square at siesta time

The Urubamba Valley near Ollantaytambo

Sierra Indian musicians on their way to a Fiesta

Masked Dancers of the Andes

'But you will have to cross one mountain range between Huancayo and Ayacucho, and another between Ayacucho and Abancay, and yet another between Abancay and Cuzco. And the road is very bad.' He excitedly described with his hand a series of wave-like motions which suggested something rather more precipitous than a giant scenic railway. 'Très dangereux! Muy peligroso!'

Our looks must have shown our reluctance to accept his warnings. 'If you do not believe me,' he went on, 'let us ask the lady over there. She is from Huancayo.'

The lady from Huancayo was one of the Peruvian Chinese whose ancestors came to the country in the nineteenth century as labourers in the sugar plantations; now, as merchants, their descendants are among the most prosperous members of the small Peruvian middle class. She had that precise and self-assured manner—just a little short of arrogance—with which we were already familiar from our acquaintance with the Vancouver Chinese, and her reaction to our project was emphatic.

'From Huancayo to Cuzco!' she exclaimed, turning to Inge. 'I advise you not to try it, señora! From Ayacucho to Cuzco there are no buses. You will have to hire a car, and if you find anyone to take you it will cost more than a thousand soles.[1] Besides, the conditions in the hotels on the way are not good for ladies! You would not like it!' There was an unanswerable finality about her conclusion.

You would not like it! How often and how exasperatingly we were to hear that phrase during our stay in Peru! On this occasion we took it to imply that we, as foreigners, were too soft to undergo the hardships which Peruvians could endure. Later we realized our error. Living in a country where status distinctions are very pronounced, most Peruvians regard them as more important than differences of nationality. A Lima man whom we met later in the Sierra remarked: 'If one of the market women up here tries to cheat you, do not think it is because you are a foreigner. She would do the same to me. In her eyes we are of the same class.' In

[1] The Peruvian standard of currency is the sol d'oro (made of a brass alloy); at the time we travelled it was worth about 5 Canadian cents, or 4d. Thus 1,000 soles amounts to nearly £17.

his turn the educated Peruvian has little dislike of foreigners, but he despises the life of the Indian. And we soon realized that when a man or a woman of this class said to us about anything in Peru, 'You would not like it,' the impulse behind the remark was one of identification; the phrase meant: 'You would not like it any more than we.' On this occasion the Chinese woman was emphasizing the fact that educated Peruvians, unless they are eccentrics, see no virtue in travel for its own sake, and prefer the conveniences of their towns to the discomforts of their roads.

Soon, from the vagueness of the answers they gave to our more precise questions, we realized that neither Señor Merida nor the Chinese woman had in fact travelled on the routes they condemned. Full of good intention, they damned from hearsay. And so we remained undecided as to what we might do in Huancayo, disinclined to abandon either of our vaguely planned routes, perturbed at the same time by the thought that the warnings we had been given might indicate real difficulties, but also a little flattered to hear what we regarded as a matter of catching the right bus, or at worst hitching lifts on the right lorries, magnified into the dimensions of adventure.

The spectacular part of our ascent into the Andes began after San Bartolome, a village about fifty miles from Lima. There the train stopped for almost an hour, to be serviced for the climb ahead, and the passengers got out on to the long stretch of sand that served for a platform. The interlude remains vividly in my mind as our first sharp taste of Andean life.

The air was bright and fresh—Alpine air—and the soft brownish-green of the winter grass mantled the massive slopes behind the village orchards. The station was as active as a plaza on a saint's day, for the peasant women had come down in their bright dresses—red and purple skirts, vividly embroidered aprons and white panama hats with great black bows—to open the daily trainside market. Some of them walked among the crowd selling the produce of their terraced gardens: green sweet lemons and brown passion fruit, plaited into long strings like Breton onions; little baskets of green cane, each containing precisely five large oranges or five chirimoyas; neat bouquets of carnations and moss roses, bound in corn leaves. Señor Merida insisted on buying a basket of chirimoyas for us to taste; they were the fruit of a species of custard-apple, and inside their tough green skin there was a whitish paste with one of those inanely sweet tropical flavours which one enjoys mildly but has no great wish to try again.

The touch of an exotic Breughel which the scene possessed was given by the impromptu restaurants that had sprung up under the trees around the station. On Peruvian trains only the first-class passengers are served meals—heavy, over-peppered lunches which take hours to eat and which reduce one to a state of somnolent indigestion. The others buy their food at the stations, and class divisions in Peru spread even to eating habits, for while we in the Pullman waited until 12.30 for our lunch, the Indians ate their dinner at 10 o'clock, one of the many habits of Inca times which contact with Spanish civilization has failed to change.

Some of the cooks at San Bartolome were roasting stubby ears of corn on sheets of tin; these were eaten with slices of soft white cheese. Others were grilling lumps of meat on skewers over little charcoal burners. 'They are called anticuchos,' Señor Merida explained. 'C'est le coeur du boeuf.' 'Beef heart!' Inge exclaimed in horror, recognizing one of her most detested foods. 'Mais c'est délicieux!' protested Señor Merida. 'The heart is soaked in vinegar, and then it is grilled afterwards. You must certainly try it.' Later, on my own, I ate anticuchos, but the experience did not lead me to count it among my great gastronomic experiences.

Most of the activity, however, went on around the tables where set meals, costing a shilling or so, were being served. The passengers sat crowded on wooden benches, eating hungrily with spoons and fingers, while the half-breed cooks scooped rice and slices of meat on to the plates with their greasy hands, and ladled out from large earthenware bowls a potato soup called chupe, which is the traditional staple dish of the Andes, made for many centuries before either the Inca or the Spanish conquest, and still serving the Sierra Indians as a protection from cold as well as from hunger. And all the time, giving the scene its final touch of strangeness, we heard around us the Quechua language of the

35

mountains, the chuckling breath-catching speech which remains the most enduring monument to the Incas, who imposed it on the rest of Peru in place of the myriad tribal dialects that had existed before their time.

2

There are mountain ranges whose nature one perceives almost at a glance. One looks at the Alps from the terraces of Berne, at the green wall of the Sierre Madre rising up from Tamazunchale to the Mexican plateau, and an immediate impression is created which acts as an enduring frame—a first view of the whole— within which all one's more particular observations can find their place.

But there is no such quick and easy way to envisage the Andes. The enormous complexity of this tangle of ranges and plateaux makes the panoramic view impossible, and even in memory the Andes remain interminable and intricate. What one recollects is not a mental snapshot, but a chaotic sense of vastness that has been accumulated in the slow process of daily travel.

The formation of the Andes seems, indeed, like a series of gigantic masks designed to make knowledge difficult. First the foot-hills screen one's view of the larger mountains beyond, and then, when the climb into the real Andes begins, it is a journey with no visible goal, a continual circumvention of vast masses of rock, scored by deep chasms called quebrados and forming high cliff faces beyond which one rarely sees even the top of the next crag. It was not until several hours after leaving San Bartolome that the actual summits of the coastal Cordillera rose into sight above the ends of the higher valleys. And by then we had already climbed so far—to almost fourteen thousand feet—that, though they were in reality much higher than Mont Blanc, these peaks seemed hardly more spectacular than Snowden or Scafell, and certainly far less dramatically memorable than the preceding part of our journey in which the train climbed up the series of steep escarpments, between five and twelve thousand feet, which the Peruvians call The Eyebrow of the Coast.

When the railway builders reached San Bartolome in the early 1870's, they found that no orthodox construction methods would take their lines up the apparently impregnable cliffs above the village, and many critics prophesied that the mountains would remain unconquered. But Honest Henry Meiggs, the former confidence trickster who planned the Central Railway, was not an orthodox railway builder. He had, in fact, almost no engineering knowledge of any kind, but he possessed the type of imagination that is stimulated by obstacles. It had enabled him to make a fortune out of lumber in the California Gold Rush; it had saved him from the San Francisco sheriffs when he was exposed—after being elected Alderman by his appreciative fellow citizens—as the contriver of a series of frauds involving almost a million dollars; it had enabled him to frustrate extradition proceedings and had brought him a second fortune as a contractor in Chile. Now it was to help him to overcome a mountain barrier only less formidable than the Himalayas. When his engineers despaired, he refused to accept the thought of defeat, and the Meiggs legend represents him declaring at one anxious conference that the tracks would go up the mountains even if they had to hang from balloons.

Under Honest Henry's bullying the engineers found a less fanciful solution—that of building what railwaymen call switchbacks. This means in practice that the railway follows the cliff face in a zigzag path, and at each point of the zigzag there is a siding where the train waits while the brakeman jumps down and throws the points. Then the engine pushes the train up the next lap, pulls it up the following one, and so tacks upward until it reaches the less precipitous slopes above.

Even the switchbacks did not obviate the need for some highly acrobatic engineering. Sometimes the line was carried on bracket-like trestles projecting from the sides of precipices, and sometimes in galleries blasted from the rock. It clambered around great open faces looking towards the distant sea, along the sides of deep quebrados where spiny agaves and scarlet wild geraniums clung in the crevices of the rocks, and over steep grassy mountainsides that were sometimes flooded with blue lupins or golden broom. Even when we had turned the last switchback, and the train had begun to probe laboriously through the higher ravines and valleys, there were still great barriers to be pierced and difficult chasms to be crossed. We went through sixty tunnels before the summit, and over almost as many bridges and trestle viaducts. The most Gothically impressive place of all was a gorge called El Infiernillo —Little Hell. Here, in a scene that would have suited the gloomy tastes of a Salvador Rosa, the perpendicular walls of yellowish rock enclosed a dark and narrow chasm through which, even in its depleted winter state, the Rimac boiled in constricted turmoil. The railway crossed El Infiernillo by a bridge, suspended fifteen hundred feet up the walls of the chasm, and reached by tunnels opening into the cliffs on either side. It was built by men hanging in cradles from the rocks above, and before it had been completed many of them died on the rocks below.

Not all the journey maintained this vertiginous quality, for each gorge cut its way through the enclosing rocks to a valley above; and these valleys changed in character with the rising altitude. The earliest were places of exceptional greenness, blessed by a damp climate which had induced the ancient Indians to populate them thickly. High up the steep mountainsides, wherever stones could be laid to hold back a few square yards of earth, the remains of their terraces patterned the slopes with neat walls like grey contour lines. Only the lower of these andenes, as the terraces are called, were now cultivated by the remaining inhabitants; the rest were left to the sheep and goats. But the white houses of this region suggested a life more prosperous than that of the cane hovels of Chosica, for they had orchards of pears and cherries, and narrow fields of wheat and dark alfalfa beside the white river, and among them stood little cairns surmounted by painted wooden crosses garlanded with flowers.

But in the higher valleys life grew harsher, and the villages more austere. I remember particularly a place called Chicla—a grey stone settlement well above the tree line. Its roofs of corrugated iron were weighted with boulders because of the high winds, but among the lichen-green rocks that spattered its rough pastures there still grew steep yellow fields of barley. The mountain road ran here, and we could see the trucks labouring up the steep gradients, while a pack train of llamas stepped slowly along a more ancient highway that wound in a faint scar along a higher hillside. Far above them, silvered like a plane by the sunlight, a white heron was flying against the clear blue mountain sky. In these higher regions, indeed, there were many birds, but most of those we saw were predators—small, pink-breasted hawks, harriers swooping low over the dry bushes, and later—wheeling and gliding, black and vast-winged over the highest crags—the first condors.

The valleys where we saw the condors were sombre places in which only a few stemless thistles varied the winter yellow of the ichu grass which covers the higher pastures of the Andes. The stillness, the dense, fuzzy shadows of the overhanging cliffs, the monotony of colour, combined to create that ominous atmosphere which one so often senses in high enclosed places among the mountains. Yet even here, as in all but the most stubbornly rocky corners of the Andes, some kind of human existence persisted among the isolated hovels of thatched boulders and the lonely cemeteries with their toppling metal crosses, for shepherds in dark ponchos stood knitting beside the railway to watch the train go by; the chullos they wore—those winged knitted caps of the Sierra Indians—gave the only points of brightness in this landscape of deadened tones.

In this region we first saw the llama at close quarters. When the train approached one of the grazing herds, the younger animals would scamper away, but their elders always stayed, standing motionless or reclining, to convey in a poising of the head on its tall neck, in a veiled look of the long-lashed eyes, an ironic mingling of disdain and interest. What impressed one most about these animals was that the features which in captivity appear most grotesque—the long, absurd neck and the disproportionately thin legs—were precisely those that now made them seem so well adapted to a land where the stony paths demand a delicate tread and where fodder grows often in places beyond the reach of any ordinary neck. Here one's faith in the appropriateness of evolution—shaken in Regent's Park—was at least in part restored.

So far I have given the impression that our journey into the Andes was taking us through a country where life was primitive and rural—a world of Inca terraces and peasant farms, of Indian shepherds, of llamas and condors. But, although the existence of most of the people who live near the Central Railway is indeed both primitive and rural, differing little from the pattern that came into being as a result of the sixteenth-century compromise between Inca customs and those of Spanish medieval peasants, Henry Meiggs did not build his railway for a society of subsistence farmers. He built it because the Andes contained copper, which needed a more efficient means of transport to the coast than the mule-trains that had satisfied the Spanish silver-miners.

High in the mountains, at about ten thousand feet, we began to see the first mine buildings clustering around their shaftheads, and long after the cultivated fields had come to an end, at more than thirteen thousand feet above the sea, we reached Casapalca, the first real mining settlement. With its sheds and its sidings and its general air of sooty mechanical drabness, this little town squatting on an eroded, rubbly mountainside might have been in Montana as easily as in Peru. But the people of Casapalca belonged only in the Andes, for, like almost all the miners of the Sierra, they were Indians who had retained obstinately the habits of the farming villages from which they came. The women still wore the vividly coloured peasant garb which was imposed by the Spaniards, and cooked on primitive stone hearths outside the dismal lines of one-roomed brick houses provided by the mining company. It was modern industry served by people in the rural dress of Don Quixote's day. Only the schoolmaster of Casapalca seemed outside this pattern of contrast as he sat on his chair in the village playground and read to the pupils who squatted around him on the cindery earth. One wondered at the devotion or resignation that kept him in this desolate little fragment of Black Country among the mountains, patiently chipping away at the monumental illiteracy of the Sierra.

Above Casapalca the summits glittered into sight like pyramids of white porcelain, and the rocks beside the railway were bearded with icicles. Here we first encountered the mountain sickness which the Peruvians call soroche; it affected many of our fellow passengers so severely and with such a variety of symptoms—nosebleeding, dizziness, vomiting and even fainting—that a white-jacketed attendant was kept busy scurrying up and down the coach with a kind of canvas wineskin filled with oxygen, thrusting its nozzle promiscuously into the nostrils of one passenger after another.

Inge seemed immune from soroche, and even maintained afterwards that she felt invigorated by the clear air of these altitudes. My reactions were curious, but not painful. I felt an irresistible drowsiness and my head lolled and nodded like that of an uncontrolled marionette, but more disturbing was my loss of the ability to talk coherently. It was a kind of disintegration of the syntax. 'Cigarette a like would you?' I would ask with the thick deliberation of the self-conscious drunkard. 'Match you a have?' I would continue, frantically making conversation to keep awake, aware all the time that in some insidious way my tongue was playing traitor to my thoughts, but unable to impose any discipline upon it. These manifestations, which were merely puzzling and frustrating to me, seemed distressing to my companions, and I remember, in my moments of clear-sightedness, Señor Merida leaning over and saying urgently, 'De l'oxygène, señor! Without it you may be very sick!' But soroche seemed to have stirred all those lessons of British doggedness that had lain happily dormant in me ever since my schooldays. Obstinately waving aside the man in the white coat and his nozzle, I told myself that I must Fast Stand, that I must Challenge the Meet, that, What Come May, I must Lip a Keep Upper Stiff.

The British spirit, or perhaps mere physical adaptability, triumphed, and by the time we reached the summit I was wide enough awake to see the last copper mine on the Pacific slope—a jumble of corrugated iron buildings clambering up a cliffside like a Pueblo village and reflected in the mirror of a tiny lake—and to read the board at Ticlio which announced that the railway was crossing the coastal Andes at a height of 15,693 feet. We were over the Continental Divide, hundreds of feet above the Matterhorn, and all the half-congealed trickles among the rocks were now running towards the Amazons and the Atlantic.

As we crossed the summit Señor Merida pointed to the peak nearest to the railway line, which was crowned by a sheet of tin painted with the Peruvian colours. 'It is named after Don Enrique!' Don Enrique was Meiggs, who still retains a faint halo of heroism in Peruvian eyes, as much for his megalomaniac generosity and his sexual prowess as for his railway-building abilities. And it seemed right enough that Honest Henry, who had changed the life of Peru by providing the first efficient link between the Sierra and the Coast, and who finally bankrupted himself and died of strain in the process, should have his monument. What one missed was a monument to all the labourers (one estimate runs as high as ten thousand) who died of accidents, of dysentery, of the gnawing verrugas fever of the Andes, and of sheer exhaustion, before Meiggs could fulfil his desire to build the highest railway in the world.

3

Down from the summit, through dry gorges and beside lakes fringed with ice, the railway descended into a wide canyon among bald white bluffs which the Indians call the Hills of the Moon. The natural cataclysm in which these rocks originated had tortured their strata into great waves that seemed to have congealed at the moment of breaking. And what nature began in the way of desolation man had completed; for it would be hard to imagine a more Dantesque marriage of original lunar starkness and artificial ugliness than the town of La Oroya which lay in this setting. The industrial buildings and the crammed rows of miners' barracks were all overshadowed by the vast smelter in which most of the ores of the Andes are reduced to their constituent metals; the black tower of its chimney rose high above the town, spreading sterility over the hills with its acrid vapours. Yet here again, blossoming garishly among all this industrial deadliness, the brilliance of the Andean dress conveyed a sense of life as obstinate and almost as triumphant as the flowers that germinate in the ruins of war. At La Oroya Señor Merida left us; on the platform he paused to raise his hand in a last salute, and then, like a man caught in a fast current, he was carried off in the rush of Indian passengers towards the buses and lorries waiting at the station gates.

Soon after La Oroya we entered that region of high valleys and pastures which is the real Sierra, and, as the canyons broadened, one began to experience the curious Lost World feeling of a primeval landscape, under a sky at once boundless and miraculously close, which is characteristic of very high tablelands. The train followed the valley of the Mantaro, a valley as bland and smoothly-flowing as its shallow winter river, and for many miles the country was almost untenanted, since most of its inhabitants had moved to the mines and the few who remained were content with tiny potato plots on the edges of crumbling adobe hamlets. The abandoned Inca terraces, rippling down whole hillsides under their grey-green veils of grass, gave the valley a grave and desolate beauty like that of a deserted city—an impression only accentuated by the pale grace of the pampas grass by the riverside and the crimson blossoms flashing like flames out of the grenade-shaped cacti.

But finally, and with surprising abruptness, the hills opened and fanned out into the wide basin known as the Valley of Jauja, the principal farming region of the Central Sierra. Jauja, a city that was old when the Incas came, raised above the plain a silhouette swelling into baroque domes and rich lichen-yellow tiles, and down the valley the whitewashed granges stood openly in the fields. We commented to each other on the contrast between these unprotected farms and the fortress-like buildings in which the owners of Mexican haciendas had protected themselves; evidently this was a more pacific—or a more fearful—countryside.

It was late in the afternoon when we reached Huancayo and

the threadbare Indian porters came shouldering on to the train, growling at each other, and almost wrenching the suitcases from the passengers' hands. But theirs was an unreal menace, a mere charade of violence; as soon as the man who marked us down as his particular clients had got his hands on our luggage he ceased to play the bandit, muttered an almost obsequious 'Ya! Ya!' when we told him to take us to the Government Hotel, and pushed a way out for us on to the platform, where he slung our two cases on his back, balanced them with a juggler's ease until he had secured the carrying rope that tightened over his chest, and then jogtrotted ahead of us across the station yard towards the Plaza.

Huancayo, as we saw it then, was a town of wide dusty streets lined with plain two-storied buildings, heavy-eaved, with open balconies below which the shops receded darkly; the general effect was one of mountain austerity, such as one encounters in some towns of the Pyrenees. Here and there the grubby whitewash of the walls still caught the rays of the falling sun and threw them back in dazzling patches of light. But in the shadow we shivered, for the air at eleven thousand feet is so thin that the cold bites sharply as soon as the light ceases to fall.

Because of this, the time pattern of Lima is reversed in these Andean towns. Life follows an almost Indian rhythm, even for those who are not Indians, and the day gets into swing soon after dawn, reaches its peak at high noon, and dwindles by sunset. It is a matter of climate rather than culture; one learns quickly in the Sierra why the ancient Andeans worshipped the sun.

In Huancayo the evening withdrawal had begun. The photographers out in the plaza were folding their tripods, the merchants from the little daily market were hurrying home, humpbacked with burdens, and as we entered the hotel a military band of Indian soldiers with tarnished brass instruments tramped towards their barracks to the beat of rattles. It was not yet six, but the streets were emptying and the town was descending into a suspension of life which, except at the time of a fiesta, afflicts every Andean town from sunset until dawn.

The Government Hotel, with its white stone façade and its wooden-screened miradors, stood out in contrast to the dingy utilitarianism of the shops and offices which occupied the other sides of the plaza. It was, in fact, a much better hotel than we had expected to find in a railhead town in the high Andes, and, since from now on we had to rely mostly on Government Hotels of this kind, it may be as well to comment a little more fully on these very useful institutions.

The idea of a state-administered inn is, of course, nothing new in Peru, for the Incas in their time built hostels, which they called tambos, along their great public highways, and any person travelling on official business was given all he needed in the tambo where he stopped for the night. Under the Spaniards the tambos, like the Inca roads, fell into decay, but never completely vanished, for the better Spanish administrators did their best to keep the old system of communications from total collapse. In 1543, for instance, the governor Vaca de Castro issued a decree providing for the continued maintenance of tambos by the local authorities, and in accounts of travels in Peru written early in the present century I have come across references to primitive shelters, still called tambos, which were maintained here and there among the Andes in small communities where no hotels existed; the ancient habit of hospitality had lingered centuries after the Incas and their roads had disappeared.

Thus, when the Peruvian Government decided during the 1930's to start a chain of hotels in provincial towns, it was following an ancient precedent of the community providing for the needs of travellers. But the hotels that emerged from this programme were very different from the old tambos, since the aim was to give not minimum accommodation, but something better than the decayed hostelries—relics of the early years of Independence—which are still all one can expect in many Peruvian towns. The programme was carried out with an energy and an imaginativeness unusual in South American public administration, where the intention so often counts as much as the achievement. Almost twenty of the hotels are now in operation; they are often run by trained European managers and employ some of the best cooks in Peru. Even the visual arts have found their place in the programme, for we found examples of modern Peruvian painting in many Government Hotels, while it was in the dining-room at Huancayo that we saw our first examples of those strange and dazzling Virgins, like golden infantas, which were painted in the seventeenth century by the Indian primitives of Cuzco.

Once we had established ourselves in the Huancayo hotel, it seemed high time to fill in the gaps in our plans which had become so obvious during our conversation with Señor Merida. We decided first to find out whether any means actually existed for travelling across the Sierra to Cuzco. The hotel clerk, a morose and abrupt man with a Spanish lisp, was unencouraging. 'It can be done,' he declared, with what seemed to us excessive irony, 'but you need a jeep—and good fortune.' He knew of nobody in Huancayo who would drive us; whatever we paid would not be worth the wear and tear on the car. In the end, after playing with our idea like a gloomy cat, he unbent so far as to admit that there was a bus every other day to Ayacucho. But, he added, Ayacucho was only a third of the way, and there were positively no buses beyond it.

Even a bus to Ayacucho was more than we had expected, and we went down to the wide street beyond the plaza from which the buses left. The camion for Ayacucho had gone that morning, the half-breed girl in the office told us; there would not be another until the day after tomorrow. But there was a man driving his car back to Ayacucho that night; he was waiting to pick up two or three passengers, and we might get seats if we wished to risk travelling after dark.

To leave immediately would mean seeing nothing of Huancayo, but we decided to talk to the driver in any case. He was a young man in khaki drill who might, so far as we could tell, have been either a mechanic or a civil engineer; in a new country one learns slowly the clues to social gradations. Yes, he was driving to Ayacucho. He was waiting for a friend and they would leave in an hour. 'A las ochymedi,' he added—at half-past eight; like most mountain Peruvians, he robbed Spanish of its sonority by dropping many of the vowels, and in this way gave it an almost Indian quality, for *ochymedi* runs more easily off a Quechua tongue than *ocho y media*.

We could come with him—he hesitated appraisingly—for three hundred soles, and if we did him that honour he might be able to find us a car in Ayacucho that was driving on to Abancay. But what if we waited and went to Ayacucho by bus the day after tomorrow? 'Ah,' smiling sadly, 'but then my friend will have gone to Abancay.' We went back to the hotel.

After dinner we drank capitanes—a mixture of vermouth and the Peruvian grape spirit called pisco—in the bar, and watched the commercial travellers playing, with a great banging of leather cups, a guessing dice game called Dudo—'I doubt you'. An American engineer with clay-covered boots was talking loudly to a silent compatriot about his troubles with the workers in the mine he supervised. Three men we had already seen on the train from Lima watched us with open curiosity. 'You talk a lot about Peruvian gentility and Peruvian tact,' Inge grumbled, 'but look at them for an example. Ever since eight o'clock this morning they've been staring at us.' 'Perhaps they're not Peruvians,' I suggested. 'They may be some other kind of South American.' Inge was not convinced, but the argument ended when we began to talk to a young Welshman at the next table.

His name was Morgan; he worked for the railway and was looking after some work at Morococha, a mining town on a branch line nearly fifteen thousand feet up. He was disinclined to talk about railways; my attempt to draw a comparison between the daring construction of the Central Railway and the more conservative attitude towards engineering which I had encountered when I worked on English railways fifteen years ago did not move him. He was not, he hinted rather broadly, an old railway hand. He had taken a job with the Central Railway because it was a way of getting to South America, and now what he was thinking about most was going home to Cardiff on his next leave.

'Do you know Porthcawl?' I nodded. 'Well, I sometimes go down to the beaches south of Lima, and when I look inland to the desert I think myself back on that stretch of coast that runs between Ogmore and Porthcawl.' As he said this I had a sudden nostalgic vision of the sandhills surging in waves up to the ridge above the grey castle of Merthyrmawr and the poachers laying their snares for the rabbits that used to swarm among the wild moss-roses in the hollows of the dunes; I had not been there for seventeen years, but the memory was so sharp and pleasant that I looked forward, with that folly which makes us wish to clothe our memories with solid flesh, to the day when we would go to the dunes of Peru and reconstruct a lost Welsh holiday.

'Why be in a hurry to go to Ayacucho?' said Morgan. 'It's interesting to go to Cuzco that way, but there's much more to see if you go through Arequipa and Puno.' I explained that we intended to travel that route as well. 'Well, don't let me discourage you. I dare say you've been told often enough what to expect. But you can't leave Huancayo the day after tomorrow. It's only Wednesday, and the great thing in Huancayo is the Sunday feria. It's the biggest market in the whole Andes. The Indians come in from all the Sierra villages, and you can buy anything from a needle to a haystack.'

'Let me make a suggestion,' he went on, after thinking for a moment. 'You can see Huancayo in a day, and you can go out to one of the villages another day. And then why don't you go to a little town called Tarma about fifty miles from here? It will give you a completely different aspect of the Andes. You go back to La Oroya on the train, and then by bus over a pass and down into a deep valley, and there you find Tarma. There's a good hotel with a swimming pool, and it's very quiet. Just right for vegetating a bit and sopping up Peruvian life, if that's what you want. To tell you the truth, it's the sort of town where I've often thought one could spend a jolly good honeymoon.'

'Besides,' he added, stepping quickly away from sentiment, 'it's very near to the jungle. You can get down to the Chanchamayo in three or four hours if the road's open. And there'd be no trouble at all about coming to Huancayo for the feria. You could just travel in with the Indians from Tarma.'

By eleven, when the barman was ostentatiously switching off lights and checking his books to remind us that the other guests had long gone to their rooms, Morgan had effectively completed our temptation. We had decided to go to Tarma in two days' time, and to postpone our journey to Ayacucho at least until after the Huancayo feria on Sunday. It was to be one of several journeys which we planned but never made. We did not see Morgan again.

4

So striking did we find the people of Huancayo, and so impressive the landscape around it, that the town itself deposited a very light impression on my memory, and even those pictures that still come into my thoughts are scenes of Huancayo life rather than scenes of Huancayo.

I remember the church, for instance, because of the plain-song of the Franciscan brothers which filled its stripped and arid interior with the massive decoration of sound. I remember the two plazas, not for music, since they did not even have a bandstand, nor for any individuality of appearance, but rather for the careful way in which the Indian gardeners applied even here the ancient Andean methods of cultivation, irrigating their plants with tiny trenches dug by the hoe, just as if they had been crops of potatoes on some mountainside terrace. And the shops I recollect are not those which were filled with imported goods from Birmingham and Tokio, but rather those that suggested a life—or a death—different in some ways from our own.

The undertaker's shop near the church, for instance, in whose window enormous white shrouds, edged with elaborate gold embroideries in Grecian patterns, were draped between candles as tall as a man and encrusted with curious arabesques in red and gilt wax. Or the small houses in back streets over whose doorways hung ragged bunches of flowers. We would look into these houses and see the Indians—men and women—drinking a cloudy brown liquid which the woman tavern-keeper dipped from a great glass jar or a tall earthenware crock of an ancient pattern whose pointed end had been thrust into a bed of sand. It was freshly brewed chicha, a kind of corn beer which has been made in the Andes ever since any civilization has existed there, and which still provides the Sierra Indian with nutriment as well as entertainment.[1] Chicha is a drink with a more noble past than one might imagine today, when it is despised by the beer-drinking educated Peruvians. Under the Incas it played a ritual part in every festival, fulfilling much the same social-liturgical function as wine in the Christian world, and Prescott talks lyrically in *The Conquest of Peru* of Pizarro and his companions being invited by Atahuallpa to 'quaff the sparkling chicha from golden vases of extraordinary size, presented by the dark-eyed beauties of the harem'. Here, as on some other occasions, that often excellent historian suffered from never having seen the things about which he wrote; chicha does not sparkle, and it is a sad and sour drink in comparison with the wines to which Pizarro's men must have been accustomed in their native Spain.

But the scene of Huancayo life which for its sheer grimness lodged most sharply in my memory was that of the public slaughter-house. We found it by chance. On the edge of the town the main street crossed a ravine beyond which the fields and the adobe shacks began, and here, in full view of those who looked down from the bridge, the slaughter-house had been built. It was divided, by a high wall that ran at right angles to the road, into a double scene, like one of those stage sets in which the spectator can see two related but separate actions going on at the same time.

On one side of the wall, the raddled butchers were dissecting the carcasses with quick, slashing movements, and on the flight of wide steps that faced them a group of women with dark plaits and swarthy, expressionless faces sat watching. Each had a basket and a large knife, and every now and then one of them would run forward, slice off some fragment of offal and take it to be weighed by the checker on his gory scales. As we watched, an old woman dragged away by its horn a flayed bull's head whose bulging, bluish eye stared up in accusation.

And well it might accuse, one felt, looking at the parody of pastoral innocence on the other side of the wall, where the cattle

[1] A fairly recent study of the Aymara Indians near Lake Titicaca, for example, showed that only a heavy consumption of chicha kept their diet from falling below the calorific value necessary for their farming work.

ruminatively waited for the axe in little byres of rough poles, thatched with golden straw. In their gentle, reclining attitudes there was all the bitter-sweet languor of a Botticelli nativity, but it was a Botticelli that had fallen into the hands of some Bosch-like apocalyptic, for the angels on the roofs of the byres were vultures, and a runnel of blood seeped past the feet of the waiting cattle to cloud the brook in the ravine.

That this scene still lives so vividly in my mind emphasizes the fact that in the Andes we were far less conscious of the presence of death than we had been in Mexican towns; macabre scenes were exceptional and for that reason memorable. The kind of mortality cult which the Mexicans inherited from the marriage of the death-oriented Spanish medieval culture with the death-obsessed society of the Aztecs, has never existed in Peru, where the Incas developed a life-cult based on sun worship. And today, even if the Peruvian Indian shows all the signs of having been beaten in spirit by centuries of Spanish oppression, one never sees him as living, like his Mexican counterpart, in a tragic mental landscape peopled by bleeding, doomed Christs and the recurrent symbols of triumphant death. Rather one is impressed by a kind of blind urge that struggles within him like a mole towards the sun, an obstinate insistence on survival in that rigorous mountain world by which his mind and his body are conditioned and confined.

It was the Indians and half-breeds, with their struggling and often vividly expressed vitality, who gave Huancayo its real individuality. The society of the Sierra is a simple and static one, where the racial divisions that came into being during the colonial era are retained more sharply than anywhere else in Peru. For there are few people in the mountains who do not observe the distinctions between its three surprisingly self-contained groups of inhabitants—the whites, whom the Indians call mistis, the cholos (white-Indian half-breeds), and the pure Indians. When this rigid pattern began to form it is hard to tell. The early Spaniards were unfastidious, and since they were accompanied by few women of their own race, readily took Indians as wives; the fact that Diego Almagro was a half-breed did not prevent many pure-blooded

Spaniards from supporting him in his assassination of Pizarro. The first qualms about miscegenation evidently appeared during the seventeenth century, when Peru was changing from a frontier society to a stable community which tried to reproduce the manners of contemporary Spain. It was then that Peruvians became eager to conceal their Indian forebears, and Salvador de Madariaga has suggested that the motive behind their anxieties was not racial prejudice so much as the fear, since many of the unions between the early conquerors and their Indian women had been irregular, of incurring the stigma of illegitimacy.

The actual result was a society as sharply divided along colour lines as any dominated by open racialist doctrines, and it was out of this situation that the cholos emerged as a third race in the Sierra. Kept apart from white society, these half-breeds developed their own exclusivism and soon ceased to interbreed with the Indians; since that time they have been content to remain the intermediate race which dominates the trade of the Andes and provides most of the artisans and petty officials of the Sierra towns.

Huancayo, as a major centre of administration and commerce, has a fairly large white population, but these mountain creoles have still the rootless air of perpetual colonizers. After four hundred years the white man—who has become so successfully naturalized in the Rockies—seems as anomalous in mountain Peru as he did in British India. It is the Indians and the cholos who are the true Andeans and who, by their massive inertia, defend the one society that is different enough from anything else in the world to be called characteristically Peruvian. Essentially, despite its white inhabitants, Huancayo is a cholo town which on market days becomes Indian.

Rather than the men of either race, it is the Indian women and the cholas (the cholo women) who impress most vividly upon one the individuality of Sierra life, and this is because they are more conservative and preserve more obstinately the colourful attributes of the past. Except in a few isolated regions around Cuzco and Huanuco, the men have largely abandoned the brilliant local costumes which their ancestors wore during the seventeenth century;

elsewhere, apart from the occasional brilliance of a knitted cap or a red sash, they are content with reach-me-down clothes from the market or murky home-spuns woven in the Indian villages. But their very drabness only emphasizes the vividness of the impression created by their women folk.

By ordinary European or even Asian standards the Andean women are rarely beautiful, though I can imagine sculptors or painters admiring their stolid, monumental qualities. Their bodies are stocky and deep-chested owing to their lungs being adapted to the mountain air, and their flat-planed faces and opaque eyes lack expression and mobility, though at their best the younger women have a glow of rustic vitality which can be pleasing enough in its own way. This applies particularly to some of the cholas; their features, though almost as Mongolian as those of the Indians, are much more finely drawn, and under the coppery skin their cheeks flush into a golden-vermilion bloom, the colour of a ripe nectarine. They reminded us often of the photographs we had seen of Tibetans, and later on we met an American who had travelled in Nepal and who remarked that, if one could transport the women of the Andes to the square of Khatmandu, they might easily pass for natives. It was an example of the evolution of parallel physical types under parallel geographical conditions.

The women of Huancayo were moved by a kind of restless vigour which made it difficult for them to remain unoccupied, and, as they trotted rather than walked through the streets, they would twirl their spindles so that even away from home they could use every spare moment to prepare yarn for weaving or knitting. But neither the activity nor the solid charms of the Andean women would have impressed one so greatly, if they had not been emphasized by the brilliant dress of the Sierra.

The most important garments of this elaborate costume are the wide, heavy skirts. By the number and magnificence of her skirts a Sierra woman's wealth and social position are proclaimed, and for this reason all she possesses must be worn at once. A well-dressed woman will carry the weight of eight or even as many as twelve skirts; the best is always on top, but it is raised as the wearer walks through the market, so as to show that even her underskirts are finely coloured and of equal value. Each skirt, except for the braid that may be sewn to its lower edges, is of a single vivid colour, and always different from that beneath it, so that every woman carries her own spectrum of favourite tints. As one might expect among the descendants of sun worshippers, most of them choose from the shades that run from crimson, through orange, to yellows as clear as primrose and as dense as ochre. Occasionally an anemone purple is worn, and more rarely blue or green, but never any sombre colour.

Above her belling cluster of skirts the Sierra woman wears an elaborately embroidered blouse, and an oblong cape, or manta, handwoven in geometrical patterns, which almost reaches the waist and is pinned across the chest. Next, there is the carrying cloth, of brilliantly striped cotton, which is slung over the back and used for any kind of burden, from a baby to potatoes for the market; like the manta, it is a relic, not of Spanish, but of Inca dress. Finally, few Sierra women go without hats, and here a racial distinction appears, for around Huancayo the Indian women wear low-crowned hats of yellow or orange felt, while the cholas prefer panamas with black ribbons so wide that at first sight they appear to be in mourning.

It is, indeed, in details rather than in general style that the costume of the half-breed women differs from that of the Indians. Cholas despise the subtly dyed handwoven materials of which the Indians make their skirts, and prefer machine-made clothes because they have recognizable money and prestige values. After we had found out the various prices of the garments in Huancayo market, we calculated that the full dress of a moderately well-turned-out chola would cost at least fifty pounds, not counting the heavy gold rings and bracelets that must accompany it; the average yearly income in Peru is less than fifty pounds. Yet I often wondered whether so great a compulsion to load oneself with brilliant clothes could be explained entirely in the prestige terms to which modern anthropologists are so attached when they deal with American Indians. Perhaps the desire to shine before one's neighbours is there, but that it should take this particular form may result from some more pressing urge to seek, in renewing the colours of the sun itself, an almost magical identification with the sources of life.

5

History flows far back in the valley of Jauja, but its tides of conquest and conflict have left surprisingly little in the way of recognizable flotsam. Of the formidable dog-eating and dog-worshipping Huancas whom the Inca Emperor Pachacuti defeated in the fifteenth century even the language has vanished. Of the great Inca city which arose at Jauja after Pachacuti's conquest hardly a wall remains, for it was built in perishable adobe, and in the valley itself four centuries of the plough have removed all trace of the pre-Columbian farmers. Even the colonial era left nothing resembling that rich deposit of architectural skeletons which still graces the Mexican plateau. Only in the people and their way of living are these successive eras of the past preserved in any substantial way; the blood of the Huancas still flows in the veins of modern peasants, the speech of the Incas lingers on their lips and the customs of long-dead generations of Spaniards are preserved curiously in their dress and their daily habits. And in this way, lacking those obvious signposts to history which are provided by durable monuments, the valley of Jauja has nevertheless an air of immeasurable antiquity, of humanization extending far into the past, which gives the landscape a hold over the imagination as powerful as a myth and as hard to define.

Into this landscape we set out on our third morning, with the aim of visiting the Franciscan Abbey of Ocopo, which Morgan had told us was one of the few interesting colonial buildings in the region. 'They won't let a woman in, except to the church,' he warned us, but since we imagined that the church would probably be the most interesting part of the building we decided to go there in any case. 'You can take one of our autocarrils out to Concepcion,' Morgan added. 'Then you just walk over the fields to Ocopo.' He made it sound very simple—a pleasant, pastoral morning's stroll.

The autocarril was an old-fashioned, wooden-seated railcar that served the villages and hamlets along the Mantaro River as far as Jauja. It took us the twenty odd miles to Concepcion for less than a shilling; it had only one class, but, by established custom, the Indian women, with their bundles and their children and their great overflowing skirts, sat together in the back of the coach, while the front was left for the few passengers who wore twentieth-century clothes. This was done so naturally, so obviously without resentment or cringing, that one could accept it without difficulty as a convenient social arrangement.

Our journey was rather like a country bus trip, casual and capricious. At any place in the open country where an Indian wished to get on or off, the conductor would stop the train. But at one point, as if exasperated by our leisurely progress, the driver was seized with an impulse of speed and sent the railcar hurtling along a particularly uneven piece of track with such swaying rapidity that the Indian women squawked with terror and even the conductor pulled frantically on the bell cord until we drew up, with a scream of metal wheels, at the platform of one of the stations.

The wide fields of the valley, as we travelled through them, were golden-yellow with the end of harvest. A hazy blue overtone hung like the suggestion of smoke over the clumps of eucalyptus. And the hills beyond were patterned with the bright chequerboards of the hanging fields, the campos colgantes, of the Indian communities; harsh yellow squares of barley alternated with the deep orange of quinoa, a kind of millet peculiar to the Andes, and the new green of potato fields contrasted with the deeper colouring of alfalfa. Above the arable lands, the grass ran like sunlight up to the grey outcropping crags against the light-filled sky.

The peculiar static grandeur of the valley was due to the dry winter air, thin and clear, which eliminated those progressive changes in tone that normally give the impression of distance. It flattened the hills into great backdrops, painted in infinite detail, and, by taking away the quality of recession, gave the whole scene a strange feeling of arrested motion, like a stage that awaits the entry of the actors.

Yet, despite this static impression, the valley was filled with activity. In some fields the stooks of harvest were still standing; in others, where the threshing had ended, families of Indians had come festively to collect the grain that had been left; they were not the only gleaners, for the harvest had attracted many birds which flew up from the stubble as the autocarril passed—white doves and plovers, a multitude of yellow and green finches, and the inevitable hawks who preyed on the grain eaters.

All this pastoral activity, the golden crops and abundant herds, had their Arcadian flavour, but it would have been a mistake to make too much of these idyllic suggestions, for almost all the valley lands and the herds as well belonged to the haciendas. The Indian peasants were either share-croppers, dividing the land's yield equally with the hacendados, or paid hands working for a few soles a day.

At Concepcion there was a platform with some sheds, a row of railwaymen's cottages outside which girls were washing clothes in a narrow canal, and a little cantina whose walls were plastered with beer advertisements. We could find nobody at the station, but a woman came to the door of the cantina, and I asked her the way to Ocopo.

'Ocopo! It is a long way, señor!'

'How long, señora?'

'At least eight kilometres.'

It looked as though Morgan's walk through the fields would be more than a quiet stroll, but we decided we had time enough to get there and back before the afternoon train.

'It is a pity,' the woman continued. 'The car from the convento came to take one of the fathers to the train, but it went back straight away.' I remembered having seen a Franciscan with a briefcase getting on to the autocarril. 'But perhaps you can get a taxi in the plaza,' she added consolingly.

Having learnt that the town of Concepcion was some way off, and that the road to Ocopo went through it, we set off up the gravel lane from the station. 'They imagine that every foreigner is incapable of effort,' I grumbled as we walked past the high maize fields and the horses grazing in their pastures, and with that we dismissed the thought of getting to Ocopo except by our own efforts. It was a dull but populous road. An old woman came out of a potato patch, bare-footed and carrying her shoes in her hand; as soon as she reached the lane, she put them on for the sake of appearance, and immediately the grace went out of her movements. Other women came towards us, each carrying some burden on her back, and, unlike the people of Huancayo, they all greeted us.

It took almost three-quarters of an hour to reach Concepcion; the road was hillier and longer than we had expected, yet it could not have been more than three kilometres, and we realized that the unexpected tiredness we felt must be due to the fact that we were not yet accustomed to the altitude.

Concepcion was a straggling, overgrown village with a few shops and the usual plaza where Indian women sat squatting before piles of undersized potatoes. A taxi was indeed standing there. Our resolution to go the whole way to Ocopo on foot was already weakening, and we agreed to find out at least what the drive would cost. The taxi was old, and the driver was slowly patching a broken window with white sticking-plaster. He wanted forty soles to take us to Ocopo and back. It was about fifteen shillings, and excessive in Peruvian terms. But, as we were to find by repeated experience, taxi-drivers in Peru have a curious, self-denying independence. By possessing cars of any kind, they belong to the lowest fringe of whatever middle class exists in their country, and they have enough pride in their position not to indulge in the bargaining which is carried on in the markets. Consequently, when one of them names an excessive price which the prospective customer rejects, his professional pride forbids him to take anything less. The driver in Concepcion refused to make even the token reduction of a few soles which would have satisfied our sense of outrage, and he returned to his sticking plaster with a finality so pointed that for us in turn it would have meant a loss of face to accept his price.

So we left him, and after two starts along wrong streets, due to our misunderstanding of directions, we finally tramped down the straggling main street in the direction of Ocopo. By the time we got to the edge of Concepcion we must have walked, counting our wasted steps, very nearly the original eight kilometres which the woman in the station cantina had mentioned, and Ocopo was clearly still a long way off. How long, we were much less certain, since Concepcion ideas of distance were evidently flexible. A pair of giggling boys in the plaza had told us that it was five kilometres. A woman in a shop had said it was seven. Now we came to a café at a crossroads and went in to drink some mineral water; it was recommended as 'altamente radioactiva'—highly radioactive—and we realized from this that the radiation scare had not yet reached the Sierra. Ocopo, the proprietor of the café told us, was still seven kilometres away. He pointed up a road that turned off the main highway and went winding towards the hills. 'From the top of the second hill you can see the convento,' he said.

We set off, but the first hill was more than enough for us. Near the top, and two kilometres out of Concepcion, we realized how insignificant at eleven thousand feet was the fact that we had been able to walk twenty miles a day with ease at sea level. Our hearts pumped laboriously, we gasped like asthmatics, and we looked wistfully over the landscape for any kind of vehicle that might have given us a lift. Even an ox-cart we would have welcomed. But the road was deserted, and we were still, if our last informant was correct, five kilometres from Ocopo. And how were we to know that even he had not underestimated the distance? We told each other the reasons why it was unnecessary to go on to Ocopo. Women were not admitted, the church had probably been as ruinously restored as that in Huancayo, etc. But in the end we had to admit that our real reason for not continuing was the fact that we could not imagine ourselves summoning the energy to go the rest of the way to Ocopo and return on foot. So we went slowly back into Concepcion; the taxi driver was still mending his window, and pointed us out to a friend as we went past, dragging the feet of our dignity.

We had not seen Ocopo, but Ocopo, after all, had been only an excuse to spend a day in the valley of Jauja, and that classic landscape had been experience enough. On the more practical side, we had also learnt the lesson, which we afterwards applied scrupulously, to rely as little as possible on our own powers of movement at altitudes which, after all, would make an experienced Alpinist move with strength-conserving caution.

6

At dawn the following day we left Huancayo by the morning train. The dew dazzled on the long tips of the eucalyptus leaves in the groves outside the city, and a train of pack donkeys was setting out into the country, loaded with striped sacks. The air was bitingly cold, and I remember looking out, as we ourselves shuddered and gulped down the hot, bitter coffee which the steward had brought us, and seeing a girl in a cotton shift standing knee deep in a stream where she was thumping clothes with a wooden paddle.

Three hours later we got down at La Oroya into the midst of a shouting pack of boys who had marked us down as obvious strangers and fought so bitterly among themselves to carry our luggage that in the end we had to interfere by main force to prevent the larger boys from tearing the cases out of the hands of those we had agreed to employ. It was only after this undignified little incident had come to an end, and we had started to push our way towards the yard where the buses waited, that I noticed the whitish blisters covering the hands of the boy who walked beside me. I never found out what sickness had caused them, but I felt a little apprehensive at the time, since I had just been reading about the dangers in this region of a kind of minor leprosy called uta, which disfigures the face by gnawing at the nose and the lips.

The Tarma bus was a small, beetle-shaped vehicle which seemed already full, but Latin Americans are expert at packing a vehicle beyond all probable capacity, and the ayudante—the jockey-capped adolescent who travels with every Peruvian bus as porter, conductor and tireless general factotum—shouted excitedly at the Indians inside until, after much shuffling of bundles, a little space appeared. We struggled on board, assisted by the hands held out to us by three creoles in the front row. Once we were seated we recognized them as the men who had stared at us so assiduously on the train from Lima and in the hotel at Huancayo. They stared at us again, two with sorrowful spaniels' eyes in coarse round faces, and the third with that involuntary and rather gay ferocity which goes with a certain type of aquiline Roman profile.

The Roman was the most voluble of the three. He immediately asked us if we knew Italian and, when he found that we did not, talked to us in Spanish, and kept talking—on and off—all the way to Tarma. We overcame our original distrust; indeed, there was nothing else to do, for even if one had been tempted to practise a frosty English withdrawal, it would have been impossible to maintain in the highly social atmosphere of Peruvian travel.

The bus drove out of the station yard, over level crossings guarded by the armed and khaki-clad private police of the mining corporation which controls La Oroya like a feudal barony, and down the grey main street to the open valley where herds of black alpacas grazed within sight of the industrial citadel. Across the Mantaro we turned up a deep canyon whose cliffs hung over meadows kept lush by a mountain stream that fell in shallow, feathery cascades from one green pool to the glassy eddies of the next. 'It's a wonderful river for trout! Jesus Christ! So big!' shouted the Roman enthusiastically, and I could believe him. But the valley was full of private-fishing notices, and at one point two Indian boys with canes in their hands slipped quickly into the shelter of a reedbed as the bus approached them.

The trout stream swung off to the north, towards the great swampy plateau of Junin; our road rose eastward over bare, smooth mountainsides; among them there were many grey circles of stone and these looked most ritualistic, but they were only the sheep-cotes into which the herds we saw wandering over the uplands would be driven at night. We climbed to fourteen thousand feet at the top of the pass. It looked like the edge of the world, with only the sky beyond; then we rode over the summit, and the valley of Tarma fell away steeply below us in rolling slopes of sere grass and red earth spattered with boulders. The road raced down vast sweeping curves, and we exclaimed in admiration, for its fine engineering was certainly something far different from the bad trails we had been led to expect in the Andes.

'Yes, it is a fine road,' said the Roman meditatively. 'Nowhere else in the Andes will you find such a good, wide, new road.'

'It is the best road in Peru,' remarked one of his companions. 'Think who made it.'

'Amigo, you have no historical perspective,' cried the Roman. 'It is the best *modern* road in Peru. That we shall all be wise to admit until the 28th July.'

His allusion to the date of the Presidential inauguration, now only a fortnight away, made it clear that the dictator Odria had been responsible for the road, but evidently there was some political story hidden in the jests. However, before we could follow it up, the Roman was pointing excitedly across the valley. 'There—there is the best road in Peru!' he shouted. 'Look! It is the great road of the Incas.'

A grey line came from the distance about half-way up the opposite hillside; the road, we could see, was supported by a wall of rough masonry. The modern highway took a further curve, and all at once the cobbled surface of the Inca road was running beneath it and had emerged on the other side, narrowing off to a path barely six feet wide which plunged into a rock cleft.

'It was the greatest of their roads,' the Roman explained. 'It ran from Quito down to Argentina. Five thousand kilometres!'

'It's still used,' said one of the other men. And down the valley a small train of llamas was indeed travelling on the old imperial highway.

Terraces began to appear on the hillsides, clasping their segments of coloured crops or rusty earth, and among them were little clusters of huts built of pebbles gathered from the fields, and thatched with straw. 'Look at them,' said the Roman, whose lively interest in such matters strengthened our feeling that he was no Peruvian born. 'They may have been built last year, or ten years ago, or fifty years ago, but they are exactly the same as the Indians built in this valley when the Incas ruled. Señores, here there is no need for archaeologists to reconstruct the past. Open your eyes, and it lives around you.' He waved his hands like an impresario, and his friends were clearly moved by his eloquence.

The road plunged quickly downwards (in less than ten miles from the pass it falls four thousand feet), and Tarma came into sight—a bowl opening among the great bald hills like a clearing in the forest, with its floor patterned in a mosaic of white walls and red tiles, of yellow thatch and green gardens, brought into curious focus by the occasional stridency of a gleaming metal roof.

The Roman and his friends huddled in consultation. 'Do you intend to visit the Chanchamayo?' he asked us. We had thought of following Morgan's suggestion to go there and I said as much. 'It is magnificent. You *must* see it,' the Roman shouted enthusiastically. 'My friends and I are leaving Tarma immediately for San Ramon. Would you join us in hiring a car?' They would be there for two or three days, he added.

We hedged politely, and muttered between ourselves. Inge, for whom the unexpectedness of an opportunity is often its great attraction, was half in favour of going, even though she could not quite overcome her initial dislike of the Roman and his companions. I, more cautious and more inclined to hang on to a plan once I have forced myself to make one, felt vaguely resentful at the thought of being pushed towards a new decision. After all, I reasoned, if we went to the Chanchamayo straight away after lunch, as the Roman proposed, we would miss the Sunday feria in Huancayo—unless we stayed in the region a whole week longer. Surely we could get to San Ramon a day or two later. Inge agreed in the end. A cloud blew immediately over our relationship with the Roman and his friends, who seemed to regard our refusal as something near to a personal affront, and under its shadow we drove down the last hill to the edge of Tarma and up the drive past lawns and tennis courts to the Government Hotel.

The hotel was a pleasant-looking adaptation of the old rambling South American country house, trapping the midday sunlight among the paved terraces and bright flower beds which the low, airy wings of the building framed within three sides of an octangle. Morgan, we felt, had been right, and our liking was sustained when we went into our pleasantly furnished room and looked out from its window at the scene which was to become a great deal more familiar than we expected before we eventually left Peru.

Ponies grazed in a small paddock below the window, and the white-smocked hotel maids were hanging out sheets that cracked in the wind. Beyond the paddock lay green market gardens criss-crossed by irrigation ditches along whose grassy banks boys were running with bird-shaped kites that soared and dipped erratically against the chicory-blue sky. And at the end of the gardens the hills began to rise, first in cultivated terraces and then in great smooth brows whose peculiar rusty colouring gained a glowing richness from the sunlight. Among the terraces little roads slanted up towards small white farmhouses, their walls splashed with bougainvillea vines and darkened by the long shadows of cypresses and the inevitable eucalyptus. The scene blended appealingly the pastoral and the naturally magnificent; nowadays, as I write of Peru in the south of France, I often find a similar feeling—and even a great deal of actual resemblance—in the little valleys behind Menton, with their terraced, roseate hills, their sparse, severe trees and their light-coloured villas.

Since the hills were so much closer together and the air did not have room to perpetrate the same illusion of flattened distance, the Tarma valley had not the theatrical grandeur of that of Jauja; it was more intimate, more on the human scale. Jauja, I decided, had been a place to stimulate one's dramatic imagination; Tarma seemed, on that first day, much more a place to live, perhaps tranquilly, perhaps even productively. Later, after two months in Peru, I came to distrust such feelings.

7

If our liking for Tarma continued after the first impression, it was not wholly because of the landscape. Unless one is by nature a solitary—and for me solitude has as few charms as it had for Cowper's castaway—one's reactions towards places are mingled inextricably with the people one meets in them, and in Tarma we were lucky enough to make a number of pleasant acquaintances.

The Ortutays were the first of them. Señor Ortutay was the manager of the hotel, a young Hungarian with a leonine face who reminded me a good deal of the American poet Kenneth Rexroth. His wife was one of the blonde Magyars, small, vivacious and very good-looking. They had both been brought up in that peculiar atmosphere, mingling cultural liberalism and political conservatism, which seems to have characterized certain regions of Hungarian life between the wars; in opinions we often disagreed with them, but tastes we usually shared, and, like most Europeans, we found ourselves in curious unanimity over the civilization of the American world.

The Ortutays had fled, separately, from Hungary at the time of the Communist invasion, had met as exiles, travelled to Argentina and then, like so many of their compatriots, proceeded to Lima. They were the first representatives we met of a new kind of foreign penetration into Peru. Where in the past the strangers used to come as speculators or as transient employees of foreign companies, with no loyalties to Peru and little stake in its future, the recent political upheavals in Europe have brought into Latin America many men and women with technical and administrative abilities who come to make a new life for themselves there. In Peru such people have been welcomed, for even the leaders of the politically radical movements realize that the more educated foreigners choose to settle in their country and become Peruvians, the more chance there may be of ending foreign economic control without disasters like that which overtook Mexico when the English and American oil companies drew out their engineers after the expropriation of the petroleum industry in the 1930's.

But the Ortutays were really much too pleasant as people for me to continue to use them as data for sociological generalizations. To run a modern hotel in any fashion with a staff of sixty barely trained Indians would be difficult, but they did it well, and, despite their manifold anxieties, managed to retain a natural charm of manner that was at times a relief from the elaborately self-conscious politeness of the Peruvians. To us they were friendly from the beginning, and their advice and help had a considerable influence on our travels in Peru.

'I will lend you a car for the afternoon,' said Señor Ortutay during our first conversation. 'There was some things in the valley which you really should see.' He mentioned a miraculous shrine and a couple of small towns already influenced by the life of the jungle. After lunch the station wagon belonging to the hotel called for us, and the cholo driver started off for the church of El Señor de Moroguay—the shrine which Señor Ortutay had mentioned.

The broad asphalt road on which we had come from La Oroya continued past Tarma for another forty kilometres in the direction of the jungle. Down the broadening valley the green margin of cultivation crept upwards on the hillsides, and maize grew instead of barley on the terraces and the hanging fields. The trees became more numerous, and the peaches blossomed in the orchards as the climate grew perceptibly milder. We passed through a small town called Acobamba which had a tiny bullring built entirely of mud bricks and roofed over with tiles, and after Acobamba the houses acquired verandas, those architectural accompaniments of a warmer and more leisured life; their posts and the balconies above them were festooned with garlands of black and purple and yellow corn-cobs.

After a while we turned off the highway and drove up a narrow cobbled lane, between banks covered with scarlet wild geranium, towards a white church in the foothills. In the steep fields beside the lane, where ploughs would have been useless, the Indians were digging their potato plots with those peculiar implements called tacllas whose design is derived from the digging sticks of the Incas, with the only difference that a steel point had been substituted for one of fire-hardened wood. The diggers levered up the earth in large dusty clods, and the women came afterwards and broke them up with hoes.

It took us a long time to get to the tiny group of cottages that formed Moroguay, for a donkey walked slowly and obstinately before us all the way, disregarding the driver's wild hooting. The church itself was very simple; its main architectural peculiarity was that it had been built against a granite cliff which formed its end wall. A grinning cretin stood in the doorway and waved us into the interior; he was the only guardian. On the bare rock above the altar was a painting of Christ, covered by a sheet of glass; it looked as though it had been done by some journeyman painter who had seen at least a copy of Raphael. But the legend claimed that one night a group of Indians, lost in a blizzard, had huddled against the cliff for what slight protection it might afford: the next morning, when they gave thanks for being alive, they discovered the painting, which had appeared miraculously during the night. Ever since then, the Señor of Moroguay, as the painting is called, has been conscientiously working wonders for the sick and the unfortunate.

Miraculous paintings and statues play a very large part in Peruvian popular religion, and most of them are representations of Christ. Outside white Lima, the Virgin plays a much less prominent part in Peru than in most other Catholic countries, and no Peruvian Madonna has a prestige that even approaches that of the Dark Virgin of Guadalupe in Mexico. This fits in with the historical pattern, for Inca religion was almost as masculine as that of the Jews in its approach to deity.

The most important of these Peruvian miraculous paintings is that of the Lord of Miracles in Lima, which has a great popular following among the Indians, cholos and negroes. It dates from the mid-seventeenth century, when a liberated negro slave made a painting of Christ on the wall of the fraternity to which he belonged. In an earthquake that followed almost immediately, the wall remained standing while all the buildings around it fell. Soon it began working cures, and it remained unharmed through all the subsequent Lima earthquakes. During the centuries that followed it became an object of almost fanatical devotion among the poorer Limans, and particularly among the negroes, who regard it as their particular charge. Such, indeed, is the painting's prestige that every year, when a reproduction is paraded through the street of Lima, the President kneels ceremonially on the bal-

cony of his palace as it passes by. A curious sidelight upon the
cult of the Lord of the Miracles is given by the fact that in recent
years the painting, evidently unable to act miraculously for its
own preservation, has been fading. In 1954 a painter was brought
from Italy to restore it, but none of the devotees seems to have
regarded it as strange that a wonder-working painting should
decay, or to have doubted that the virtue inherent in the un-
touched original would pass automatically into the restored
version.

The Lord of Moroguay, of course, represents an advance on the
Lord of the Miracles, since it is supposed to have originated, not
from a human but from an angelic hand. I could not glean any information as to its real origin or how its legend sprang into being.
But what seemed to me most interesting about the shrine was the
fact that it had not been exploited in the same way as similar
shrines in other Catholic countries. There was no pretentiousness,
no commercial organization. A line of ugly Victorian painted
vases, filled with peach blossom, stood on the altar, and three
peasant girls prayed before them; the cretin mopped and mowed
in the doorway and a car drew up from which two tight-skirted,
high-heeled women from Acobamba came tottering in to make
their devotions. There was not a priest to be seen.

After Moroguay the trip was disappointing. Palca, the town at
the end of the road, had certainly an atmosphere, but it was the
rather mephitic atmosphere one breathes so often in marginal
communities. The dusty square had its palm trees and its decrepit
bandstand, and slatternly girls in low-cut blouses stood like
characters in a cheap film outside the bead curtains of the only
café; there was a feeling of lassitude, of wilting the midday hours
away, which might have seemed authentic against the green background of the jungle, but carried a suggestion of the bogus in the
setting of bare Sierra hills from which we had not yet emerged.
'Where does the forest begin?' I asked the driver. 'Just five or six
kilometres down the road,' he said. But he had clearly no intention
of going there, and we turned back towards Tarma.

The town of Tarma, which we explored for the first time on our
return from Palca, was a place of greater individuality of character

than Huancayo, and this may have been due partly to its physical compactness. The streets were narrow; they ran up and down the little declivities that broke the surface of the town; they wound and twisted at times in defiance of the orthodox gridiron pattern so usual in South American towns, and they were always liable to peter out in bits of waste ground populated with chattering birds or in deserted gardens where the roses were being crowded out by bluegum saplings. And the deceptive houses, neat and gay from the outside under their fresh white or blue or pink washes, but often gloomy and ill-furnished and earth-floored within, sheltered a host of artisans—cabinet-makers, wheelwrights, saddlers, shoe-makers—who carried on their trades in workshops open to the air. And yet, though so much of its life belonged to a pre-mechanical age, Tarma had less real feeling of antiquity than the country around it; it had been easier among the terraces of Moroguay to remember that this was a valley where the armies of Pachacuti had marched in conquest and where in the middle of the eighteenth century the rebel Juan Santos Atahuallpa had defied the Spaniards for a decade in the name of Indian freedom.

In fact, if any age was reflected at all emphatically in Tarma, it was that of Peru's most recent dictator. A new cathedral of white marble glittered over the plaza, and on the far side of the gardens an equally new municipal hall stood framed between the monkey-puzzles and the date palms. Each bore its grandiloquent legend declaring that the foundation stone had been laid by the President General Odria. And as we walked on through the streets we passed a succession of other new buildings. There were two hand-some modern schools; down by the old iron-roofed shed that served as a market an imaginatively designed hall was almost ready to take its place; near the hotel a large hospital in an anti-septically functional style had been built to supersede the graceful infirmary of cloistered patios and gardens on the main street. The town had inherited the infirmary from some departed religious order; though doubtless crowded and unhygienic, it was certainly the most pleasant-looking building in Tarma.

Such a profusion of new structures in a town which hitherto seemed to have remained content with its nineteenth-century public buildings was strange enough to excite our curiosity. It was obvious that Tarma had been particularly blessed by the departing government of President Odria, but the reason why was not so evident.

Later on, in the hotel bar, Señor Ortutay introduced us to a young Peruvian engineer who was working in the Sierra. We joined them and described our afternoon and our impressions of the shrine of Moroguay. Then I began to talk about Tarma, and asked why there were so many new buildings in the town. Ortutay hesitated. Robles, the engineer, grinned. 'It was all part of the President's programme to improve conditions in Peru,' he said. 'Unfortunately the programme went lopsided in Tarma.' I realized from his manner that he had said as much as he intended to say for the moment, and I changed the subject by asking for some advice on travelling to the Chanchamayo.

'You won't be able to go before Tuesday,' said Ortutay. 'They are building a new road and four days of the week it's closed for blasting.'

'Why on earth do you want to go there?' said Robles. 'If you wish to see the jungle there are much better places than the Chanchamayo, where the trees are scrubby and the rivers are small.'

'Why don't you go to Tingo Maria?' said Ortutay.

'Tingo Maria! Where is Tingo Maria?'

If any place ever trapped us by sheer euphony, it was Tingo Maria. As soon as we heard the name, our minds made themselves up, and all that our companions could tell us in its favour was subsidiary in our thoughts to the notion of a fragile but exotic beauty which the sound of its name had set echoing there. However, we still respected the practical problems of the road, and we listened carefully to what we were told about the four hundred kilometres of mountain and jungle travel towards the north-east that stretched between Tarma and Tingo Maria, which lay on the banks of the Huallaga, one of the great tributaries of the Amazons. We decided to leave for Tingo Maria in two or three days, and Señor Ortutay promised to find out what he could about transport. Then he left us.

'It might be a good idea to take a walk out of doors,' said

Robles. 'Have you seen the hotel zoo?' The sun had already sunk below the high hills when we went out with him, and the valley was filling, like a great water-trough, with shadow and cold. He led us around the back of the hotel to a little enclosed lawn which contained a few rough cages of boards and wire netting and, over in a far corner, a shrine of pebbles like a rustic grotto. The only uncaged animal was a vicuña, slender, fawn-coloured, and looking like a deer whose neck had grown out of all proportion and whose head had developed that expression of a supercilious camel which is common to all the llama family. It seemed to enjoy its spoilt captivity, and when we entered the enclosure it was playing a strange game of hide-and-seek with the Indian boy who looked after the animals, leaping around the cages on its thin legs and flashing its long neck from side to side like a mad periscope to detect the next move of its playmate.

None of the other animals imitated the vicuña's gaiety. A little coatimundi had curled its striped tail over its pointed head and was sleeping in a corner of its cage. A young fox stood shivering in the entrance to his kennel and barked in anger when we looked at him. In the biggest cage a condor sat with great wings drooping down on each side and pointed head thrust forward; all the majesty of the soaring sky bird had gone from this creature of dull plumage and mean aspect.

'He is sad for his mountain-tops,' said Robles. 'Even a condor is fond of his home, and so is a dictator.' He paused and then laughed. 'And that is the answer to your question about Tarma. It is all very simple. President Odria is a native of the town. He went away as a little bare-footed cholito, he made himself a career in the army, he watched his chances carefully, and one day he returned as the dictator of Peru. You must admit that it was only natural that he should wish to impress the people who had known him as a poor boy. That is why Tarma has so many fine buildings. And that is why this hotel is so good. Odria built it for his own pleasure. While he was in power it was often very inconvenient here for the hotel guests, for as soon as the Señor Presidente wished to take a holiday they would all be told to leave. Odria would come on a special train from Lima to La Oroya, and drive down his fine new road to occupy the hotel. And I mean occupy in the military sense. You see the little building beside the gates to the drive? And the two penthouses on the roof? There the guards would watch day and night—machine guns ready—whenever he was in residence.'

In this tale of a dictator's magnanimity, this showering of benefits by a returning hero, there was a touch of the mental attitude of the Arabian Nights. By transforming his native town, Odria was giving concrete expression to the change in his own situation. Yet his actions were also in that patriarchal tradition which characterizes rulers in those countries where political morality sees very little wrong in a man of power looking after his own—his own class, his own friends, his own region.

Robles summed it up with the mild cynicism that we were to hear in almost every Peruvian voice when the talk turned towards politics. 'The moral is that each town in Peru should provide a president in its turn,' he remarked, 'and then in the end every place will be as well off as Tarma. But it will take a long time before all of them can be satisfied, and in the meantime there is much bitterness. You should hear what is being said in all the little towns of the Sierra. Once they envied Tarma. Now they gloat. When Odria is gone, they say, the people of Tarma will begin to feel the bite from his enemies.'

'Do you think Odria will really go?' I asked.

'Of course he will,' said Robles. 'He will go, but those who follow him will be very wise if they leave alone the good things he has done and concentrate on setting right the bad things. Perhaps they will. But I do not know whether we can expect it.' He shrugged his shoulders and led us back to the hotel.

8

The next day, Sunday, we caught the early morning bus to the Huancayo market. It took us over a cross-country road that revealed very dramatically the perils of driving in the Andes once one leaves the few main highways. Deceptively, the road began in a mild gravel lane leading out of Tarma into a dank valley where a stream gabbled over its cascades among meagre thickets of willow trees. But soon it narrowed into a dirt track, scooped and gouged by the rains, and barely wide enough for a single vehicle. This mockery of a road began to climb the steep wall of the valley in a series of hairpin bends, so sharp that the bus could not take one of them in a single turn. Each time there had to be a series of complicated backings and creepings forward, during which the outer wheels would churn and manœuvre within inches of the precipitous verge. A slight miscalculation in steering, a barrow-load of earth crumbling away from the edge that looked so insecure, and nothing could have saved us from crashing far down into the valley.

At such moments we realized that the warnings we had been given about Andean roads by people like Señor Merida had not been all exaggeration. As if to emphasize the lesson, one of the sharpest corners was decorated by a cluster of small wooden crosses, on some of which wreaths of paper flowers were still decaying. 'A truck went over,' the driver explained, grinning. 'Many Indians were killed.' The light way in which he talked of the tragedy did not strike me as callous; rather, it seemed to express a stoical acceptance of danger and a relief that—this time at least—his own cross had not been among those thrust into the treacherously loose earth beside the road.

Eventually, travelling through serpentine villages of white mud houses and over bushy slopes that were fragrant with a kind of yellow acacia, we climbed to the high, bare grasslands on the top of the range. The long curves of the open pastures were broken, here and there, by grey traces of the Inca roads and by ragged outcrops of rocks from which, as we approached, small mountain birds would burst in twittering clouds. On the other side of the pass the road fell in serpentines into a valley bright with abundant quinoa. Here the villages were more compact and also more dirty than those near Tarma, and their people had a formidable naturalness of manner. Once a magnificently dressed young peasant woman who had got on at one of these villages asked the driver to stop the bus. She stepped down, spreading her crimson skirts about her like the corolla of a gigantic poppy, and squatted unconcernedly in full view of us all; a moment later, rising and lifting her skirts clear of the ground with an adroit twist of the hands, she walked back to the bus, not without dignity. The Indians looked on indifferently, some half-breeds laughed, and the driver, as he released the brake, muttered: 'Son animales!' with all the contempt that divides the mountain cholo from the Indian.

When we reached Huancayo, the feria was already in full swing; it had transformed the town almost unrecognizably. This was the largest market in the Andes, and possibly the largest in Latin America. Multitudes of Indians had come in from the haciendas of the valleys and from the communities of the mountainsides, travelling by truck and bus, on horse and donkey, and often on foot, driving their slow trains of llamas through the early morning darkness or toiling down the mountain paths with their own backs burdened under the produce they hoped to sell. And they had turned Huancayo, from the cholo town it was on any weekday, into an Indian fairground where one tramped among crowds in homespun for whom the twentieth century existed mainly as a source of wonder.

Many of these Indians were members of villages still organized on the ayllu system which was already old when the Inca dynasty began. Under this system the land belongs to a commune (or ayllu), and it is re-divided regularly so that each adult in the village gets his fair portion, while many tasks like house-building for newly-married couples are shared by the group. The ayllus are mostly self-supporting; they grow food primarily for their own consumption, with the potato as the basis of their farming, and they weave their cloth from wool produced by their own sheep. In the markets they sell only the scanty surplus of subsistence farming, and buy such useful or colourful objects as they themselves cannot make. There are nearly five thousand such communities in Peru alone, and many in Bolivia.

Some of the people of the ayllus whom we saw in Huancayo were far more primitive than the valley Indians with whom we were already familiar. Often they were almost unbelievably dirty, and poverty did not seem to be the cause, for some of the most expensively dressed, the most heavily loaded with gold rings and bracelets, were among the least washed. Physically, even, they seemed a different race, leaner, smaller, darker. The women were often bare-footed, the men shod in hairy pieces of llama skin drawn together roughly by leather thongs. With their hair unkempt over their timid, shifting eyes, these people would flit agitatedly from stall to stall, chattering in Quechua among themselves, and occasionally, if they felt courageous, bringing out to some dealer a phrase in a Spanish that sounded outlandish even to our ears. At lunchtime many of them crowded around the hotel to gaze through the dining-room windows at the strange manners of the creoles; under their blank, persistent gaze one felt like a fish in an aquarium on Bank Holiday.

What struck me immediately on looking at the stalls in the market was the enormous quantity of manufactured goods that had found their way into the mountains. The displays of cheap cloth and ready-made garments alone stretched for hundreds of gaudy yards. There were sellers of furniture, of mattresses, of great tin chests painted as gaily as gypsy caravans, and of plaster figures of Santiago valiantly flourishing his sword against the heathen. Only here and there, in this flood of modern shoddiness, did one come across the native craftsmanship for which the feria was once celebrated. The potters, who still contribute so much to Mexican and Guatemalan markets, had almost vanished, routed by the triumphant vendors of enamel ware, who stood shouting by their stalls with chamber-pots on their heads. Even the better handwoven cloth (which is still made in considerable quantities) did not reach the market, and we tried vainly to buy some of the beautiful materials which the Indian women wear. There were, indeed, some gourds carved in relief pictures of the mountain farmer's life which had a stiff Egyptian quality, and some wooden spoons from the jungle with geometrically patterned handles. But these scanty examples only emphasized how far craftsmanship has decayed in Peru since the eighteenth century. During that time there has been no growth of any kind within the Andean Indian culture, but only a slow draining away of the creative impulse in the imitation of set styles, followed, in the end, by the decay of these styles themselves under the impact of modern mass-production.

Yet, if the Indian no longer practises to a great extent the craftsmanship of the Inca days or of the first stimulating period of contact with Christianity, his life is linked with the past in ways which are perhaps just as fundamental, and there are aspects of a market like that of Huancayo which have undoubtedly hardly changed at all over the past four or five centuries.

We saw this, for instance, in the products which the peasants had brought in for sale in the vegetable market. In almost every case they were the fruits of plants already grown in this region when the Sun God shared with his worshippers the crops of the Andean terraces. Maize and beans and potatoes—all native to the Americas—were there in an amazing variety of strains and colours. Of the potato alone five hundred types are said to be grown in the Andes; the most prized in Huancayo was a small yellow variety to which the women would draw our attention, shouting at Inge: 'Las amarillas, señora! Las amarillas! Son buenas!' But more curious were the tiny dried potatoes that looked like grey, semi-translucent pebbles. These had been subjected to the most ancient of dehydration processes, and, by means of alternate freezings and sun dryings, had been reduced to about a fifth of their normal weight. Potatoes of this kind, which keep indefinitely, are called chuño, and once they were a great staple of the granaries in which the Incas kept supplies of food as a precaution against famine. Another tuber we saw at Huancayo, where it seemed almost as popular as the potato, was shaped like a Jerusalem artichoke, but its ivory skin was blotched and mottled with red and purple. It belonged to a plant called oca, which is peculiar to the Andes, where it has been a popular food for millennia.

If, in health, the Sierra Indian eats and grows almost exactly what his forefathers did, in sickness he remains just as faithful to tradition. A whole section of the market was occupied by native healers, or curanderos, and to look at their stalls was to slip back into the magic-ridden nightmare of medieval medicine. There were, of course, many seeds and leaves which doubtless had some curative value, for the modern European pharmacopoeia is largely indebted to the discoveries of Peruvian Indians. But the curanderos regard herbal medicine as only secondary; sympathetic magic is the real basis of their healing. Their stalls were cluttered with such ingredients of the witches' sabbath as snake-skins and armadillo shells, hides of foxes, paws of porcupines and bodies of freshly killed condors. All of these had a place in the lore of the Inca medicine man; the broth made from a young condor, for example, was strongly recommended for the relief of feeble-mindedness. But some fragments of European magic seemed also to have been adopted, for the curanderos sold spiral gold rings on which written charms had been engraved; these seemed indispensable to both the Indian women and the cholas, and we noticed that even the poorest peasant from the remote hills would wear at least one of them.

The curanderos of the Sierra are a feared and honoured profession—a profession which is almost a cult, with its traditions, its ritual and even its Mecca, for the best healers, feared as sorcerers and valued as counter-sorcerers, come from the village of Collahuayas in the Bolivian altiplano. In the past the Collahuayans would wander over the Sierra from Quito down to the Gran Chaco; stricter frontiers have doubtless restricted their journeys, but still their methods dominate Andean folk medicine. Their secrets are guarded, so far as the Indians are concerned, by terror, and, so far as strangers are concerned, by silence. Usually we found the Indians in the markets quite willing to talk about whatever merchandise they might have for sale, but this was never the case with the curanderos, and to the most elementary queries about the names of plants or seeds they would always reply with a hostile: 'No sabe! I don't know.'

But heresy creeps even into Indian medicine, and the Collahuayans have their unorthodox rivals in the Sierra markets; these are Jivaro Indians from the Amazonian forests, who have as great a reputation in the jungle as the men of Collahuayas in the mountains. The Jivaros are a venturesome people, and many of them find their way into the Andes and even down to the coast, where they live by selling remedies made from jungle plants. There were two of them at Huancayo, a middle-aged shaman and a youth who acted as his assistant. They had the kind of picturesque oddity which the real curanderos lacked. They wore the striped toga called cushma which is characteristic of their tribe; on their heads were basketwork coronets, and bands of black and white beads were crisscrossed over their chests like ribbons of distinguished orders. They were nimble men, with mobile, knowing faces, and they enticed the duller mountain Indians with a miniature circus which any self-respecting Collahuayan would have despised. Two monkeys played tricks, a coatimundi was pulled out of a sack and put back hurriedly when he refused to perform, and a young boa-constrictor with magnificent orange lozenges was induced to wreathe himself torpidly around the shoulders of the assistant. Finally, the shaman himself went through the vivid pantomime of a man, in the extreme agonies of toothache, gaining miraculous relief from applying an infallible mixture which the assistant immediately began to hawk among the crowd, in sealed envelopes bearing the medicine man's photograph. It was one of those occasions when two worlds slip together, for the Jivaro shaman's peculiar antics reminded me vividly of a Negro quack who haunted the Shropshire markets in my boyhood, selling mandrake root as a universal panacea.

The nearest thing to a universal panacea in the Andes is the coca leaf, which is used, not for the exceptional ailments of the flesh, but for the hunger, exhaustion, cold and boredom which are the daily sicknesses of Sierra life. One hardly travels a day from Lima without noticing the Indians chewing ruminatively on their green quids as they hump their burdens through the streets of the Sierra towns, but it is in markets like that of Huancayo, where most of the coca-trading goes on, that one realizes the role this mild narcotic plays in the lives of millions of Peruvians.

Coca is a state monopoly, but the actual selling is done by chola women, whom we saw in Huancayo, sitting as solemnly as Rhadamanthus before the brass scales on which they carefully weighed out the small, dried green leaves. They had many customers, mostly of the poorer class of Indians, who would buy their coca by the double handful and thrust it into woven pouches; afterwards, they would often go on to other merchants who sold the prepared lime which the coca eater carries with him in a bag made from a bull's scrotum. A pinch of the lime, taken with each wad of leaves, helps to release the narcotic quality of the coca.

So far as we could see there is no attempt at a serious control of coca consumption. The state makes a middleman's profit, but the Indian appears to buy as much as he can afford. This is one of the ways in which Andean life has actually changed a great deal since the days of the Incas, who used coca moderately for its pain-killing and euphoric qualities, but supervised its distribution so that the people should not become addicted to its use. The Spaniards, however, found that it was profitable to grow coca and sell it in unlimited quantities; they also found that with coca an Indian will work more, endure worse conditions, and be content with less food. With such manifest advantages to be gained from free distribution, the Spanish authorities never gave serious thought to control, and the present universal coca-eating of the Sierra dates from the elegant age of the Viceroys. No Peruvian government, of any political tinge, has since been prepared either to abandon the profit it can gain from coca or to risk the Indian unrest that might result from restriction, and among educated Peruvians there is still a great deal of disagreement as to whether coca-eating is really harmful.

As we walked on through the feria, observing, comparing, ex-claiming and clicking our camera with a diffidence which lost us all the most revealing shots, we moved to the noisy throb of Andean music, blaring crudely from the cheap cantinas, which celebrated the weekly arrival of the Indians by playing records of Sierra music. It was a strange music—quite unlike the Spanish-Negro style of the coast; wild and melancholy, curiously complex in its rhythms and so oriental in its tone that for a moment, when first we heard it, we imagined that some Chinese bar-keeper must be playing nostalgically the songs of his own country.

The music from the loudspeakers was so distorted that we could hardly distinguish the instruments that were being played, but we soon had an opportunity to listen to living Sierra music, for when we entered the main plaza we heard the mountain rhythms once again and saw that one pavement of the square was occupied entirely by makers of musical instruments, the one craft that still flourishes without diminution, since it is in music more than in anything else that the vitality of the Indian past is preserved.

In one group sat the men and women from the hill villages which specialize in drum-making; softly and in curious little rhythms they beat their instruments of llama skin, listening intently and carefully adjusting the strings whose tightness determined the pitch. Beyond them sat the makers of the quenas, the short cane flutes whose shrill notes add the eerie background quality to the Sierra dances. And finally, flourishing their great instruments over the heads of the other musicians, there were the men who had brought from the jungle villages along the Ucayali the larger bassoon-like quenas, at least ten feet long, which need strength to hold and skill to play; we saw many men lay them down with disgust after producing no sound worth the name of music, but in the hands of experts they gave a deep sound like that of a long Tibetan trumpet, so rich and at the same time so dolorous that it seemed to express more effectively than any other music the feeling of melancholy which accompanied one's delight at all the coloured gaiety of the sunlit Andean world.

Gaiety and melancholy: as we walked that afternoon among the thousands of Indians from all the strange inhabited corners of the valleys and mountains, among men and women from the edge of the jungle and the edge of the snowline, we realized how much these qualities were combined in the nature of the Andean people as well as in their music and their country. They strike one at first as a sad race, but the stony gravity of their faces can change abruptly into laughter, and that night, as we drove back to Tarma, we caught a glimpse of this other aspect of a people for whom the burdens on their backs seemed so often the best of symbols. On the edge of a village which we passed just as the light was failing, the beat of drums and the shrill of quenas was starting up, and we could see the women whirling into the wild and monotonous course of the huayno, that spinning, skipping, skirt-swirling mountaineers' dance which is the favourite of the Andes. In comparison with the people we had seen all day, these seemed transformed into the personifications of freedom from care. And yet there were many who still danced with the burdens on their backs.

PART II

Descent to the Forest

I

Our journey to Tingo Maria began with the morning bus from Tarma to La Oroya; there we took a camioneta—an overgrown station wagon holding a dozen people—to the mining town of Cerro de Pasco. From Cerro de Pasco, which lay about a third of the way to Tingo Maria, we would have to trust to chance, since the transport of the Andes is in the hands of small local companies and nobody in Tarma could tell us what might run on roads fifty miles away. All they could say was that there would always be something—a bus or a coca truck returning to the jungle—which would take us farther along the road.

The first part of the journey went smoothly enough, and the only discomfort we experienced was caused innocently by an Indian who sat beside Inge in the camioneta from La Oroya. He was a shy and inoffensive man, but he held in his lap a covered basket full of chicks from which arose a stench so pungent that Inge found it almost a physical torture to breathe. I was in the acute stage of a cold which the chilly air of the previous night had aggravated to the point where I was unable to detect even the rankest smell, so that the obvious solution would have been to change seats at the first stop. But we were both so anxious not to give any appearance of race or caste prejudice that we did nothing of the kind, and Inge endured her discomfort until the Indian got down at a village half-way to Cerro de Pasco. Remembering the incident, I wonder at our punctiliousness, and I also wonder whether the Indian would have been sensitive enough to detect any insult in our changing places, but I think that if we were again in such a situation in a country of strong social prejudices we would probably act in the same way.

From La Oroya the road climbed to the high plateau of the Pampa de Junin. It was a vast moorland without trees or even the smallest bush, lifted fourteen thousand feet above the sea, ringed by magnificent saw-toothed ranges which eventually knit together in the Nudo de Pasco, and overhung most of the time by leaden snow-clouds. Country of this kind is known in the Andes as puna, and its principal vegetation is the tough ichu grass. Cultivation is difficult, for on the puna even barley will not ripen, and the only crop we saw was some hardy variety of potato.

Because of the difficulties of agriculture, the inhabitants of the Pampa rely almost entirely on their herds. Near to La Oroya there were several large sheep and cattle ranches, fenced off as carefully as American ranges, but as the ground grew higher and more swampy, the pastures were abandoned to the Indian rancheros, a race of horsemen, wrapped in great brown ponchos, who rode across the country after their tiny herds on fast and wiry little ponies.

Despite its poor vegetation and its harsh climate, the Pampa was surprisingly well-inhabited, like every corner of the Andes where the Indian feels he will be left in peace. The rancheros had fenced off small fields with dry stone walls, and in these they grew their tiny patches of potatoes and kept whatever animals they did not allow to roam the open puna. Each farm had a small square house of pebbles or, more often, of turf, and a barn of the same materials, usually circular in shape, with a high conical roof. The prehistoric dwellings of the Orkneys must have been very similar to these barns, and the whole aspect of the bare little farmsteads on the stark moor, with dark piles of peat standing before the houses, reminded one of the descriptions of primitive Scottish crofts in the days before the great migrations from the Highlands.

Life in the farmhouses was probably as elemental as it was on the bare puna, for the houses rarely had even an opening where a window might have gone, and, though the wind was extremely cold, I saw no smoke rising from the dwellings. The women cooked out of doors, by slow and smoky turf fires; what they cooked, apart from potatoes, I do not know, but there were so many guinea-pigs browsing about the farms that these animals must have formed an important part of their diet.

Like many pastoral peoples, the Indians of the Pampa lived

mostly on scattered holdings, though there were signs of a social life binding them together. Here and there in the open country, for instance, we would pass little chapels dedicated to the Lord of the Miracles, an appropriate enough object of worship in this desperate landscape, and there were also isolated cemeteries where the graves were marked by square piles of stones, each crowned by a cross and framing an oven-like hole, charred with candle smoke and used for placing offerings to the spirits of the dead. Sometimes the crosses were surrounded by many broken bottles, mementos of the graveside orgies which in the Andes often follow immediately after a funeral.

Even the two places on the Pampa which were regarded as towns —Junin and Carhuamayo—were merely sprawling rural settlements, where every house stood in its own field and the plaza was a stretch of rough ground on which the rancheros tethered their horses when they visited the municipia. Everything in these towns was drab and joyless, for the melancholy of the landscape had entered so far into the people's minds that they seemed to have no desire for the colour with which other Andeans brighten their lives, and even the women dressed in dull tones that harmonized all too well with the dark pastures.

It was when we were going through this region that we first became aware of the careful watch which is kept on travellers in Peru. When we had booked our seats for the camioneta in La Oroya, the women in the transport office had asked our names, our passport numbers and our ages. We thought the requests curious, but since it is the custom for regular transport services in Peru to ask the passengers to take out insurances costing a few pence (an eloquent enough comment on Andean roads!) we imagined that the information would be needed in this connection.

In Junin, however, the camioneta drew up before a building where two officers of the Guardia Civil, the semi-military rural police, stood watching the road. They were both, in that region of stunted people, tall men in grey uniforms, jackbooted and spurred, with revolvers at their belts and cavalry sabres clanking on the cobblestones as they walked towards us. The driver pulled out a paper which, as I looked over his shoulder, I saw to be a list of passengers, presenting all the information we had given about ourselves. He handed it to one of the guards, who ran his finger down it and then stepped up to look into the camioneta. His eyes rested on us for a moment, and I heard the driver say, 'Si, los extranjeros, señor Guardia.' The guard nodded, made some remark to his companion, and then waved the driver on. The same thing happened at Carhuamayo and again on the edge of Cerro de Pasco.

This was our introduction to a procedure which became so familiar by the time we left Peru that, unless it was accompanied by some special incident, we accepted it as part of the routine of travel. At first we associated it with the régime of General Odria, and thought of it as a dictator's device which would pass away with his departure. But the Guardia were just as zealous in their inspections under the democratic Prado, after he came into office a fortnight later. Perhaps out of fear, our fellow passengers were usually disinclined to talk very freely about the practice. Some said that it was a check on smuggling, but the Guardia were clearly much more interested in people than in goods, and I think those who suggested in rather veiled terms that the inspections were political in nature, aimed at tracing possible revolutionary agents, came much nearer to the truth. Every Peruvian government lives in fear of its own people, and in countries where this happens the functions of the police are wide and their power is great. It would be hard to imagine men who appeared more conscious of that power, or more proud of it, than the Guardia Civil, a force created by the dictators of pre-war years and actually trained, until the beginning of the last war, by Italian Fascist officers; they were the only group of Peruvians for whom I felt an enduring dislike.

North of Junin dark, peat-stained pools broke the surface of the monotonous puna, and soon we came to the Lago de Junin itself, which filled a great dip in the plateau twenty miles long and several wide. Dense, dark-brown reedbeds stretched far out from its shores, and as we approached them the ducks and waterhens flew in large noisy flocks over the water in the direction of the strange basaltic formations on the lake's farther shores which are known as the Forest of Stone.

Beyond the lake the gap between the mountains narrowed sharply and the Pampa ended in the bare valley where Cerro de Pasco is situated; a town of 20,000 people which flourishes—if one can apply such a word to its grim industrial existence—at 14,300 feet, some two thousand feet above Lhasa.

Cerro de Pasco has a long history, and, more than most Peruvian towns, it still shows the various stages of its development. Coming down the hill where the American engineers live in their modern clapboard bungalows, we entered the narrow pot-holed streets of the original Spanish settlement. Many of the shops and run-down posadas had been mansions in the Colonial days and they retained their massive oak balconies and great carved doors opening through rococo archways whose gracefulness had long become decrepit. Centuries of grime had sifted over them and centuries of mountain weather had bitten into their surfaces, so that Pasco, a handsome town in photographs, seemed as sad a sight in the unflattering mountain sunlight as a beauty who has surrendered to the years.

The original Pasco was built on the profits of silver. The first mine was opened in 1630, and for a while, until Potosi excelled it, this was the most prosperous silver town in South America. Like many of the Spanish settlements, it combined a superficial gracefulness of life with extreme misery, and travellers in the early nineteenth century still saw the ore from the mines being brought to the surface by Indian porters. By this time, however, the mine-owners had realized the need for modernization, and their efforts to obtain machinery resulted in a minor epic of the Industrial Revolution which in its way was as curious as the story of Honest Henry Meiggs. James Watt, who was first approached, claimed that it was impossible to make engines which could be dismantled into parts small enough to be transported into the Andes. But Trevithick, the gigantic Cornish wrestler who invented the loco-motive, accepted the contract, designed the engines, which were adapted to the low atmospheric pressure of these altitudes, and persuaded Hazeldine, the Bridgnorth ironmaster, to build them.

Then he shipped them in parts on the South Sea whaler *Wildman*, which sailed around Cape Horn and docked at Callao, where a great mule train was formed and, accompanied by Trevithick, climbed the narrow pack trails which were then the only roads in the Andes, crossed the divide at almost seventeen thousand feet, and reached Pasco with enough parts left, despite losses over precipices on the way, for Trevithick to set the pumps going.

By the mid-nineteenth century the silver mines were almost worked out, and Cerro de Pasco began to decline. But when it was nearly a ghost town, copper became a vital industrial metal, and at the turn of the century Pierpoint Morgan and his associates bought up all the important mining claims in the Central Andes and formed the Cerro de Pasco Corporation. Today, for a hundred miles along the spine of the western Andes, from Casapalca to Cerro de Pasco itself, the word of the Corporation is very near to law. Two large towns and several smaller settlements are virtually under its control; it owns a private railway 150 miles long, five hydro-electric power stations and a million acres of ranches; it operates its own system of hospitals, schools and department stores, and it has the privilege of exemption from custom duties. Next to the Army and possibly the Church, it is the most powerful single organization in Peru. Like most corporations of its kind, it lies open to many obvious criticisms, and yet its influence has not been wholly negative, for it has given the miners better treatment than they would have received on the native haciendas, while its efforts to provide health services and schools have set standards which eventually may move the Peruvian authorities to emulation.

Despite all these changes, Cerro de Pasco had acquired surprisingly little of the atmosphere of a modern industrial centre. The mine buildings lay outside; the town itself, with its hilly, miry streets, its crowds of Indian women, its market, might well—but for its peculiar sooty decrepitude—have been the centre of a purely agricultural region.

The camioneta drove uphill into the plaza. It was the end of the trip; the driver, knowing we wanted to reach Huanuco, the next large town on the way, circled the square, shouting at the buses and trucks that were getting ready to leave. None of them was going to Huanuco. 'They say there will be a bus at three,' he told us. 'Be sure to take it, señores! Pasco is not a good place to stay the night.' He rubbed his hands and shuddered with simulated cold before he drove off.

It was not yet noon. We walked through the plaza, past the shabby little shops, past the coca-sellers, past the old woman with the mangy green parrot that told fortunes by picking out slips of paper, and round and round the dejected flower-beds where only a few stunted daisies defied the rigour of the climate. It was the ugliest spot we ever reached in the Andes. Even the Pampa de Junin had a magnitude in its desolation which stirred some melancholy response in one. But this windy denuded square, with its mean buildings, was as ugly without redemption as a prison yard. To have to stay even for three hours seemed insupportable, and we made ourselves all the more gloomy by trying to imagine the state of mind of people who chose, for the sake of a career or a living, to inhabit such a place as Cerro de Pasco for years on end. 'If Shelley had seen this,' commented Inge, 'he would never have said Hell is a city much like London.'

On our third turn of the square a Civil Guard stepped out from behind a lorry. He had a moustache of theatrical ferocity, and we expected at least to be asked for our papers and to be questioned about our reasons for travelling. But the guard merely asked us where we were going and then, when he heard we wished to reach Huanuco, said that he would find us some way of getting there. In a moment he was back. The persuasive powers of a member of the Guardia Civil are evidently greater than those of a mere camioneta driver, for he told us, with great self-satisfaction, that we could travel on a bus that was leaving almost immediately for Ambo. Ambo, he explained, was a town well on the way to Huanuco, and between the two places there were buses running all the time.

We had already enough experience to distrust such glib assurances, but we decided that even if we got no farther than Ambo, it could not fail to be better than Cerro de Pasco. The bus, we found, was a curious hybrid vehicle of a type common in the

Andes. On the chassis of an ordinary truck a local wheelwright builds a great oblong superstructure, which gives a lumbering, top-heavy appearance, obviously decreases stability, but at the same time allows a much larger cargo to be carried than that for which the truck was originally intended. The front part is roofed over and fitted with four or five hard benches; the back is open, and is loaded with whatever merchandise the driver picks up on his way.

Like boats and railway engines, all these dangerous-looking vehicles have their own names, and that which went to Ambo was called the King of the Mountains. It was almost full of Indian women and children, but the driver quickly cleared the seats beside him, and we arranged ourselves there with difficulty, since the benches had been fitted to suit the Indian figure, and the extra two or three inches in the length of our legs condemned us to a fidgeting discomfort all the way to our destination.

Edging from the plaza, the King of the Mountains drove out past the rows of miners' barracks and took the road towards the final pass over the Nudo de Pasco, beyond which we descended steeply beside a little stream that was grey and polluted from the sludge of the mines. It was the beginning of the Huallaga, that great Amazonian tributary which we were to follow for the rest of our journey.

The bus ground on down the narrow gravel road and swung awkwardly, with all its great superstructure creaking, around the bends. At the sharpest of them the little monkey-faced driver would quickly and surreptitiously cross himself and glance up at the shrine of the Lord of the Miracles that was attached to his windshield before he grappled with the wheel as fiercely as if he were wrestling with a demon.

We were descending from bleakness towards warmth, from the treeless monotony of the high plateaux towards the fertility of the montaña, and almost every twist of the road brought some new plant or bush to vary the texture of the hillsides and the cliffs around us. Soon we entered a series of ravines whose high and often overhanging walls were furred over with large glaucous leaves and pitted with caves. One of the larger caverns had been transformed into a shrine; within its darkness a whole galaxy of candles glittered, accentuating the natural fretting of the roof so that it looked like some vast creation of Gothic fancy. Occasionally, when the ravine broadened, we would see tiny pastures hanging high above the road, so steep in appearance that one wondered how the few sheep grazing there could fail to drop into the chasm. And once every two or three miles there would be a stone hut, tucked into some angle of streamside meadow, with llama skins drying on the ground beside it and a few tiny terraces clinging like swallows' nests to the rocks.

Out of the gorges we emerged into a rufous country of conical hills where the adobe houses were as red as the land itself and even the river, purged at last of the clouding impurities from the mines, had taken on the purplish tinge which in childhood one attributed to the rivers that were said to run with blood after historic battles. Rain had fallen—the first we encountered in Peru—and in the damp fields peasants were out working with tacllas and hoes, preparing the earth for sowing and tending the green lines of plants that shone freshly against the bright, wet earth. At first the fields were planted with potatoes, interspersed with rows of melons and of white-flowered beans. Later, it was the soft green of young maize that covered the terraces, and this was a sign that we had left behind us the harsh climate of the tablelands.

All the time, through the ravines and the red hills, the voice of Flores went on softly behind us, with an amiable and ultimately wearying persistence. Flores was, apart from ourselves, the only non-Indian passenger, a young cholo in a blazer and a panama hat who had got on the bus at the petrol station outside Cerro de Pasco, with a jealously clutched briefcase as his only luggage. Immediately he introduced himself—Miguel Flores, a proud native of Huanuco and an employee of the Corporation. He held, I imagine, some clerical or minor supervisory position; certainly he told us dutifully that the miners were all contented and that nowhere—in Peru at least—could any man hope for a better employer than the great American company.

But these, I suspect, were *pro forma* declarations, since, once Flores had made them, he was not interested in talking at any length about the Corporation or anything else so familiar. He was one of those half-educated, miscellaneously read men, still common in the provincial towns of Peru, who hunger and thirst after knowledge as others after righteousness. It is men like these who buy up the old-fashioned autodidactic literature which is published in Lima and sold in large quantities in the smaller towns; facts are their bread and wine, holy and sustaining at the same time, and they have an almost magical belief in the power conferred by the mere accumulation of scraps of learning.

Flores clearly regarded us as an almost miraculous windfall for a man in the ardent pursuit of knowledge. He began by telling us that he spoke Spanish, Quechua and a little English, and gave a virtuoso display of the learning he had already acquired by declaring that English and Quechua had more in common with each other than either with Spanish, and by proving it with examples. To us, who knew no Quechua, it sounded most plausible; it also served to establish Flores in our minds as a serious young man. From this point he could follow his two main lines of attack. First he wanted to find out what we, as foreigners, thought of Peru. Secondly, he was intent on gathering whatever facts he could about the countries we already knew.

Flores had too much Peruvian politeness to accept without giving, and he offered some crumbs of information in return for the loaves he expected of us, but he managed so well that now I recollect very little that he actually taught us during the hours in which we talked to him. On the other hand, he had all the half-conceited desire of the man in love with facts to impart them to those he regarded as more ignorant than himself, and he used the occasion, not merely to satisfy his own curiosity, but also to enlighten the Indian women who sat around him. Thus our conversation took on a curious pendulum quality.

'Ah, Canada!' Flores would say. 'You come from Canada! Now they tell me that Canada is a cold country, with much ice and snow. Is that true, señores?'

'Not entirely,' I would answer, and tell of the hot summers in the prairies and the warm winters of the Gulf of Georgia.

'Verdad?' Flores would exclaim with almost childish astonishment. 'So it is sometimes hot in Canada!' Then, having absorbed this amazing piece of information, he would turn to the Indian women and repeat, with urgency, 'They tell me it is hot in Canada!' And the Indian women, who clearly had not the least idea what or where Canada might be, would stare and giggle, and chatter together in incomprehensible Quechua.

'Tell me,' Flores would continue, 'is it a fact that there are penguins in Canada?' And so the interrogation would go on until he had satisfied himself as thoroughly as possible on the fauna of North America, on the way in which the Rockies differed from the Andes, and particularly on the political status of Canada, for, like many Peruvians, he thought that the independence of the British dominions was a myth and that the Commonwealth operated in the same way as the Spanish Empire of the eighteenth century. I still doubt whether he really believed my explanation that sharing a monarch does not necessarily mean sharing a government.

But, most of all, Flores enjoyed discussing Mexico, and here he was seeking, not facts for their own sake, so much as some kind of assurance that Peru meant something within its own Latin American world. 'And which do you prefer,' he asked, after a few tentative questions; 'Mexico or Peru?' Clearly our answer would mean a great deal to him, and yet it was a question which even now neither of us could answer simply. But we had already undergone the softening influence of Peruvian behaviour. Why hurt the feelings of this pleasant young man—and possibly damn for ever in his eyes the manners of the English—by refusing him on some abstract grounds of sincerity the answer he expected? 'Of course we prefer Peru!' I declared impulsively. 'Verdad!' shouted Flores. 'You hear! They say Peru is better than Mexico.' And then began the relentless questioning as to why we preferred Peru, and we retreated from one slippery generalization to the next. Mexico was more violent than Peru. The Peruvians were more friendly than the Mexicans. The Andes were more magnificent than the Sierra Madre. Pulque was worse than chicha, and pisco was better than tequila. And with every fatuous step we sank in our own esteem, we clearly rose in that of Flores. The three of us would travel together all the way to Huanuco, he declared, and then he would find some way of reaching Tingo Maria the next day, so that, to show his friendship, he could have the privilege of introducing us to the jungle.

Meanwhile we stopped in a little town of yellow adobe houses called San Rafael. Flores and the driver led us into what they described as the only possible restaurant. It was a low room with an earthen floor, lit only by a wide doorway, and there we sat around a large table covered with gaudy oilcloth—the driver and Flores, Inge and I, and one of the Indian women who seemed a little more prosperous and sophisticated than the rest. The other passengers waited in the bus for our return; they, like the Incas, had dined in the morning. The food, which was cooked on a battery of Primus stoves, was surprisingly good—a thick, piquant chupe, and then a well-seasoned dish of lamb and rice. With an execrable cup of coffee—which we took against the advice of Flores, who drank manzanilla tea himself—it cost about eighteen pence each.

The proprietor of the eating-house was something of an original. He was an old sergeant of the Peruvian army, and he claimed—though I could not follow his rather incoherent explanations—to have served at some time in his career beside the British. To convince us, he stood by the table and bellowed: 'Ri' turn! Lef' turn! Stan' eesee!' And then he went on to make in Quechua a series of what were clearly rather malicious anti-British jokes; Flores and the driver laughed immoderately, and we sat smiling in the sickly manner of those who know they are the butts of incomprehensible jests and have resolved to put the best face on the situation.

San Rafael was the end of the real Sierra. Beyond stretched hot hills covered with prickly pear or yellow with ripening maize. Ambo, which we reached at about four in the afternoon, was a pleasant white town, with a green, bushy plaza where the King of the Mountains ended its journey. A band was playing down the street, and the square was full of honey-coloured, pigtailed girls in gaudy satin dresses, and youths in blue serge trousers and white shirts; fashions had changed, and the people were lighter and more slender than the Indians of the plateau. We had descended more than 7,000 feet and, though there were still another 6,000 to go to the Amazon valley, for the first time in Peru we had the feeling of a tropical country.

As we got down from the bus, the band began to march up towards the plaza. 'It is the music of our Lady of Carmen,' said Flores. 'It is her fiesta,' said the driver, 'but there is no bus for Huanuco. Perhaps there will be one tonight.' 'It might be Mexico,' I said, forgetting Flores. We gestured to each other with resignation. Flores seemed touched for the honour of Peru. 'There is no need to stay,' he said. 'Let us share a taxi to Huanuco. It will only be forty soles.' We agreed, and Flores hurried off to telephone, while we watched the fiesta procession approaching.

It was very small and simple in comparison with fiestas we had seen in Mexico. The band marched first, in white shirts and big straw hats, playing lilting tunes like those of Basque peasant dances; next came a company of boys carrying paper Judas figures on long canes, and then a group of men who fired rockets into the air as they walked. Behind trotted the crowd, and many among them, I noticed, had red eyes from some kind of ophthalmia. The band marched on to the steps before the church, and played its loudest; the rockets whooshed upwards and the sticks fell clattering into the plaza; the girls put white and pink camellias in their black hair. Then the boys began to plant their Judases in the flower beds. Around each cane a Catherine wheel had been fixed, and one of the men ran forward to light the first of them. The wheel spluttered and flared, the stick began to spin, drunkenly, and as the paper Judas caught fire it fell to the ground with an angry fizz while the crowd cheered.

That was all we saw of the fiesta, for Flores returned to say that he had found a friend with a taxi. Everything was arranged. All we had to do was to wait for a lady whom the driver wished to take with him. They arrived a moment afterwards, but the lady, a fat, exuberant chola, was accompanied by her daughter and an old and silent man whose relationship to her or to the taxi driver we never discovered. All of us packed into the small, old-fashioned car, but still it was a great deal more comfortable than the bus.

As we approached Huanuco the valley levelled out into the borderland farming country which lies between the real Sierra and the forest-covered slopes of the montaña, as the jungle is called in Peru. It was the country of great sugar estates, and every few kilometres we would pass the massive quadrangle of a hacienda. On one side of the square would stand the sugar mill and the tall-chimneyed aguardiente distillery, and on the other sides the warehouses and stables and the manager's quarters; the heavy wooden yard gates would be open to let in the trucks and ox-wagons loaded with cane. Outside the quadrangle, in monotonous rows, were the labourers' quarters, which consisted of a small, bare cubicle, with unglazed window spaces, for each family; so far as we could see from looking into those whose doors were open, they contained no furniture.

Outside one of the haciendas stood a group of Civil Guards, with rifles in their hands, while women were coming in from the fields. The driver's lady friend gave a snarl of disgust as we passed the guards, and suddenly pulled out of her pocket a police whistle which she put to her lips. The driver seized her hand and for a moment the car swayed while they struggled, and Flores looked back anxiously through the rear window at the Guardia. Then, almost at once, it was all over and everybody was giggling nervously. 'What was happening at the farm?' I asked a moment later. Flores looked a little uneasy and nobody answered the question directly. But the driver, a little while afterwards, spoke into the air. 'At that hacienda the workers get two soles a day,' he said, 'or three if they are lucky.'

At Huanuco we dropped our fellow passengers one by one. The old man got out, as silently as ever, at a street corner, the woman at a florid little bar by the plaza. Outside our hotel the driver asked us to pay for the whole party; we were so annoyed by the silence of Flores that we discourteously reminded him of his own suggestion that he should pay his share. He did so, but his opinion of us was obviously impaired. However, he assured us that he was our amigo, and declared that we would certainly see him in Tingo Maria the next day.

On that first evening in Huanuco we saw little of the town—

barely enough to gain more than a general impression of long, narrow streets running for an immense distance from small plaza to small plaza, streets which seemed crowded with Chinese restaurants and tailors working in open doorways, and which were flooded with relentless sound, for the Huanuco municipality, in fatherly anxiety for the happiness of its people, had fixed loud-speakers to the lamp-posts, from which, inescapably, the music of the Sierra blared and echoed through the air from morning until long after dusk. Huanuco must also have been a garrison town, for there were many soldiers about, and I carry as my clearest recollection of Peruvian military life the picture—which at times I find it hard to convince myself is not a caricature—of an immensely fat colonel whom we saw coming out of the Prefecture with two thin, tall tarts clinging to his arms; the trio seemed to belong to the fancy of some Marxian cartoonist rather than to the real life of a remote Sierra town.

That evening chance brought us back to the subject of the great haciendas. An American and an Englishwoman, both elderly, were talking over their coffee and across three tables in the hotel dining-room. The woman came of a family of English planters and had just sold her land in the valley; the man was either the owner or administrator of some hacienda. They were exchanging recollections of a former landowner who had died, almost penniless, in Lima. 'He never knew how to manage his money, ma'am', said the American, with a kind of nostalgic indulgence. 'He could have been the richest man in the valley. He was for a time, in fact. But instead of keeping it at that, he wanted to live like a prince as well.' 'And he succeeded. You must admit that,' the woman interrupted. 'Indeed he did, ma'am. Why, when you went out to his place in the old days, you were literally lifted off your horse by his lackeys, and every moment of the day—and of the night as well if you wanted it—the servants were there to wait on you hand and foot. But he wasn't content with that, ma'am. He had to be different from the rest of us. Anyone could have plenty of Indian servants. But he was the only one to import an orchestra all the way from Europe. Yes, every winter for years on end, ma'am. And fifty dollars a time he'd spend on favours for the ladies.'

In that snatch of conversation a whole era, hardly past in the Andes, came alive to us. Combined with the taxi driver's remark on the condition of the workers (which later I had ample chance to confirm) it gave the picture of a primitive colonialism at once more rapacious and more innocent than that of the great modern corporations, which eschew the unthinking enormities of the past and seek to bind by chains of petty kindness.

2

All the roads that lead from the Sierra into the deep valleys of the montaña are so narrow that, in theory at least, they are single-track routes. One day traffic goes down to the jungle, the next it comes up to the Sierra; on Sundays the roads are open in both directions and travellers surrender their lives into the hands of the Lord of the Miracles. Flores had already warned us of this arrangement, and we had found that, unless we wanted to spend two further nights in Huanuco, we must leave the next morning for Tingo Maria.

At nine o'clock we stood waiting outside the hotel. The commercial travellers went off into the town followed by boys carrying their sample cases; a priest cycled past with a solar topee on his head and his soutane flapping to reveal white legs in khaki shorts; a persistent little shoeblack persuaded us to employ him and made a great virtuoso play with brushes and polishing cloths which alone was worth the pence he charged. A dozen buses and camionetas circled around the plaza, bound for various Sierra villages, and at last, after half an hour, an even more battered hybrid than the King of the Mountains drew up before the hotel.

It was the Tingo Maria bus, and it was called The Centaur. The driver, a tall Spaniard with gold teeth and a blue silk shirt, had so far managed to collect only four of his passengers, and now we set off to pick up the rest at their homes in what, we gathered, was the accepted Huanuco custom. One old woman sent out a message by her daughter to say that she would not be ready for half an hour. Would we come back? We did. We also drove three times around the jail in search of an address of which neither the driver nor the lounging prison guards had heard, and four times we went back to the depot in one of the plazas to pick up the stragglers who might have arrived there in the interval. At last the list was almost complete. 'Only Don Miguel Flores and Señora Irma,' said the driver to the ayudante. 'Ah, so he's coming after all,' I said to Inge, and we both felt moved by the constancy and forbearance of our companion of the previous day. But the fat, middle-aged man who shook hands jovially in all directions and shouted, 'Ciao! Ciao!' was nothing like him; Flores, we afterwards learnt, was one of the common names of Huanuco.

'And now Señora Irma,' said the driver. We drew up outside a dressmaker's shop; three women burst out on to the pavement in a miniature tornado of screams and giggles, and stood there embracing and kissing loudly. Wiping their eyes demonstratively as the señora came on board, her companions sobbed, 'Feliz viaje!' But the señora's attention had already shifted to the driver who, with gold-glittering smiles, installed her in the seat of honour beside him.

Señora Irma was a woman of thirty, with a soft moon face which, except for her very handsome dark eyes, was appealing mostly for its manifest good humour; it was a face to melt and fuse into laughter, and there was laughter also in the quaking revelations of the señora's tight and exiguous satin dress. Señora Irma was clearly a card. She was also, we were soon to find, a peril.

For a while, after leaving Huanuco, the road skirted the Huallaga, now a wide and powerful stream, but eventually left its course to take a cross-country direction leading towards the Carpish range which rises between Huanuco and the jungle. It passed through a corrugated country of low mountains separated by lateral valleys, and at the best of times the constant climbing and descending would have made driving difficult. But the risks we ran in The Centaur were complicated not only by the driver's obsessive tendency to take curves at top speed on the wrong side of the road and his absorption with Señora Irma's handsome eyes and ivory bosom, but also by the fact that a number of Indians had ignored the ban on travelling towards the Sierra that day, so that more than once we met a truck unexpectedly on a blind corner and our driver turned away from Señor Irma's charms barely in time to avert a crash by violently swinging the wheel and manœuvring through what seemed some impossibly narrow space between the other truck and the road bank, while the bushes lashed through the open window at our faces.

More than any other region in Peru, the country through which we now passed reminded me of Mediterranean Europe, as if the spirit of Spain had taken here a more enduring root, not only in the compact, well-cultivated little farms among the dry hills, but also in the people, who were half-breeds and might have passed easily for dark Spaniards or Portuguese. They wore a distinctive local dress of coloured satin shirts, white cummerbunds and dark trousers, full at the knees and tapering down to tight ankles bound with string; they had thonged leather sandals and dark hats of soft felt, and carried striped ponchos carefully folded on their left shoulders. They looked jaunty and earthily elegant, like characters from D. H. Lawrence; the women had an orientally subdued appearance which was created largely by the white shawls they draped over their heads and shoulders. Even the architecture carried its Mediterranean suggestions, for the adobe of the houses had been cast in moulds which produced Romanesque arches and Grecian columns, and from a distance a village of mud nestling on a hillside would look deceptively like some ancient stone hill town of southern France.

Beyond this Mediterranean enclave the last small valley rose up between dry hillsides of cactus and agave towards the pass, which was guarded by two low, scrub-covered peaks. And then, as The Centaur coughed its way through this undramatic portal, the great Amazonian jungle was suddenly surging below us, and the wooded hills of the montaña swept down in range after range of rounded peaks until the green of the vegetation turned into the blue of distance. And beyond the blue one knew that there lay Iquitos and Brazil, and the forest flowing on for its two thousand unbroken miles to Belem and the Atlantic.

From the descending curves of the road we looked down on the jungle as we might have done from a low-flying aeroplane—upon the silk-cotton trees bursting upward like domes of malachite through the green chaos of palms and bamboos and tree ferns, upon the flame trees opening their great umbrellas of vermilion flowers towards the sun, upon the clambering lianas and the sword-leafed epiphytes crowding the branches of the great trees. It was like hearing for the first time, played by an orchestra, a symphony which one has heard on records a hundred times. The themes were familiar, almost hackneyed. Hudson, Bates, Waterton—all that these nineteenth-century travellers wrote on the Amazonian chaos of life rushing upward to the sun I had read so often in childhood that almost every detail they brought to life in their writing had become part of an imaginary world which now arose from the past as I looked at the real forest around and below me. Yet the fact that I was seeing what in this sense I had expected did not diminish the delight of looking at it for the first time in all the colour and magnificence of actuality.

One aspect alone of the montaña was unexpected. All my reading about the Amazonian jungle had led me to believe that, while at ground level the forest is almost completely silent and seems devoid of animal life, the tops of the trees are full of activity. And so I imagined that, since we saw it from above, we would have the kind of opportunity which travellers in the jungle rarely experience; I expected to watch families of monkeys bounding along the branches and gaudily coloured parrots and trogons fluttering among the equally brilliant flowers of the blossoming trees. In fact, we saw nothing of the kind. Not a monkey bounded, not a bird fluttered in all that still sea of foliage; only the big yellow butterflies glided over the flame trees and settled on the mauve ground orchids beside the road. Why there should have been this absence of life I cannot explain. The activity on the road might have frightened away the shyer animals, but the lack of birds for so many miles was much more difficult to understand.

On the jungle side of the Carpish range the road became more difficult than ever, and the wayside crosses were frequent; twice we saw lorries overturned in the forest below us, and several times we edged past small landslides which groups of conscripts were clearing away. It was not yet the rainy season, but already the hillsides were sodden with springs whose water undermined the road and sometimes turned it into a miry streambed, from which the liquid mud would spirt up between the shrunken floorboards of The Centaur and drench our legs.

At midday we stopped at a hill hamlet called Tambo Duran, high above the Chinchao river. It was one of the makeshift settlements that in recent years have sprung up along the new roads into the jungle, and its principal building was a rough inn whose jukebox sent harsh music pealing out over the forest and whose mercury vapour lighting blazed on the sunlit terrace where lunch was served. We were surprised to see electricity at all in such a remote place, but this was typical of the unevenness with which the facilities of mechanical civilization have spread in Peru. For in other respects the village was still primitive. The garbage was cast behind the houses in untidy heaps where the vultures—the first birds we saw in the jungle—searched and squabbled; the guests—including a bemedalled touring general—came out of the inn to urinate against its walls; the village women carried water to the houses in pails hanging from heavy yokes. Yet in some way every house gained at least part of its living from the intrusion of modernism represented by the road. A few were minor eating houses, with worn tables under a cane awning; the rest were mean little booths selling fruit and a few groceries. But many of the people must also have had land in the cleared areas which speckled the valley below, for coffee dried in the sun beside the bamboo walls and two horsemen came riding up on a hill path and left their horses standing in the shade as they went into one of the houses; their beautiful gaucho saddles were heavily tooled and studded with silver.

From Tambo Duran it was only a mile or so to the easy slopes where the cultivation began—orchards of oranges and mangoes and papayas, fields full of great shuttlecock heads of pineapples, groves of red-berried coffee, and skeleton coca bushes, stripped as clean of leaves in the recent harvest as if a plague of ravenous caterpillars had passed through them.

Then the road dipped; we left these sunny gardens and entered the thick jungle in the depth of the valley. The forest pushed its tangled branches and lianas over the banks of the river, and sometimes they grappled together overhead, so that the sun shone only intermittently; occasionally there were open spots where slanting rock faces came down to the water, but even these were so moist that they nourished thick coverings of ferns. The air was heavy, tangible, smelling of vegetation. From time to time, we passed some tiny hamlet of huts built on piles, with an open shed for a restaurant and, instead of a church, an image placed in a dripping mossy niche by the side of the road.

The Huallaga, when we met it again at its junction with the Chinchao, had become a wide tropical river, split by sandbanks where the driftwood of past floods had piled in grey ragged heaps. The valley widened out towards Tingo Maria, and cultivation returned in the ragged clearings hacked out of the forest by Indian farmers. These were jungle Indians, small, brown-skinned people who seemed puny after one had become used to the barrel-chested folk of the Sierra, but civilization had replaced their native dress or undress by the ragged drill trousers and shapeless cotton dresses which seem everywhere Christianity's gift to the jungle. In fact, apart from the Jivaro medicine men who performed in the markets, we never came across a jungle Indian who wore his tribal costume. As the roads and the aeroplanes push into their country, these people quickly adapt themselves to something resembling the white man's manners or else, in the case of the more independent tribes, depart into some even deeper corner of the forest.

3

In Tingo Maria we awoke from the daydream created by the melody of words. There was none of the fragile beauty its name had evoked in this new settlement which the humid climate had already given the appearance of indefinite age. The houses were half-finished bungalows in which the people squatted untidily, or completed buildings so weathered in a couple of soaking rainy seasons that they might have been standing for half a century. Down the main street there were a few crudely finished concrete buildings and open-fronted shops, and trucks loaded with lumber and bananas and square bales of coca stood ready to take the mountain road before dawn the next day.

It was ugly—and unexpectedly familiar. For despite the jungle background and the muggy air and the chaotically mixed population, which ranged from the blondest German to the blackest Negro, I was reminded immediately of the raw little Canadian frontier towns on the edge of the northern wilderness. And the resemblance was appropriate, for the jungle regions like that around Tingo Maria are in fact the frontier lands of Peru, the areas whose barely exploited resources may solve many of the country's most urgent problems. At present Peru is in the anomalous position of a country as large as France, Spain and Italy combined, with a population roughly equal to that of Portugal, which does not grow enough food to sustain its own people adequately. Less than 3 per cent of its area is cultivated, and much of this is devoted to export crops like sugar or cotton, or to coca, which serves only as a consolation for hunger. Shortage of water on the coast and climatic difficulties in the Sierra make it unlikely that in these regions there will be any great increase in arable land; the montaña, on the other hand, covers more than half the area of Peru, its land is fertile, its climate is good for such vital Peruvian crops as sugar, maize and rice, and there is no lack of water. Future agricultural development clearly lies in the jungle valleys, and successive governments have tried to populate them by building roads and offering free gifts of land.

But, although it is fairly generally recognized that the raising of the Peruvian standard of living depends on the development of this jungle frontier, there is as yet very little of the popular demand for land which created the great movements to the North American West. Few white Peruvians are interested in being working farmers, and even the land-hungry Indians of the Sierra fear the jungle climate and are so distrustful of the unfamiliar that

106

most of them would prefer poverty in the shelter of their own communities to risking an independent existence in a new environment. Consequently, the number of people who travel down the new roads to settle in the jungle is comparatively small, and many of these prefer the easy life of trucking lumber and coca to the hard work of clearing plantations. At the same time, population pressures in Peru are likely to increase so quickly that the settlement of the montaña will soon be the only solution to the recurrent food shortages of the Sierra. And then, no doubt, Tingo Maria will be something more than the raw, sultry village that, when we saw it, so grossly belied the music of its name.

The Government Hotel stood about a mile outside Tingo Maria, at the end of a drive lined with blossoming flame trees. The woods had been cut back to leave a large stretch of meadow running down to the river, and here had been built a collection of single-storied wooden buildings on piles which at first sight suggested Kipling and Victorian summer stations in the Himalayan foothills.

The Centaur drove hooting up to the main building, and three white-coated houseboys ran forward to meet us as we climbed stiffly down. They were obviously disappointed to see that all we carried was an overnight bag and a typewriter. On the hotel veranda we had to push our way past a crowd of women who sat around wicker tables, playing cards in an atmosphere of boredom that caught one almost physically by the throat. They looked at us with an avid, hostile curiosity; perhaps they were justified, for, paying too little attention to the extreme changes of climate which any long journey involves in Peru, we had set off from Tarma in the clothing appropriate to a sharp Sierra morning and had taken nothing else but a change of linen; we must have looked very incongruous as we sweated up the steps of that jungle hotel in our heavy tweed suits, splashed with the mud thrown up through the floorboards of the bus.

The hotel was crowded with holiday-makers from the mining towns, and we had to stay in a pavilion on the edge of the forest—a long shed, divided into a double row of barely furnished cubicles whose walls gave only an illusion of privacy, since the ceilings consisted of wire mesh, above which a long loft carried every sound from end to end of the building. Dead flies and spiders hung on the wire, and the cubicles smelt of rotting leaves and neglected changing rooms. Water dripped incessantly in the dank shower compartment. As I stood there, looking and sniffing around in distaste, the thought occurred to me that Svidrigailov's bathhouse would have been very much like this. I noticed that the mosquito screens on the windows had holes in them large enough for bluebottles to sail through; the houseboy remarked, a little too glibly, that it was not mosquito season, but we carefully plugged the holes with paper as soon as he had gone.

Yet when we left this depressing shack and walked down to the river we entered a setting whose extraordinary beauty justified all the music of Tingo Maria's name. As wide as the Thames at London, but far more swift and troubled, the Huallaga ran north towards its junction with the Marañon 300 miles away. It was divided by a long island whose thick lozenge of forest came solidly to the very edge of its wide yellow beaches; around the island's far point the two forks of the river joined in a turmoil of white rapids, and on the far bank the forest rose to a great ridge that culminated in two conical peaks, completely covered with vegetation except where limestone cliffs broke in white bands through the clambering jungle. It was the presence of these peaks that gave the scene much of its beauty, for with them the forest seemed no longer a wall of impenetrable depth and density; instead, it acquired variation and perspective, and took its place in the receding series of planes formed by river and mountain and sky.

We walked afterwards into the jungle near the hotel. The groves of tall trees, with smooth unbranched trunks and spreading tops, had the kind of crepuscular and rather ecclesiastical solemnity which one sometimes encounters in large beech woods. There are few lianas and the undergrowth consisted mostly of dwarf palms and a great many varieties of those dully impressive plants with enormous glossy leaves which in recent years have become almost a cliché of interior decoration. They looked just as lifeless in the jungle as in a modernistic flat, and we were much more pleased with the extravagant flowers—a crimson lily with many blossoms on a tall drooping stem, and a magnificent red variety of the bird-of-paradise flower.

Even here, walking through the paths near the open river, we saw little animal life. Some gulls and a few large grey kingfishers populated the riverbanks, and among the trees squawked black-and-yellow birds like gilded magpies. Once there was a flurry among the philodendrons and a large pewter-coloured lizard, almost a yard long, raced across the path to the opposite thicket. But these were all the wild creatures we saw, and the heavy plungings we heard in the undergrowth turned out to be either Brahmin cattle that had wandered out of the pastures of a nearby agricultural station, or the husbands of the card-playing ladies, whom we met returning in full tropical kit, with solar topees, field-glasses and snake-boots. The snake-boots were needed, we gathered, because Tingo Maria has a particularly poisonous species of small viper. We saw no snakes, but in such an atmosphere of precaution we felt at times rather apprehensive as we walked around in our low-sided shoes.

With night the jungle lifted its mask of silence. A heavy wind sprang up before twilight, groaned drearily for a while in the tree-tops and sent dead branches crashing down beside our pavilion. Then it dropped abruptly, and invisible birds began to call. Finally, as dusk closed in, the nightly Aristophanic opera of the frogs, the toads and the insects began, louder by far than in Guayaquil.

The evening was moonlit, spattering the hurrying stream of the Huallaga with white, and etching the two sugarloafs in dense silhouettes against the pale, steel-blue sky. Large, clumsy bats flapped over the lawns as we ate dinner on the veranda facing the river—a dinner of jungle products, beginning with a chupe of some hard-fleshed river fish, going on to stewed lamb with a yam called camote and a non-poisonous species of manioc called yuca (not to be confused with yucca), and ending with pineapple which was more delicious than any I had ever eaten. Between the chupe and the camote, or perhaps between the yuca and the pineapple, the solemnity of the meal was broken and the singsong Peruvian voices were stilled by the sudden appearance of a little girl in pyjamas with blonde pigtails who came racing on to the veranda shouting in ecstatic Cape Cod English, 'Jeannie's locked herself in the lavatree! Jeannie's locked herself in the lavatree!' A young mining engineer's wife got up and followed her, and another woman began suddenly to tell, in a piercing and almost hysterical voice, the story of the even worse predicament of some unnamed little boy. 'He was playing around, and he put his foot in the John, right down in the John. And he couldn't get it out. And they had to come with a hammer and break up the John.' When her friends laughed she took this for incredulity and repeated, blushing, 'It's true. It really happened. They broke it up with a hammer.' It sounded like nature imitating Hemingway.

Dinner was the last of our pleasures that day, for the night that followed was the worst, or perhaps one of the two worst, we spent in Peru. The beds in the pavilion were not merely damp, but positively wet from the humid atmosphere, and they also felt as if they had been stuffed with potatoes. And all night long there was not a moment of quietness. The jungle chorus continued deafeningly until after midnight; then it was silenced by a violent and equally noisy rainstorm. And when the rainstorm had ended the man in the next cubicle began to snore—no ordinary snore, but a kind of gasping, rattling yell that sounded like the agony of strangling. Unfortunately the strangling was repeated at regular and frequent intervals—about once every half minute—throughout the night, while we lay awake totting up the seconds in mounting suspense. Twenty-five—twenty-six—it must be near now! Twenty-seven—twenty-eight—here it comes! The appalling sound would bray out, and for the instant one's tension would slacken, only to mount again as the next half minute drew near. The few occasions when the regularity was broken were even more distressing, for then, after counting thirty, one was left in jangling suspense until the snore finally broke out and allowed one a temporary subsidence into relief.

We slept little, and almost made up our minds to leave Tingo Maria in the morning. If we stayed, it would mean another two days before the road was open again—two days of delay in getting to Cuzco, which we began to feel it was high time we visited. And what could we do in these two days? Buy some snakeboots and sweat through the birdless paths of the jungle? Wander in the village which we disliked? Tramp around the agricultural experimentation centre? In the middle of the sleepless night they all seemed pointless occupations.

When we got up next morning, very early, our doubts were almost dispelled by our first sight of the new beauty which the jungle had assumed. The trees glistened after the night's rain, and the sun shed its dazzling miniatures in the drops hanging on the big spiders' webs. Over the sugarloaf peaks the draperies of cloud still hung, and the light mist rising from the river was just thick enough to give an enticing air of remoteness to the island and the shores beyond. The air was cool, and some brown birds were singing like thrushes.

We were delighted and our minds began to change. Then, at breakfast, we met D., who was sitting two or three tables away in the almost empty dining-room, for neither the card-playing ladies nor their snake-booted escorts were yet about. D. was young and tall, with a dark, long Castilian face drooping to flesh around the mouth. He looked at us with interest. He smiled at Inge, and then, somewhat as an afterthought, included me in the radius of his benignity. Next he shouted across the intervening tables. 'Are you going to Huanuco this morning?' Evidently that was the only reason for rising early in Tingo Maria. 'If you are,' he continued, 'you could drive with me.'

Here was opportunity offering a solution to all our wavering doubts. If we went with this stranger we should no longer have to lie awake in damp beds listening to strangling snorers. We should not have to fill two days with rather pointless jungle activities while the monuments of the Incas awaited us in Cuzco. On the other hand, we had no idea in what we might involve ourselves. The stranger might be a bad driver, which meant a great deal on these roads. He might equally well be a tedious extrovert to whom we should be tied for several hours of driving.

We hesitated, and D., putting his own interpretation on our doubt, shouted in English: 'You—pay—nothing. Is gratis!' We were so amused and nonplussed by this remark that we accepted, paid our bill, thrust our pyjamas into our bag, and quickly joined D. at the pickup truck which he was driving.

4

We had no cause to regret our decision. D. was a fast but good driver and, since his small vehicle could turn the sharp corners relatively easily, we reached Huanuco in time for lunch, a good three or four hours sooner than we might have done by bus. And during our five hours of rambling, erratic conversation, we were able to look more deeply than before into the attitude of at least one type of educated Peruvian.

D. was, I imagine, as pure a creole as one is likely to meet in Peru. His mother had been a Peruvian, his father a Spaniard, and he himself had a curious vestige of the plummy Madrid accent. But by birth and by upbringing he was a Liman, and, though his occupation as a salesman had forced him to wander over the rest of Peru and to take some interest in the country beyond his city boundaries, one felt that he still looked at the Sierra and the Montaña from outside, with curiosity and wonder rather than with sympathy.

This emerged in his love for stories about the marvels of the jungle, marvels which usually had a romantic and often a sexual element. Within our first hour together he had told us luridly of the Amazonian fish whose body is said to be exactly like that of a woman—he was evidently referring to the manatee—and of the other fish, microscopic in size, that gnaws into the sexual organs of swimmers and can be removed only after terrible operations. He dilated on the magnificent blonde women of the jungle near Iquitos, bred of the intermarriage of German immigrants and Indian women. And he told us of a village in the hills of the montaña where, as he said, 'Los mujeres son muy, muy hermosas —the women are very, very beautiful—and once a man goes there he never returns.' He lingered wistfully over the thought of this Andean Venusberg, and then went on to other stories—of the image on a mountaintop near Huanuco, whose wounds were always fresh and unhealed, and of the valley near Tomay Kichwa where neither doctors nor curanderos went because the Indians cured all ills by a single secret herb called, in Quechua, 'This plant is more mighty than God.'

D. laughed a little at his own tales, yet, like many tall-story tellers, he seemed at times almost to believe himself. Certainly, in his way of speaking, there was always the suggestion that these things should not be dismissed rashly, and he was not the only white Peruvian from the Coast to talk to us of the montaña as a region so alien that almost anything, however outlandish, might happen there. Some at least of his stories had a long tradition behind them, for the villages of beautiful women clearly derived from the accounts of the settlements of female warriors first given by the Conquistador Orellana in the sixteenth century and later accepted as substantially true by travellers as responsible as Humboldt, La Condamine and Richard Spruce. With such a weight of opinion behind this legend, it is not surprising that modern Peruvians should still amuse themselves by telling its garbled versions.

However, the only story which D. was ready to defend categorically was that of the miraculous bleeding Christ. He had seen it for himself, he maintained, and he knew doctors who had investigated it and had come away convinced that the statue exuded authentic and human blood.

D.'s insistence on including the marvellous, in at least some form or another, in his system of beliefs was all the more striking since it ran parallel to a very rational attitude in matters of everyday life, as if he were intent on keeping a sharp line between the realm of Caesar and that of whatever in his mind was the complement of Caesar. His rational leanings had clearly been nurtured by five years of medical studies at the University of San Marco, until his career was ended in a way which, as he described it, brought us face to face with the reality of life under a South American dictatorship.

Though D. had not been a member of any political party, he had, like many of his friends, been drawn into the activities of the student federation, which had taken its stand in defence of the freedom of speech and writing. Slowly D. had risen to a position of responsibility in the federation at a time when the students were among the few groups of Peruvians showing a clear opposition to Odria's dictatorship. Soon the secret police began to purge the universities of so-called subversives, and, two years before the end of his courses, D. was expelled.

So long as the dictatorship remained, he had no hope of resuming his studies and becoming a doctor. He also found that few people wanted to employ in any capacity a man on the political black list. But eventually, thanks to his medical training, he found a job selling pharmaceutical supplies for a Swiss firm which could afford to be a little independent. 'For the last three years I have been travelling through all the small towns of the Sierra and the Montaña,' he said. 'It is tiring, and I am a man of Lima; I prefer my own city. Yet I was very fortunate. Many of my friends who were also expelled could find nobody to employ them.'

Would his prospects not be better, I asked, now that the dictatorship was coming to an end? 'Perhaps,' he answered. 'But it is late to realize the dreams I once had. I am married now, and I have a child. But at least I shall no longer have a black mark against me.'

Yet D. was not so enthusiastic as one might have expected about the collapse of the dictatorship. Like Robles, he had no doubt that Odria would go, and that his departure would mean a relaxation of many pressures. It would be possible to speak and write freely, and to go about without fear of being overheard by the secret police who, in Odria's heyday, had been everywhere in Peru.

'But the freedom to speak is not everything,' D. went on. 'You must have seen what kind of country Peru is—a country of terrible inequalities.' And, with that intensity of self-criticism which we met often among Peruvians, he enlarged on the theme. There were, he said, not only the obvious inequalities between landowners and labourers, between mine-owners and miners. Even within the classes the pattern persisted. Labourers in Lima got ten times as much as they did in the Sierra. Some Indians were rich, owned land and fleets of lorries, and ground their fellow Indians even more closely than the whites had done. The desire to exploit people less fortunate than oneself had become a Peruvian habit, D. insisted, and the change urgently needed was not the departure of a man like Odria and his replacement by a man like Prado, but a new approach to social relations in general.

'You have heard all about Odria,' he said. 'But do you know who the new President Prado is? I will tell you. He is a conservative, and he is one of the great landowners and financiers of Peru. There are few people in this country richer than Prado. He was President once before, and he did nothing to attack our real problems. But there is no Peruvian government that has yet dared to curb the power of the hacendados and the foreign mine-owners, because the army is always behind the capitalists. Ten years ago we had a President named Bustamente who tried very timidly to reduce the privileges of the foreign corporations. The army swept him away and put Odria in his place. The same thing would happen again. The generals and the landowners and the capitalists —they all hang together in Peru. And that is why it does not help a great deal if Odria goes and the old attitude remains. For a few years we shall have a little freedom, and that is good, but the inequality will continue, discontent will grow up again, and another general will make it an excuse to take power.'

His reasoning sounded very much like that of the exiled leader of the radical APRA[1] party, Haya de la Torre; there was the same anti-capitalism, the same stress on the baneful influence of the foreign corporations, and, knowing the influence which de la Torre had wielded over the students, I suspected that D., even if he were not an APRA member, must be sympathetic to the party's viewpoint. But in a country where political repression is endemic

---

[1] APRA, as it is generally called, is the Alianza Popular Revolucionaria Americana, a left-wing party, founded in the 1930's, outlawed by Odria in 1948, and legalized again after his departure in 1956. Originally it was internationalistic and quasi-Marxist, but both these tendencies have weakened in recent years. Its followers are usually called Apristas.

there are certain discretions one naturally observes (I observe one of them in talking of D. by an initial which is not even his own), and, since at this time APRA was still an underground organization, it would have been indiscreet to ask whether he was a member.

'But you sound very pessimistic,' I said instead. 'Do you think there is no chance of escaping from the circle?'

'Peru changes all the time,' D. replied. 'A new generation is growing up, and it may find a way out. But do not ask me what the way will be. It will depend on the world outside as much as on us.'

We ate lunch with D. in Huanuco, and agreed to meet again when we all reached Lima during the following week. Señora D. did in fact ring us up in our hotel, but it was to say that D. had been kept in the Sierra; his truck had broken down on the road to Ayacucho.

5

We went on from Huanuco the next morning, returning over familiar ground through Ambo and San Rafael. As far as Cerro de Pasco the journey was uneventful. There we found that the cold was even more intense than two days before, and on the Pampa de Junin the wind began to buffet heavily against the front of the bus and the sky was weighed down with dull grey clouds.

Soon the storm broke, first in hail, rattling in volleys of stones like mothballs on the roof of the bus and whitening the Pampa around us. The hail eased off, and lightning cut the air in jagged bolts which seemed to dart from the low clouds in every direction. Then, while the thunder kept up an almost uninterrupted roll of muffled drums, snow began to fall and the wind quickly whipped it into a blizzard. It reminded me of a sandstorm through which we had once travelled in the Californian desert; there was the same unnatural and ominous darkness, the same almost total lack of visibility on the road ahead, the same violent and insinuating wind which in California had blown the sand into the tightly closed Greyhound bus, and which now projected the snow in jets of fine white dust through all the cracks of our ramshackle, groaning vehicle. We huddled under our raincoats and soon looked like squat snowmen, while the melting snow-water from the roof dripped rustily through the defective ventilators on to our heads.

The rough surface of the road was quickly covered and became almost indistinguishable from the marshy land around it. A slight miscalculation in driving might take us into a mountain bog or, just as easily, into collision with some approaching vehicle. The young Indian driver, who can hardly have been more than eighteen and looked as scared as any of his passengers, switched on a little red lamp beneath his shrine to the Lord of the Miracles, and crossed himself frequently as he sat hunched over the wheel and peered into the invisibility ahead. He went by fits and starts, stopping now and again for the ayudante to jump out and hastily scoop some of the snow from the clogged windshield, and then for a while scurrying along almost blindly at what, in such a wind, seemed an extremely reckless pace. The Lord of the Miracles watched over us. We neither ran off the road nor met a single car until, almost at sunset, the storm blew itself out.

Well after nightfall we reached a roadside eating house on the edge of La Oroya. Owing to the storm, we had missed the bus to Tarma; the next would not leave until after ten, and by that time, we knew, there would almost certainly be no rooms left in the Government Hotel. We ordered some beer and asked the waiter about the chances of hiring a car to Tarma. 'On a night like this, señor! It is snowing up in the pass. I don't know whether anyone will want to go.' Five minutes later he said that he could get us a car for a hundred soles. 'Very cheap, señores!' In fact, it was very dear, almost twice the customary price, but our desire to get back quickly to a shower and a change of clothes was so strong that we were about to accept when a man sitting at a table near the bar waved a cautioning hand and shouted, in English, 'No! Do not take it! Let me explain to you!'

We went to his table. He had a fleshy intellectual face rather like that of Oscar Wilde, if one can imagine an olive-skinned

Wilde with sombre eyes. 'I too am going to Tarma,' he said, 'and if it is necessary we can share a car, though we will not pay a hundred soles. But let us wait a few minutes, if you don't mind joining me while I finish my dinner. We may find some driver who doesn't want to be paid at all.'

He laughed softly, and asked us why we were travelling. 'Ah, so you are a writer, señor! Then in a sense we are in the same trade.' 'Are you a writer yourself?' I asked, pleased at the thought of meeting a Peruvian colleague. He laughed and shook his head. 'No, I am only a servant of literature, a mere traveller in books.'

A book traveller seemed an even less likely person than a writer to encounter at night in an Andean pass, and I was surprised when he told us that his business lay mostly in the small towns of the Sierra, which I had not associated with literary interests. 'But I do very well,' he assured us, and named a figure for monthly sales which I remember as being unexpectedly high. He explained this by saying that, though the really literate Peruvians were a small proportion of the population, they were usually avid readers. This he attributed to the fact that Peru was not yet a country of specialization. Education tended to be liberal, even classical, and people read to broaden their knowledge over a wide field rather than to deepen it along some narrow path. 'I hear that in North America the great slogan is do-it-yourself,' he said. 'In Peru one could describe our attitude as learn-it-yourself.' And with that he opened his folder of prospectuses and showed us the kind of books he sold—selections from world literature and potted biographies of the great, summaries of operas and digests of great novels, universal histories and, above all, the *Autodidactic Encyclopaedia*.

It was the mental food of the age of the self-educated genius, the age that had Ford as its hero and Wells as its prophet. I was reminded of Flores in Huanuco as I thought of the clerks and shopkeepers preparing their minds for greater things during the long evenings when the streets of the Sierra towns became lifeless and glacial. But this absorption with dehydrated classics was no substitute for living literature, and I asked the bookman about the situation of Peru's own writers, its modern poets and novelists and playwrights.

He shook his head. 'That is a different story. I don't handle books of that kind, but I can tell that it is not easy to be a writer in Peru, at least while one is still alive. You must have heard of our great poet Cesar Vallejo. Now that he has been dead for twenty years you will see his poems for sale everywhere in Peru, but when he was alive he earned very little from his writing. It is the same with all the arts. Few painters or musicians live by their work in our country. They must have either independent means or posts which give them a little leisure for their own work. I have travelled in North America and I know that it is different there. The North Americans despise their artists and often pay them very well. In South America we respect artists, but we let them starve.'

Inge asked him when he had been to North America. A moody look passed over the bookman's face, and then he smiled. 'Ten years ago, señora, when I was in the consular service. I have not always been selling books.' He paused, and then, evidently realizing from the nature of our silence that he had aroused our curiosity, he continued: 'I served for twelve years in the consular service—in Berlin, in Berne, in La Paz and in Washington. I never heard of any complaint being made of my work or my conduct, but six years ago I was quietly told to leave the service. I left, just as quietly, because at that time it would have been dangerous to protest. It was all for political reasons. My fault was that I was a man without politics. I neither opposed nor supported the government of General Odria. But at that time it was not always enough to keep quiet. My post was wanted for a friend of the government, and, as I had no powerful protector, I had to go. I don't complain now. Since that time I have arranged my life in another way which I find just as satisfying. But let's say no more about these dismal things. There has been a change, and if we do not expect too much from it we shall probably not be disappointed.'

Again, for the third time in a few days, we heard that note of cynicism, underlying the feeling of relief, which was so characteristic of the Peruvian mood during these last days as the dictatorship quietly faded towards its end.

The bookman soon found an acquaintance who was driving to Tarma and was willing to take us with him. We saw this benefactor only as a head and shoulders outlined against the windshield, and heard him hardly at all, for he spoke rarely as he drove his car up the snowy hills over the pass and down the slippery curves into Tarma. But we felt grateful to him when we walked into the Government Hotel just in time to take the last free room.

Later, in the bar, the bookman talked to us of his home in Arequipa. 'I am glad you are going there,' he said. 'It is a green city—the only green city of Peru.' And he went on to tell us of his children and, through some tale about one of his sons, came to religion. He was a devout Catholic, and he spoke of his feelings with evident sincerity, but with a mystic's inability to communicate whatever illumination he might have received. He was the only Peruvian who ever talked to us of religion in terms of experience. We never learnt his name.

6

For the next two days we stayed in Tarma. Robles, the engineer, was still there and invited us to spend the Sunday with him. I remember it as one of those smooth, leisurely, talkative days which shine like calm, well-stocked pools in the currents of a period spent in almost constant movement from place to place.

In the morning we went to the Tarma market, which was modest in comparison with Huancayo; it had its own curiosities, however, which Robles, peering and probing, revealed to us. An old Indian woman was selling chips of a peculiar crystalline stone. 'It is used for roasting corn,' our companion explained. 'They make the stones red hot and place the corn among them, and by the time the stones are cool it is ready to eat.' Two men sang a melancholy ballad to the tune of a guitar, and Robles stood with his head birdlike to listen, and told us that it was a conventional Quechua song about love and betrayal—a kind of Andean equiva-

lent of Allan Water. And when a massive chola started bawling in
dialect and set the Indians around her laughing, he remarked: 'She
is selling pencils; she says that they must be good because her
grandmother used them.' But even Robles could get no answer
from the local curandero, who became so annoyed with our prying
presence that he shouted angrily at Inge for handling a string of
beads on his stall. 'They are always afraid that white people will
expose them,' was our companion's explanation, but it seemed to
me that the man might quite honestly have believed in his own
magic and have thought that our infidel hands would contaminate
its instruments.

From the curandero's stall we went on to the new cathedral, as
tawdry within as Sacré Coeur, and filled with praying Indians from
the villages. Robles, who had genuflected elaborately before the
high altar, muttered anti-clerically as we came out. 'The cathedral
is in the hands of the black priests, and in Peru it is the black
priests who hate progress.' By the black priests he meant the
secular clergy, and he insisted that he admired the Franciscans.
'They are brave men,' he said. 'They will go into the jungle with
nothing but a breviary, and a knife to cut down fruit from the
trees. They will live like the poor Indians to whom they preach.
And they are no more afraid of reason than they are of the beasts
of the jungle. With a Franciscan you can discuss any controversial
subject, and he will argue with you honestly. But the black
priests are bigoted and corrupt. Reason is nothing to them.
Authority and money are all.'

Robles was a liberal, philosophically and politically, and as we
drove up to La Oroya, where we intended to have lunch, he came
back, like almost all the people to whom we had talked seriously
during the past two days, to the political situation in Peru. But he
was not content merely to dilate on the more sensational aspects of
the departing dictatorship—the secret police, the terror against
critics, the midnight arrests, the banishments and the penal
islands—all the gloomy commonplaces of South American political life. He sought rather to explain the forces behind these manifestations. The tragedy, according to him, was that Peruvian
politics had been dominated for twenty years by two irresponsibi-

lities, that of the generals, who were concerned principally with the interests of the military caste, and that of the Apristas, who for years had been the only dynamic left-wing group.

Basing my opinions on the rather partisan accounts of writers like John Gunther, I had assumed that the APRA party, that shadowy clandestine power, represented a liberalism which had been tempered by social-democratic theory and driven underground by military tyranny. Robles denied this. According to him, APRA represented nothing so much as a confused attempt at unity among elements which opposed themselves during the 1930's, for various and not always creditable reasons, to the ruling conservatives. The movement had included people of every political tinge, from Liberals to Communists; it had embraced honest idealists and time-serving politicians out of favour, as well as the *lumpen* element of professional pistoleros which adheres traditionally to every Latin American revolutionary party. APRA's usefulness, he maintained, had passed with the days of social unrest before the war; since then it had declined into cynical opportunism, and the final betrayal, in his eyes, had been the part which the Apristas had played in the recent elections, when, rather than support a genuine liberal whose success might have endangered their own regaining of popular support, the self-styled revolutionaries of the underground organization had given their votes to the conservative Prado in return for a promise to legalize their party. Such arrangements between parties of opposing views had been common enough, Robles remarked, in old-style Latin American politics, but they represented precisely the kind of opportunism that discredited the older politicians in the eyes of his own generation.

We lunched in a village called Huaymanta on the main road through the Andes, and as we ate our chicken chupe and rainbow trout, and washed them down with a passable Peruvian Chablis, Robles returned to the question of politics, and assured us that he felt confident of the future. Events would force progress; and the newer generation would learn from past errors. 'Today Peru is in the hands of a transitional generation,' he explained. 'Many of them have ideals and good intentions, but they are used to doing whatever they can according to the whims of dictators. They have piecemeal minds, with no sense of co-ordination. I will give you an example. You remember the new hospital in Tarma? While you were away last week a whole company of generals and politicians came from Lima to inaugurate it. Now the hospital is open, but it is not ready to receive a single patient. It has no equipment, no beds, no staff, no money. It is a product of men who have not grasped the need for progress to advance on all fronts at once. But that is what we young Peruvians realize. We are not political men. We don't belong to parties or engage in conspiracies, but we have revolutionary ideals just the same. We intend to change society sensibly and peacefully so as to bring good to all the people, and to do that we must co-ordinate and plan.'

What Robles had to say—and I have greatly condensed the conversation of a whole lunchtime—represented an attitude we were to meet fairly often among young educated Peruvians. He himself was a good example of the rising generation. He was clearly a competent engineer, but he did not have the narrow mind of a specialist. He saw his function within the context of society as a whole, and he wished to use his abilities to bring more abundance into that society.

This kind of disinterested realism is what countries like Peru need more than anything else, for in the past there have been too many well-intentioned projects which have foundered in a sea of oratory and incompetence. At the same time there was something disturbing about R.'s almost technocratic attitude. He appeared to envisage an élite of engineers and planners which would create a new Peru very similar to the welfare state organized by the princely caste of the Incas—who also were engineers and economic planners. Indeed, the very nature of Peruvian society, in which an educated minority lives beside a great mass of peasants who are mostly illiterate and almost completely indifferent to political life, seems to invite this kind of caste attitude even among the enlightened, and it is quite possible that the next stage in Peru may be that in which a trained hierarchy will rule, benevolently but securely, over an ignorant populace.

It was not only of politics that we talked as Robles drove down the valley to Palca in the afternoon, and as we sat at the last hour of sunshine in the hotel garden and watched the humming-birds shimmering like green metal over the reddest of the flowers. Robles discussed the Indians and their dances, and the difficulty which a white man experiences in following their rhythms as well as their thoughts. He told of the strange ritual fight between a bull and a condor which he had seen staged by the Aymara on Lake Titicaca. He told of his youth in Lima, and of the time when he had gone on a surveying party into the jungle and had been seized by an indescribable terror to find himself alone in the trackless forest.

And all the time our relationship was bathed in that congeniality which Peruvians so often have the power of inducing on the slightest contact with other people. I have known no nation more imbued with the idea of friendship, and never, in so few weeks, have so many people said to me, 'I am your friend!' and meant it —at the time of speaking—with the utmost sincerity. But customs in friendship vary as much as customs in love, and our ideas of a relationship that grows into maturity would be dull to most Peruvians, who see friendship as the offspring of inspiration, the sudden flowering of sympathy between two people. If, for us, there is Love at First Sight, for Peruvians there is certainly Friendship at First Sight, and any stranger who is amiable enough to be classed as 'simpatico' is likely to find himself the object of such a feeling. Robles fell into Friendship at First Sight with both of us; 'You will always be my friends,' he insisted.

But a corollary of the Peruvian conception of friendship seems to be that, if it can spring up immediately, it can also be contained within the intense moments of a single experience. The swearing of an eternity of friendship by a Peruvian does not mean that, if his mind is taken by some new experience tomorrow, he will not follow it and put one out of his mind. We saw Robles again, but it was clear that for him the freshness had gone out of our relationship, which had blossomed like some magnificent desert flower for just a single day.

I have no thought of condemning this attitude. I believe it is full of feeling and sincerity, and that it affords a pleasant complement to the more enduring relationships which we prefer. Indeed, it probably provides the best kind of friendship a traveller can encounter, for it eases his way like the bright fire of hospitality without leaving any trailing obligations behind it. Everyone has experienced those relationships, contracted in the chance intimacy of holidays, which are unwisely prolonged to languish like some sad bluebird brought into captivity. These are the transient friendships that really die; it is the others, whose intensity is confined within its own place and time, that live intact in the memory. And for that one day in the valley of Tarma I still count Robles in the company of my friends, though it is unlikely that I shall ever see or hear of him again.

PART III

Children of the Sun

I

To reach Cuzco by way of Arequipa we had first to return to Lima, and this time we travelled by the road which, except for a few relatively minor deviations, followed the same route as the railway. It was a journey through familiar country, and only one incident made any deep impression on me. At a village called Matucana in the western foothills the gravel mountain road came to an end and the camioneta driver decided to stop for lunch before the last smooth hours of driving down the paved highway into Lima.

We bought some oranges in the only shop and ate them as we sat with one of the other passengers in the shadow of a great wooden cross hung with emblematic ladders, spears and trumpets in commemoration of the Passion. Our companion, who had occupied the seat next to Inge in the camioneta, was a middle-aged woman with the hag-ridden look of a small shopkeeper's wife. 'You are lucky to be able to travel so far from your home,' she said to us, after having inquired where we came from. 'You have no children, señora?' she added, turning to Inge. 'None,' said Inge. 'Ah, then you have been saved enough, you have been saved enough,' she said in a peculiar, muffled voice. It was an unexpected remark, since Peruvians are usually so fond of children that a childless couple is regarded as unfortunate.

However, the reason for it became evident when she told us why she herself was travelling. Her two sons had been conscripted, one after the other, and both had been sent to serve in the jungle, where the elder had contracted leprosy, and the younger had been attacked by some sickness which the doctors had evidently not yet diagnosed. She had just been to visit them in San Ramon, and now she feared that she would never see them again as the healthy young men who had gone away from home. It was obvious that she had been driven hard by these misfortunes, and yet it was only against fate that she complained. That any human agency might be in part responsible for the sorrows she had suffered through her children she did not wish to admit. We felt pity for her and clumsily expressed our sympathy, and yet it was impossible to repel completely the atavistic shudder which the traditional dread of leprosy inspired. We knew well enough how exaggerated is the fear of contagion which many people experience towards this disease, yet neither of us could help wondering a little anxiously whether the woman might have had some physical contact with her leper son.

On this occasion we spent in Lima only the day that was necessary to make our arrangements for going to Arequipa on the first stage of our journey southward. We found that the most convenient way of getting there was by collectivo. This is a kind of long-distance taxi, carrying five passengers who pay individually for their places, and, next to the aeroplane, it is the fastest means of travel in Peru. Collectivos run to most corners of the country where there is a possible road, and the agencies that control them dominate a whole street in Lima close to the University. There we booked our places to Arequipa for 140 soles each—about $7.00 for a journey of 640 miles, including picking us up at our hotel in Lima and delivering us to our destination in Arequipa; transport at least is still cheap in Peru. 'Please be ready by 5.30,' the Chinese clerk who ran the agency said apologetically. 'It is a long drive for one day.'

To strengthen our knowledge of the ancient civilizations whose monuments we would see on this journey, we spent the rest of our day in Lima at the Museum of Archaeology, which is situated in an old palace in the Lima suburb of Vieja Magdalena. The Museum was founded during the 1930's by Julio Tello, one of the first Peruvians to make a serious study of the pre-Columbian cultures of his own country. Until Tello first became active thirty years ago, educated Peruvians had shown very little interest in anything that preceded the Spanish American society to which they regarded themselves as belonging, and they had left the important work of reconstructing the past before Pizarro's arrival to foreign scholars, particularly North Americans like George Squier and Hiram Bingham, and Germans like Alexander von Humboldt, J. J. von Tchudi and Max Uhle. These men built up the archaeological background to the Inca empire, and it was they who demonstrated that this most famous of Peruvian cultures was only the last in a series of high civilizations that had flourished in the Andes and on the adjacent Pacific coast over at least three thousand years.

Tello followed the clues of his foreign predecessors with imagination and tenacity, and to him we owe the recognition of the importance of the early religious culture that centred on the mountain temple of Chavin at the time of the Peloponnesian wars, and also the discovery of the famous necropolis of Paracas in the southern desert. But, despite his discoveries and his contributions to the theory of Peruvian pre-history, Tello had his faults as an archaeologist. He belonged to the old school that was more intent on digging out splendid objects than on patiently recording their relationship to the site in which they were found, and he has often been accused by more meticulous workers of destroying important data in the excited desire to bring out the treasures which he discovered. To an extent their criticisms were justified, and Tello's merit lay more in the imagination that led to his discoveries and to his brilliant generalizations than in the power of taking pains which is just as necessary to the working archaeologist. He was a great collector, an inspired interpreter and an indifferent accumulator of facts. The museum he created reflected these characteristics.

The ideal museum should collect, instruct and give pleasure. The Lima Museum had been efficient at collecting, for by now its cellars were so packed with ceramics and textiles, gathered from the coastal tombs, that the recent Peruvian laws which forbids the export of archaeological finds was already becoming an embarrassment rather than an advantage. But the display of these great accumulations was most ineffective. The remarkable ceramics of Moche and Nazca, for example, were so crowded into badly lit cases that it was hard not only to appreciate their merits but even, in some cases, to distinguish clearly their shapes and designs, while explanatory labelling was rare and, where it existed, vague.

Yet some of the artifacts of the ancient cultures were splendid enough to triumph over every fault of presentation; one did not need the seductive display techniques of a modern museum to admire the magnificently embroidered mantles in which the 400 chiefs of Paracas had sat for more than a millennium, buried in the red sands of a remote desert peninsula. Who these people may have been, and even in what cities they lived before coming to Paracas for burial, are among the unsolved mysteries of a Peruvian past that is populated by such enigmas. Their mantles, which perhaps were only used in death, are large—about eight feet long and five feet wide—and consist of loosely woven rectangles of cotton cloth on which the design is embroidered in the wool of the alpaca. This design is usually composed of a complex pattern of mythological beings, formalized animal figures and, more rarely, geometrical motifs, but it is the extraordinary harmony of the colouring that brings the deities to life and gives each garment something of the warmth and movement one sees in the best of European medieval tapestries. Yet this comparison is perhaps misleading, since the Paracas people never paint a naturalistic picture or tell a story, as the tapestry-makers so often did; their designs are emblematic, but superimposed on the pattern itself there is a magic of texture which derives partly from the extraordinary delicacy of the weaving and partly from the almost iridescent bloom which the mantles acquire from their exotic combinations of soft and subtle colours. Apart from certain Persian brocades, I have seen no textiles so beautiful as these products of a people without a known habitation or a name that has survived.

Among the other chaotically displayed exhibits we did eventually see, by dint of hard searching, examples of many aspects of the pre-Columbian cultures, from the great carved steles brought from Chavin by Raimondi and Tello down to such purely utilitarian objects as the quipus or bundles of strings which the Incas used for their accounts and their chronicles, and the bronze knives with which the Chimu and Inca surgeons operated on warriors' skulls beaten in by the star-shaped maces that were the favourite weapons of ancient Peruvian hand-to-hand fighting. The pre-Columbian healers must have been skilful surgeons, for a high proportion of the trepanned skulls showed by the growth of new bone that their owners had lived long after their operations, which moreover were probably carried out under one of the earliest of anaesthetics—a strong infusion of coca leaves.

But, interesting as quipus and dented skulls may be in their own ways, it is principally gold that one's imagination tends to associate with the Inca legend—the golden suns of the great temples, the golden gardens of Cuzco, the golden vessels in which Atahuallpa and Pizarro pledged each other at their first and fateful meeting. Much of the Inca gold disappeared when the vessels and statues collected for Atahuallpa's ransom in 1532 were melted into ingots by the Conquerors, but a great deal was hidden at that time, and in recent years golden objects from both the Inca and the earlier civilizations have come to light in considerable quantities. We expected to find at least some of them on exhibition, but in fact, we saw none, and on our way out we stopped at the office to ask whether a collection of Indian work in precious metals actually existed.

A young clerk answered us with a look of amusement. 'But yes, señor! We have the best collection in the world.' We asked then where it was exhibited. 'Oh, it is not *exhibited*,' he replied, laughing openly at what he evidently considered to be our innocence. 'No, no, it is all locked away in our strong rooms.' 'Then can we arrange to see it?' I asked. 'It would be difficult, señor. You would have to ask the director, and he is not here.' And, consolingly, he went on to say that eventually the museum hoped to show its gold in a specially built tunnel where it would be properly protected against thieves. So we left without having seen a single piece of Inca gold, nor, for that matter, did we see any in the rest of Peru.

2

At half-past four the next morning we were awakened by the hotel porter ringing up to tell us that the Arequipa collectivo had arrived. Owing to some inexplicable whim it was an hour earlier than it should have been. We sent the driver away, but barely had we finished dressing, when the car again drew up outside the hotel. It was still only five o'clock, but the driver insisted that, as he had still other people to collect, we should go as soon as possible. We resigned ourselves to starting without breakfast, loaded our cases on to the roof of the car, and set off.

For at least half an hour longer the driver searched through the spreading residential suburbs of San Isidro and Miraflores. In the darkness, lit by rare street lamps, the new, expensive villas of these quarters had a curiously insubstantial appearance. Their variety of style, ranging over the ages and the continents, was so catholic that, in the total stillness of the pre-dawn hour, they might have been the deserted structures of a film set equipped with buildings for every possible plot. Gothic, Tudor, Spanish Colonial, Le Corbusier modernistic—everything was there. At a sham highland castle we picked up a middle-aged man with many suitcases, and at the servants' entrance to a miniature Venetian palazzo a young man in a cricket cap, with only a haversack, was waiting. Finally, outside a little suburban transport agency, we collected a girl with a child in her arms, and our list was complete.

We started on the day's journey, heading towards the open desert. But all at once a dispute broke out between the two men in the back of the car about the seats they had booked. The driver stopped, and the argument spread. Both men claimed to have booked corner seats; so, a moment later, did the girl with the child, and nobody was willing to take the least desirable seat in the middle. The two men blustered ineffectually for a while, and then it was found that the girl had no right to be in the car at all. She had booked her place on a collectivo belonging to another agency, and had got into ours by mistake. But her own car must have gone by now, and she could not afford to pay a second time. The chivalry that is latent in most Peruvians was aroused. Turn a girl with a baby out on to the road? But no! Let her stay! Let her keep the corner seat about which there had been so much bitterness a moment before. Everyone agreed on it, and the driver, after gently reproaching the girl, got back into his seat and drove on.

Half an hour after dawn we had reached a coastal village where we stopped for breakfast in an open-air restaurant under cane awnings which was filled with truck drivers and the passengers from a bus starting on the long, two-day run to La Paz in Bolivia. Above the gabble of their talk the great Pacific breakers crashed and beat on the long open beach beyond the restaurant; we could see the spray leaping in high white fans, and beyond it the sea heaving grey-blue under the grey sky until the clouds came down in mist to form a false horizon a mile or so from the shore. On the other side of the road the sandhills sloped down, dirty yellow, broken by spurs of ochre rock. It was the beginning of the desert, and it was bitterly cold.

The restaurant was the rendezvous where we met the other collectivos that were making the trip to Arequipa. There were three of them and for the rest of the day they travelled in convoy, so that there would always be help at hand in case of a breakdown which, in this waterless country with few settlements, might involve at the very least some serious inconvenience. The driver of one of the other cars, a young mulatto with a green eye-shade, acted as pilot of the convoy, and at his signal we started down the Pan-American highway which runs through the desert and the mountains to Arequipa and Chile.

The coastal desert is one of the great geographical factors in Peru. From Tumbes, almost on the Ecuadorian border, it stretches 700 miles south to Lima, and from Lima another 700 to the Chilean border, where it extends for hundreds of further miles into the terrible nitrate wastes of Atacama. The existence of this extraordinarily arid land, 2,000 miles long but rarely much more than a hundred wide, has fascinated men ever since the days of Indian myth-making, and the people who inhabited the coast before the Incas came down in conquest from the Andes explained it by a legend which is the story of the Deluge in reverse. According to them, the first creator, Kone, made an imperfect race of men and women, and gave them a fertile Eden on the coasts of the Pacific. They sinned, and to punish them Kone forbade the rains to fall; Eden became a desert. But then, as among the Gods of Hellas, there was dissension in the heavens, and a younger God Pachacamac drove Kone away, turned the survivors of the first human race into beasts, and created a better humanity. It is true that Pachacamac failed to withdraw Kone's curse of drought, but he had endowed his men with an intelligence that enabled them to triumph over circumstances, and so, in the midst of the desert, flourished the most sensitive civilizations of Peru, the great cultures of Nazca and Paracas, of Moche and Chimu.

To Pachacamac, at about the time when the Roman Empire was falling apart, his worshippers erected a great pyramid south of Lima which became a centre of pilgrimages from all over the Andes. So great was Pachacamac's prestige that even the conquering Incas refrained from taking his idol to Cuzco, which was their usual custom with the Gods of conquered peoples; instead, they diplomatically claimed that Pachacamac was a coastal manifestation of their own creator God, Viracocha, and so, when the Spaniards arrived, Pachacamac—the town named after the God— was still the Delphi of Peru, to which even the Inca himself, the living God, sent for oracular advice. Here, in search of treasure, Hernando Pizarro hastened at his brother's orders after the murder of Atahuallpa, but already the sacred gold and silver had been taken away, and the tradition that 400 llama loads of it were buried in the sands around the temple has tantalized treasure hunters down to the present day. But if Hernando Pizarro found no gold he had the satisfaction of destroying Pachacamac's image, and the cult disappeared with the God. The Spaniards tore down the stones of the temple for their own buildings in Lima, and the pyramid crumbled into the shapeless hill of adobe bricks which we passed that morning a few miles down the desert road.

After the Indian legends had vanished it took another three centuries before a more rational explanation of the Peruvian desert was offered by Alexander Humboldt in the discovery of the current that bears his name. The Humboldt Current is a cold stream which swings out of the Antarctic and flows for 2,000 miles off the Pacific shores of South America. It cools the prevalent winds, which then pass over the warmer earth, so that, instead of the condensation that is usual when moist winds hit the land, a process of absorption takes place; as a result, rain never falls in this region from century to century.

Monotony is the prime characteristic of all deserts, and the landscape through which we travelled during the daylight hours developed very limited variations on a simple theme of sand and bare rocks and sea. Wide plains of firm sand merging into the long beaches where the high waves broke beside the road; corrugated dune land where the sand blew and drifted in smoky wisps across the road; dry rocky hills from which we would look down on the blue ocean receding into a pearly distance; ugly wastes of pebbles like great moraines: we went through all these differing types of country, but the whole land was united in its aridity and its emptiness, and the changes of mood came principally from the subtly varying colours, as the tints of the sands and rocks modulated from yellow towards orange, and then deepened to the dull reds and sombre purples of the ancient lava beds.

But if the land in this region was desiccated and lifeless, the sea was populous. The cool waters of the Humboldt Current harbour fish of many kinds, and these in turn encourage great numbers of sea birds which give an incongruous sense of life to the desert coast. As we drove along it thousands of terns and gulls wheeled over the inshore waves and brown pelicans flapped like clumsy experimental birds from the morning of evolution. But most numerous of all were the guanays—the guano birds. At first sight, because of their white chests and almost upright walk, the guanays looked like slender penguins, but at a second glance one recognized certain features—the long bill sharply hooked at the tip and the heavy, low flight over the water—which suggested cormorants in disguise. The guanays were venturesome and stupid; they would stroll solemnly from the beach to the highway, and waddle in front of the cars like old men at street crossings, with no evident sense of danger and without the least idea that by flying a few yards they might save themselves from the destruction which, on certain stretches of the road, had left hundreds of them dead on the verges, attracting the only land bird one sees in the desert— the vulture, that adaptable scavenger which is at home in every altitude and in every climate of Peru.

Every forty or fifty miles the dead surface of the desert would be cracked by a small river running down from the Andes and nurturing its narrow line of vegetation. But even these attenuated oases followed a pattern which in its turn became monotonous. Between beds of gravel a scanty dry-season stream would find its hesitant way, and thickets of yellowish reeds and jade-green canes would cluster along its banks, but there were few trees in the valleys— some palms and Peruvian peppers and a scattering of flat-topped carob trees where the desert met the edge of the moist land. The cultivated areas of level ground beside the rivers were devoted to cotton or maize, and most of the hamlets consisted of little square huts of cane or of reed mats, the products of the oases themselves. Characterless as they were, we welcomed the valleys for the coolness of their green colouring after the dazzle of the desert.

The first town, many miles down the coast, was Pisco, which we saw from the hill road that by-passed it—a miniature white city with a blue handful of harbour in which a cruiser floated. Beyond Pisco the road turned away from the sea and, to reach the oases of Ica and—fifty miles on—Nazca, it ran inland on a long arc which curved 150 miles through the desert before it came within sight of the ocean again. The terrain was now more hilly, but still completely barren, and all the emptier because there was no longer the changing blue of the sea to give its varying element to the landscape.

Both Ica and Nazca, formerly the centres of ancient civilizations, are now busy agricultural towns, nondescript and utilitarian, surrounded by sugar plantations, orange gardens and cotton fields snowy with the blossoms of tiny bushes stunted by the recent droughts. Here the people were less homogeneous in appearance than those of the Sierra, owing largely to the presence of many Negroes and zambos—the descendants of Indian and Negro interbreeding. Distinctive local costumes seemed to have been abandoned, and only the wide-brimmed straw sombrero which both men and women wore gave their dress a touch of individuality. Most of the people looked poor, and so they doubtless were, for the irrigated land in these oases belongs to haciendas which employ the local population as peons, and the sugar barons of Ica in particular have traditionally bad names in Peru for their treatment of labourers. Nevertheless, despite an obvious lack of material blessings, the people of these towns looked more light-hearted than the Indians of the Sierra; they had mobile faces, they sang and smiled, and there was a litheness about their movements which one rarely sees among the mountain people. This apparent difference in temperament may be due partly to the influx of Negroes, but it may be linked with an older past, for the original inhabitants of this region seem, in comparison with the megalomaniac Incas, to have been a modest and sensitive people, delicate in taste and endowed with a sense of humour.

Nazca was the centre of the more interesting of these desert civilizations. We went through the town around midday and stopped to eat lunch in a chifa—a Chinese restaurant—run by a mummified old man and a family of sluttish girls. It was, I think, the dirtiest eating house I have ever entered; the table-cloths were stiff with the spilt food of innumerable past meals, and the flies crawled over them like an Egyptian plague, so numerous and so persistent that in the end, knowing they would always return, we gave up trying to whisk them away. We ate what seemed to us moderately safe dishes, creole soup and scrambled eggs, and hoped for the best. As it happened there were no after effects; indeed, it was one of the ironies of our journey that when, later on, we suffered from dysentery, we could never trace it to the more filthy restaurants where we so often had to eat.

There were no ancient monuments to be seen in Nazca. The civilization that flourished there raised no great temples, built no palaces or walled cities, constructed no roads of conquest, and appears to have had no organization resembling the great theocratic systems which governed the realms of the Inca and the Chimu. Its relics are those of an unaggressive and democratic people, whose tombs show little difference in wealth, little distinction between the sexes, and few signs of a privileged military or ecclesiastical caste.

The Nazcans, indeed, seem to have been unimpressed by thoughts of worldly glory, and to have been content with drawing from the desert a living that would give them leisure to produce beautiful objects. They were excellent farmers, and not only utilized irrigation but also, in places where they could not get water, evolved a dry farming technique similar to that of the Nabateans in the classic days of Palmyra, starting off the seed with a couple of fish heads and keeping it growing by tapping the heavy dews of the desert. Their textiles were pleasant and competent without quite reaching the superb quality of those of Paracas; they excelled in ceramics, but as painters rather than as potters, for they used simple shapes and concentrated on painted designs applied to the polished surfaces. They portrayed stylized animals and birds and anthropomorphic beings; their work had a softness of colouring and a lightness of touch exceptional even in Peruvian ceramics, and also a humour which gave many of their linear figures a whimsical suggestion of caricature. Klee would have understood the Nazca painters very well, and William Morris might have found their life nearer to his ideals than that of medieval England. But all this is now a matter for museums, and little of the old culture is left around Nazca except for the good humour of its people, in which one likes to imagine that the last heritage of a graceful past may be retained.

From Nazca the road returned to the coast, and here we passed through the one part of the desert that had a dramatic and appalling individuality. It was a volcanic region, a group of hills and natural arenas of pierced and twisted lava which projected into the sea in headlands where the beating waves had isolated tall needles of rock and scooped great portholes out of the reddish cliffs. For several miles the landscape was as grotesque and tortured as if the angels had found a second Sodom to scarify with their rains of fire. And yet this burnt-out inferno was more inhabited than most other parts of the desert coast. Indian families had built sheds of pebbles among the scarred rocks and little chozas of mats down by the narrow beaches. And the life they had made themselves, in this most unfriendly of environments, was not merely that of fishermen, for there were often goats and sheep tethered close to their huts; how they fed them, unless on seaweed, I cannot imagine. Once, in a valley of dead boulders where there seemed to be no people living, we even met a large white bull walking quietly

along the road; in that setting it looked like some creature of mythology, as if the Metamorphoses were about to receive a new tale
of the adventures of Jove, seeking this time no earthly maiden but
some sad being of desolate Hades.

Later we returned to the monotonous alternation of wide
beaches and high tumbling dunes, and this continued until we
left the seashore at Camana. The only place I can remember at all
clearly in this stretch was noticeable mainly for its effort to defy
the limitations of the landscape. It was a small fishing port called
Chala, built on a hill overlooking a golden beach; its houses, and
even its church, were made entirely of planks, and all these
buildings were painted in gay, definite colours and hung over with
drying nets.

It was dark by the time we drove inland towards the mountains;
a full moon gave a baroque emphasis to the outlines of the stony
foothills. The road was wide, well-paved and to all appearances
safe, yet it was here, and not on any of the perilous mountain
roads, that our wanderings in Peru came nearest to a premature
conclusion. In the hope of making up for lost time—since we
were at least three hours late—the driver was travelling quickly.
We entered a narrow canyon which lay so completely in shadow
that, after the clear moonlight of the open road, we could distinguish nothing beyond the reach of the feeble headlights; a moment
afterwards we saw a single light approaching on the far side of the
road and imagined that it belonged to a motor-bike. Suddenly,
within a few yards of it, we saw that the light was in fact on the
off-side of a lorry, towards which we were driving at sixty miles
an hour. With a quickness of reaction astonishing after 500 miles
on the road, our driver wrenched the wheel violently, sent the
car spinning towards the verge so that it missed the lorry by a
bare inch, and then, with another sharp pull of the wheel, swung
it back on to the crown of the road. For one second, as the front
of the lorry loomed ahead, death seemed inevitable; for another
second it appeared impossible that we could escape without
crashing into the side of the canyon, and when everything was
over, it was hard to believe that we were really alive and riding
still towards Arequipa. Possibly because the incident happened so

quickly, everyone on the collectivo took it very calmly. Only the child, unaware of the real danger, cried fretfully because it had been jerked awake. The driver merely breathed out in relief, crossed himself, and muttered, in regard to the other driver, 'Too much chicha!' Yet at the next village he waited for his colleagues of the convoy, and together they went into a chapel by the road-side that was lit by many votive candles, and knelt for a long time before the altar.

An hour or two later we crossed the last sandy, scrub-covered hill and looked down towards Arequipa. Behind the city the ring-ing volcanic mountains shone tawnily under the moonlight—high among them the tall white cone of Misti which, in the vastness of its isolation against that ultramarine sky, resembled the poetic vision of Fujiyama, etched on one's mind by the hands of so many Japanese artists. Under the mountains the moon picked out in sil-houette the cypresses and eucalyptuses which stood like black companies of watchmen at every quarter of the city, and silvered the campaniles and the tiled domes. The street lights glistened like water throwing back the moonlight in the depths of a forest. Never did a Peruvian city seem so beautiful at first sight, or so tranquilly inviting, as Arequipa after that long day in the desert.

Yet there were many discouragements in the way of our enjoying it. They began with the Guardia Civil. The sentinel at the post on the edge of the city took the driver's list of passengers, and re-turned after a moment. He looked into the collectivo. 'Come to the guardhouse, señor,' he said to me. I got out of the car, and Inge followed me. 'Only the señor,' said the guard. 'Ah,' said Inge resourcefully, 'but the señor's Spanish is very bad.' The guard thought stolidly for a moment, and one of our fellow passengers said hurriedly in broken English, 'Is better you go, señora. Sometimes difficulty. . . .' Clearly he thought that a witness was desirable in an interview with the Guardia, and we walked together towards the guardhouse. My mind, always fertile in anxiety, throbbed with possibilities. Had a rumour of my anarchist youth come home belatedly to roost? It hardly seemed likely that it would settle in far-off Arequipa. Had one of the people to whom we had talked politics been after all a secret police agent? I could imagine none of them in the role of an informer. Then perhaps a case of mistaken identity?

I was still pondering the last possibility when we entered the guardhouse. Two officers sat at a desk with a volume like a large ledger open before them; three heavily armed guards stood around the almost bare room. The elder officer, fat and moustachioed, pointed to a couple of chairs. The younger, fair-haired and Gothic, took up a pen and leaned expectantly over the book. They looked slowly through our passports, pondered over our visas, and asked why we were visiting Arequipa. And then, without any of the accusatory questions we had expected, the interview was over. The two officers rose and shook hands ceremoniously; the younger opened the door and hoped we would enjoy the city. Nothing could have been more polite than their behaviour, but this left us all the more puzzled by what seemed a pointless interview. Later, when we got back to Lima, we were told that during the few days before the inauguration of the new President a particularly close watch was being kept on travellers in Peru, and that the arrival of two foreigners late at night in a provincial city was in itself un-usual enough to arouse the suspicions of the Guardia; the ques-tionnaire, according to this interpretation, was merely a harmless face-saving procedure designed to allow the officers to take a close look at us before they allowed us to enter the city.

However, the politeness of the Guardia did not prevent our resenting this kind of roadside interrogation, and we apologized to our fellow passengers for the delay with an acid comment on the procedure that had caused it. 'It happens often,' said the man who had already spoken to us; 'it is what we expect.' He spoke in a mollifying tone, as if reproaching us by implication for kicking against the inevitable. But, unlike him, we had not been born in a country where travel had been carefully supervised ever since the days when the Incas placed guards at every bridge to make sure that their subjects were not wandering without authority, and our feelings towards the Guardia became even more bitter when, a quarter of an hour later, at eleven o'clock, the collectivo drew up outside the Government Hotel. For there another grey-uniformed officer moved out of the shadows of a eucalyptus tree and stood beside the car looking silently at us and at each piece of luggage as the driver handed it to the hotel porter. He was still watching as we went through the door into the foyer of the hotel.

After eighteen hours of travel we were tired enough to feel mildly paranoiac about an arrival accompanied by double attentions from the police. Our gloom deepened when we found that, though we had wired for a reservation, the hotel was so full that we were allotted a dim little room in an old, rarely used wing. Moreover, since the kitchen was closed, all we could get to stay a ten-hour hunger was a corned-beef sandwich which the night porter prepared after a good deal of persuasion and a tip. As we sat champing the thick hunks of bread and stringy meat, shivering from exhaustion and cold, dismally regarding the dim lamps and the worn chenille bedspread, we forgot the Arequipa we had seen from the hill an hour before. Eden had faded, as it fades so often in travelling; instead we felt ourselves in a purgatory of disillusionment, and the prospect of all the miles that remained to be travelled appalled us.

3

Yet we left Arequipa after all with the feeling that it was the most pleasant town of Peru, and even now, more than a year later, when I remember our journey, I realize that if I ever return it will be mostly for the sake of two cities—Iquitos, which we never saw, and Arequipa, of which we saw too little.

The change in our attitude began as soon as we left the decrepitude of our room the next morning and looked out from the hotel terrace at the bell-towers of the city and the mountains beyond them. The moonlit city of the night before was reconstructed in our minds, but gilded by the mellow sunlight and the soft air of a summer's morning in the middle of winter.

Everything now seemed so pleasant that we decided we would like to stay in Arequipa longer than the day or two we had originally intended, and we went back into the hotel to see whether there might be some chance of our being given a better room. The manager, Dr. Schaale, was a pleasant, paternal Austrian, who later did us many of those small kindnesses which sound trivial when one tries to describe them but which mean a great deal when one is travelling in a strange country. At the moment he apologized, and I am sure with genuine regret, for the room we had been given, but insisted that he could do nothing better. Indeed, even that room he could let us have only for another night. On the next day, the 27th July, he explained, the city would be invaded by people coming from all over southern Peru for the Independence Day celebrations. This year there would be more than usual, brought by curiosity, since, if the Army decided not to accept the new President, the trouble might well begin in Arequipa, which is the traditional starting point for military coups in Peru.[1] 'By the 28th you won't find one room in the town worth taking,' Dr. Schaale remarked.

We found that he was right, and we had to reconcile ourselves to spending a single day in Arequipa before we went on our way to Lake Titicaca. And it was doubtless this very shortness of our stay that gave our experience of Arequipa its peculiar, tantalizing intensity.

Indeed, Arequipa has always pleased travellers by a freshness of atmosphere and character which is due largely to the fact that it belongs to none of the extreme climatic zones of Peru, but lies between the Sierra and the coast, 7,000 feet above the sea and almost as much below the tableland of Titicaca. Its air is light, yet dense enough to hold the warmth of the sun much longer than the atmosphere of the Sierra; the coastal mists never reach it, and rain rarely falls, yet the land is green under its clear sky, for long ago the Incas trapped the waters of the River Chili and built the irrigation system which makes Arequipa a city of trees and gardens in a lush farming valley. When Francisco Pizarro arrived on Assumption Day in 1540, even his toughened heart was so moved by this temperate land of perpetual summer that he christened the new city Villa Hermosa.

[1] Both Sanchez Cerro in 1930 and Odria in 1948 began their uprisings by 'pronouncing' in Arequipa.

The Spaniards liked Arequipa, and nurtured with fine buildings this remote settlement which, until fifty years ago, could be reached only by the mule tracks over the mountains. Even today Arequipa is predominantly a creole city, with a strong Castilian tradition-alism which is personified in the many blue-sashed seminarians and heavily braided officers one meets in its streets. Yet, for all its conservatism, Arequipa is not primitive in the same way as the half-Indian towns of the Sierra. It is clean, it smells mostly of food and of flowers, it has attractive cafés and fairly sophisticated shops, and its buildings are graceful enough to mingle well with the almost excessively dramatic background of bare pointed mountains.

The attractiveness of Arequipa's Renaissance mansions and churches, and of the eighteenth-century arcades that surround its plaza, is due largely to the stone from which they were built. It is a white volcanic stone, called sillar, which is flecked delicately with small fragments of black ash and which weathers into a pale, warm grey that softens and enriches the light it reflects. The best of the surviving buildings erected in this stone during the colonial era are the Church of the Compañia, built at the end of the seventeenth century, and the neighbouring Jesuit Cloister, which was added during the very early years of the eighteenth century. Both are examples of that strange renaissance of Indian art—the last burst of a dying fire—which followed the conversion of the Inca dominions to Christianity. In Cuzco and Quito the movement produced its inspired schools of painting, but in Arequipa it turned towards sculpture, and the façade of the Compañia Church, as well as the walls and pillars of the Cloister, are covered with an elaborate pattern of relief carving which was done entirely by Indian craftsmen.

At first these closely worked walls strike one as a gauche imita-tion of the Churrigueresque style which flourished luxuriantly in the churches of so many Latin American countries. In fact, how-ever, the carvings in Arequipa are quite different from the pro-ducts of that late baroque school, and in origin they are American rather than European. Their creators were not concerned with the heavy patterning of light and shade which gave movement and depth to the Churrigueresque fantasies in stone. Instead they carved shallow relief for the purpose of surface decoration, and their work is wholly two-dimensional in feeling; shadow is used only to outline forms and never as an element in the design. The patterns are characteristically Indian, both in manner and motif. Even their lines remind one of pre-Conquest reliefs, for there is a tendency to flatten the extremities of curves and to produce half-squared circles and spirals similar to those which one sees in both Chimu and early Aymara carvings.

Even more unexpected than the survival of an Indian manner of carving is the richness with which native life and even pagan traditions are represented on these Jesuit walls. Among the crowded reliefs, which leave hardly an inch of wall undecorated, the men and women, the plants and animals of the Indian world are all represented. Llamas and pumas, guinea-pigs and snakes—all of them appear in a kind of Noah's Ark pageantry, but there are also such ritualistic symbols as corn-cobs and coca leaves, and often, bringing in their echoes of Inca ceremonies, the feathers of various sacred birds. Even more curious is the frequent presence of the sun and the moon, the very symbols of the most powerful of the pagan Gods, now brought prominently into the decoration of a Christian building. Nothing could show more eloquently the evangelistic eclecticism with which Catholic missionaries in that period set about their task of conversion.

In this desire to win the souls of the Indians by sweeping into the new cult every symbol that might have meaning for the Indian mind, there is something reminiscent of the nineteenth-century evangelists appropriating the songs of taverns and music halls, of General Booth asking why all the good tunes should be left to the Devil. But while, with unerring bad taste, the Salvationists and their kind always borrowed from the Devil his ugliest inventions, this pagan hymn to Christianity which the Jesuits inspired their converts to carve on the walls of Arequipa achieved a lyricism that was rarely present in pre-Christian Peruvian art.

It is true that the carvings on the Jesuit buildings had already some of that overdrawn fragility which is often the sign of an artistic tradition at the moment of decadence. Yet to look at them now, 200 years later, as representing the last important period of Indian art, is to measure the descent into apathy that has made the Andeans of today into a people virtually without art.

This fact makes all the more tragic the indifference with which such work—or any work of the past—is treated by modern Arequipans. What beauty the city has, apart from its setting, it owes mostly to the remaining colonial buildings, but there is little attempt to organize their preservation, and for the most part they are left to the caprices of their owners. Even in the Jesuit Cloister we found that, far from any effort being made to maintain intact this exceptional example of Indian-Spanish art, the buildings that gave on to the Cloister were being used as lawyers' and architects' offices, and the carvings themselves had in some places been covered with coatings of cement, applied in such a way as to imitate a facing of dressed stone.

We saw only one colonial mansion in anything like its original condition, and that belonged, not to an Arequipan, but to an English mine-owner and his American wife, who welcomed us very hospitably when we went there on Dr. Schaale's introduction. The house, like most of the older mansions in Arequipa, was built around a cobbled central patio, and, as they led us through the high, barrel-vaulted rooms, our hosts told us the history of their effort to re-create the kind of dwelling that might have flourished in Arequipa during the high days of the Spanish Empire. When they bought it, the house had been half-ruined; for many years it had stood empty because of one of the legends one often hears in Latin American towns about a former owner who had fallen under the ban of the Inquisition and whose dwelling was therefore an ill-omened place to inhabit. 'In a way that was a good thing,' remarked Mrs. W. 'It saved us the trouble of clearing away all the nineteenth-century rubbish that would otherwise have been there. The main thing was that the walls were so well built that they stood up against a long period of neglect. And the carvings were still amazingly fresh when we cleared away the grass and the ferns. You'll notice that they are all Indian work.'

And indeed, when we saw the rich decorations of the windows

and doorways, and the friezes that here and there remained on the bare inner walls, we recognized the same low relief style that we had seen on the Jesuit buildings. But the secular house-builders had left less to the fancy of the artisans, for the motifs which appeared on this mansion were those that would have suited the tastes of a Spanish hidalgo two centuries ago—the flowers and garlands and lutes, conventional images given an unexpected freshness by their exotic Indian lines.

'We had to rebuild some of the vaulting which had fallen,' Mrs. W. explained. 'And after that we began to look for doors and furniture to match the house. We drove and rode all over the countryside to hunt for whatever we could find in old granges and farmhouses.'

We examined the wood carving, which was done mostly in elaborate and almost Moorish geometrical patterns. 'Surely this is Spanish,' I suggested. 'No, most of it is by Indians,' Mrs. W. replied, 'but it does resemble southern Spanish work. There were some Spanish craftsmen in the beginning who taught the Indians, but the Spaniards soon felt that manual work was undignified for white men, and so the Indians have carried on alone ever since.' Mrs. W. went on to explain how, apart from style and finish, one could be fairly sure of telling the local Arequipa woodwork. 'You look for straight, thin grain,' she said. 'That belongs to a kind of willow which grows in the valley. In the days when everything had to be brought here by mules it was hard to import wood, so the carpenters used whatever was at hand, and they soon found that willow was the best local wood for carving.'

Apart from the furniture, the W.'s had collected Indian textiles and pottery and a number of Cuzco primitive paintings, whose intense velvety colourings glowed within massive gilded frames, which had been set with hundreds of tiny glittering mirrors. All the objects belonged to the brief Spanish-Indian renaissance that had produced the house itself, and the W.'s had brought them together with such tact that the house was not merely a private museum, but had also retained the feeling of a dwelling in use which made it easy to imagine some eighteenth-century creole living there a cultured life that might well have tempted the hostile curiosity of the Holy Office. The one saddening aspect of the house was that it had been left for foreigners to re-create a heritage about which the real heirs—the Arequipans themselves—seemed mostly unconcerned.

That evening, as we left the Casa W. and walked back along the streets of walled gardens towards the hotel, the blue of the sky was darkening, and already the daylight was becoming transmuted into the cold luminescence cast by the rising moon. Slowly, in the classical harmony of pale light and dense shadow, the city on which we had first looked was re-created around us. Only the fragrance of the datura, thickening as the evening lengthened, reminded one of the taste of summer in the hot streets of the afternoon. The cycle of our day in Arequipa was completed.

4

From Arequipa to Lake Titicaca one can travel either by rail or by road; we followed the example of the Peruvians who, whenever they have a choice, seem to prefer the slow security of the mountain trains to the perilous discomforts of the collectivos or buses. So, getting up once again before dawn, we set out to catch the Southern Railway's thrice-weekly train to Puno.

The Southern Railway, I should explain, is one of those curious disconnected fragments, like the line from Lima to Huancayo, that make up the anarchic railway system of Peru. It starts at a small seaport called Mollendo, about ninety miles south-west of Arequipa, runs up to Lake Titicaca, where it connects with the boats to Bolivia, and then turns north-westward towards its terminus at Cuzco. At no point does it come within less than 200 miles of the Central Railway, its closest neighbour to the north, which in turn is unconnected with the half-dozen smaller railways that trace their autonomous ways up the river valleys of northern Peru. All these lines ending at the sea are in fact relics of the age when railways were built to serve the interests of mine-owners and exporters rather than those of Peru as a whole.

Outside Arequipa the fields were lush with young crops and running with water from the morning opening of the irrigation channels, and the encircling volcanic peaks seemed anchored in a lake of green. But as the hills rose above irrigation level the ground turned abruptly into a hot, marigold-yellow waste on which grew strange cacti with angular limbs like spider-crabs, covered with translucent golden spines and studded with topaz-yellow flowers. For a while the mountain settlements were close together, their characters changing progressively as one climbed towards the cold. At Yura, a decayed spa village about 9,000 feet up, the women came along the train with bananas and chopped sugar-cane. At Uyapampa, three or four hundred feet higher, there were apple orchards and green terraces and a few pine trees, but already, under the eaves of the houses, grey brush was piled instead of firewood. The land was becoming parsimonious, and soon it merged into a glacial country of rocks and leafless bushes, a country that some-times broke into unexpected colour when yellow cushions of rock roses blossomed among the dead scrub or lupins lapped like blue water around the green-lichened boulders. Once, like a message in this unpopulated wilderness, a life-sized kneeling figure of Christ was painted on the rock wall of a cutting; it had been done by some workman in the black and white paints used for marking the railway mileposts, and it had a haunting, almost Byzantine quality of line, tightened by the stress of feeling.

On the highest of the uplands the brush straggled to an end, and the smooth ichu meadows gave grazing to flocks of sheep and alpacas. The mountains were populated once again, but the villages were little more than nondescript huddles of pebble houses. At one of them, late in the morning, the train stopped its hour for the Indian passengers to take their meal in the thin bitter air that had hung long icicles on the station water-tower.

This time the Indians who crowded around the food-sellers were mostly Aymara, members of a large tribe that inhabits both the Peruvian and the Bolivian sides of Lake Titicaca; we had already encountered them in Arequipa, where many have migrated recently owing to the drought in the southern Sierra. The Aymara have always been a stubbornly independent people. After the Incas had subdued them militarily, they were one of the few Sierra tribes to keep their own language in defiance of the conquerors' attempt to impose Quechua. In Spanish times they were the most stubborn fighters in the great Indian revolts of the 1780's, and today, more even than the Quechua peoples, they resist assimilation and regard themselves not as Peruvians or Bolivians, but only as Aymara, united by tradition and habit across meaningless frontiers.

Even among Peruvian Indians, the Aymara seemed to us an exceptionally ill-favoured tribe—squat, thick-waisted and heavy-featured, with sallower skins and more sullen expressions than the people of the Central Sierra. The women showed these characteristics most emphatically, and one rarely saw among them that look of florid vitality which sometimes takes the place of beauty among the Quechua women. I always hope, doubtless naïvely, to find in a people with a name for independence some kind of likeable aura that will arouse more than a theoretical sympathy, but with the best will I found it hard to see anything congenial in the Aymara. Yet almost certainly their very unlikeability is part of the strength that makes them so tenacious of independence. A people more charming, more pliant, more open to sympathy might long ago have lost its individuality. And so perhaps, in seeking the noble savage, we must change our ideas of nobility and expect, not some naked Sir Galahad, but the Indian who, sullen, dour and suspicious, contrives by these unpleasing qualities to survive where gentler and softer races have been submerged.

In dress the Aymara did not differ greatly from the Indians we had already encountered. They followed the same general style imposed by the Spaniards in the sixteenth century, except that the multiple skirts of the women were shorter than those worn around Huancayo and—most striking of differences—the Spanish peasant hats worn in other parts of the Sierra had been replaced by the English bowler, which has been the feminine fashion around Lake Titicaca for a good many decades, and is now worn in a variety of colours that would startle a Bond Street hatter. Little girls are inclined to sport red bowlers, staid matrons prefer brown and race-track grey, and the younger women have a giddy taste for bright yellow hats, worn low over the sulky brows at the jaunty angle of a music-hall masher.

Through the afternoon the train meandered on over the highlands, stopping at tiny hamlets, drawing into sidings to wait for the goods trains that came crawling down from Lake Titicaca, their roofs crowded with ponchoed men whose gaudy eared caps were pulled well down over their necks because of the cold. The siesta mood set in, sweeping the Pullman like a numbing vapour, and heads lolled in drowsiness or turned to books as an escape from the repetitiveness of the landscape. Two trousered and cameraed girls—later we found from the Puno Hotel register that they were Chileans—read the poems of Cesar Vallejo and Max Brod's book on Kafka in a Spanish translation. Vallejo and Kafka seemed outlandish enough on this isolated plateau to provide an excuse for a conversation, but the girls themselves carried an armour of youthful self-sufficiency that deterred us both from the attempt, and soon we retreated into our own books—Inge into *Buddenbrooks* and I into *The Devils*.

To return to Dostoevsky in this setting was disturbing, for even though I had been looking at Indian life in much the same way as Beebe had looked at the fishes of the deep sea, I had felt the impact of its rather elemental simplicity strongly enough to make the over-complexity of a novel like *The Devils* stand out in exasperating clarity. It appeared, despite all Dostoevsky's avowed anti-intellectualism, the product of a mind of devious sophistication and contrivance. I regretted not having brought a volume of Turgenev instead, for I suspect that *A Sportsman's Sketches* would have seemed far more sympathetic in this pastoral and primitive setting than anything by Dostoevsky, that child of the city and all its distortions.

I am sure, of course, that exceptional circumstances of this kind necessarily affect one's reaction to almost any book above the level of mere distraction. Significantly, of the half-dozen volumes I took to Peru and read scrappily in hotel rooms and on the dull stretches of journeys, that which absorbed me most was a translation of Herodotus. The world of the ancients, and particularly the Persian Empire, came amazingly alive against the Andean background, and in the Greek historian's final analysis of how the strength of the Persians declined once they had deserted their harsh life as mountain warriors for the luxury of the valleys and plains one found much of Peruvian history explained. For the Incas and the Spaniards alike, hardy men from the meagre table-lands, experienced the same weakening corruption as the Persians of Herodotus when empire came as the deceptive reward of their valour.

At last, undramatically, we crossed the pass of Crucero Alto; it was somewhat over 14,500 feet. Now the parched torrent beds began to converge on the great self-contained basin of Titicaca. As the country sloped gently down towards the flat altiplano that surrounds the lake we passed large shallow lagoons—populous with seagulls and ducks—which lay in the hollows between soft hills 'like the Sussex Downs. The settlements became larger and more characterful than the stony hamlets of the mountaintop. Santa Lucia was a village of whitewashed houses surrounding a ruined church; there the girl hawkers came along the train selling little sugar men like the magical pottery figurines made by the ancient Peruvians. And at Cabanillas we felt ourselves, for the first time since Arequipa, in a town rather than a village, but a distinctively Indian town; the houses were painted pink and orange and white, and the train passed down a wide main street shaded by great eucalyptuses. The women of Cabanillas paraded in scalloped jackets and red and yellow skirts embroidered with black ogee figures, and it was the men who twirled their spindles as they watched the train.

Nearer the lake the terraces of cultivation began to score the hillsides once again. But even as one passed them at the speed of a train, the signs of the drought that had gripped this part of the Sierra like a year-long winter were evident enough, for many of the dry fields grew nothing at all, and many of the smaller farmsteads had already the look of abandonment, as if the countryside were gradually becoming depopulated.

It was not until after dark that the train started down the branch line from the junction of Juliaca towards Puno and the lake. Already, as dusk fell on the eve of Independence Day, the celebrations had begun. At one country station a procession of schoolboys came down to the train, carrying lanterns in the shapes of ships and aeroplanes and other emblems of the modern cults of material progress. And then, swinging down to the lakeshore, the line skirted the Bay of Puno; in the distance the lights of a town scribbled their shuddering reflections, and rockets rose and burst into stars that cracked the glassy blackness of the bay. We had arrived in Puno.

Since the Government Hotel in Puno is only a short walk from the railway station, it is the custom there to hire a porter rather than take a taxi. We engaged the first youth who came up to us, and he set off with our bags, and stopped all at once in the shadow of a doorway. 'Pay me before I go on,' he said. 'I want ten soles.' I was too surprised to think immediately what to do, and before I had even answered him a voice with a German accent shouted, 'Ha, what is this?' and a fair-haired man whom I had seen already on the train ran forward, grabbed the youth by his jacket, flourished a massive fist under his nose and bawled: 'Picaron! Rascal! Pick up those cases and go on your way!' Cowed, the boy did as he was told, and scuttled ahead. 'Give him two soles! That is enough!' the man said to me, and then he proceeded to introduce himself and his wife, a dark and attractive creole. His name was Weiss; he was a Swiss from Zurich, who had lived for some years in Peru. 'You cannot let these fellows get away with it,' he grumbled. And when, at the hotel door, I gave the boy five soles, which seemed a fair price according to Peruvian standards, he laughed and shook his head. 'You are spoiling them. It is no good. They must be kept in their places.'

5

Out of the waters of Lake Titicaca, says one of the ancient Inca legends, the creator god Viracocha made the sun and the moon. At that time there were already men living on the earth, but they were like wild beasts, uncouth and miserable. When the sun looked down he had pity on them, and sent his son Manco Capac down to an island in the lake to teach them the arts of civilization. And, says the legend, it was Manco—that Andean Prometheus— who went from Lake Titicaca over the mountains to found the Inca dynasty at Cuzco.

For modern archeologists the lake is almost as fascinating as it was for the Indian myth-makers. No evidence actually supports the idea that the Inca civilization itself originated anywhere but in the valley of Cuzco, from which it emerged during the fourteenth century to dominate the Andes. But long before then the altiplano around Titicaca had been the home of a great early civilization which built the massive temples of Tiahuanaco on the Bolivian shore at the time when the Byzantine Empire was at its height, and whose cultural influence affected even the Moche and Chimu peoples in the deserts a thousand miles to the north.

As had happened with the early peoples of Paracas and Nazca, the very name of the Tiahuanaco civilization was lost in the systematic remaking of oral history by which the Incas sought to suppress the racial traditions of conquered peoples and to impose their own myths with an efficiency that anticipated the remakers of history in Orwell's 1984. Yet the awe which the great lake inspired in the minds of the Andean peoples forced even the Incas to accept its sacredness and to give it a place in their traditions, in much the same way as Virgil incorporated Troy in the tradition of Rome.

To this day Titicaca has remained for Andean Indians a Huaca, a sacred place, and the sense of its mystery has transmitted itself to those modern scholars who are inclined towards the more romantic interpretations of world history. Like all the ancient American civilizations, that of Tiahuanaco has been linked with the lost continents of Atlantis and Mu, as well as with ancient Egypt. It has also been identified with the mysterious Biblical land of Ophir, while, according to yet another version of South American pre-history, it was invaded by the Mongols and Manco Capac was the child, not of the Sun, but of Kubla Khan. Finally, recognizing the simplicity of the Aymara language spoken around the lake, certain philological enthusiasts, like Onffroy de Thoron, have claimed that this was the very speech of Adam and that the basin of Lake Titicaca is in fact the situation of the original Earthly Paradise, the birthplace of man.

One approaches a place that carries such a weight of myth and romance with a certain undefined expectation. But it would be a poetic exaggeration if I were to suggest that, when we stepped out of the hotel in the morning and crunched over the frozen puddles towards the lakeshore, I felt within me any recognition of Titicaca's god-haunted past. Over a piece of sandy waste land the railway sidings spread towards the beach and the jetty, and out in the bay an old steamboat was moored; it was the *Yavari*, which the ubiquitous Henry Meiggs, when he was planning the Southern Railway in 1868, sent up through the mountains in small pieces on muleback. Great yellow reed beds closed the neck of the bay to a narrow channel, and beyond them the pale blue waters of the lake itself rippled coldly towards the distant white ridges of the Bolivian Nevadas. The arid hills swept in brown folds down to the shoreline, and no tree broke their bareness. What beauty the lake had was almost cruelly severe; after the jungle, after green Arequipa, such massive simplicity froze and appalled one. And yet the sheer strangeness of this miniature sea, more than a hundred miles long, spreading its wide waters on a level with some of the most formidable peaks of the Alps, gave at least the sense of awe. It was no Earthly Paradise, but it was a landscape hard enough to drive men towards civilization and chill enough to make them seek the fatherhood of the sun.

On our first morning we were content with our brief shoreside visit to the lake, since we intended to spend the rest of the day in Puno seeing the Independence Day festivities. Outside the hotel, on our way back, we ran into Weiss, who was going for a walk in the town and asked us to accompany him. His wife, he told us, was sick from soroche, the mountain sickness; she was a Lima girl, and perhaps it had been unwise of him to expect her to take to the mountains. 'What makes it worse, we are on our honeymoon,' he lamented, and went on to speak of his wife with such feeling that for the moment we forgot the rather poor impression which his behaviour towards the Indian youth had given us on the previous evening.

Puno was a dour mountain town of brown stone houses roofed with corrugated iron; its few trees grew grudgingly in the thin air of the altiplano, its buildings were neglected, and the patterned courtyards of black and white pebbles for which it was once celebrated had mostly been cemented over to avoid the trouble of maintaining them. But the façade of the cathedral, carved by the seventeenth-century Indian craftsmen, was very handsome, and quite different from the churches in Arequipa, since the decoration consisted of a group of saints in deep relief, carved with an angular stiffness that bore a naïve and distant cousinship to the figures of Chartres. Here too the native motifs appeared; one saint was shown accompanied by a tame puma, and on the great cross of green wood that stood beside the main door there was a sun at one end of the transverse beam and a moon at the other.

As we walked about the town I was reminded of a remark Mrs. Ortutay had made in Tarma. 'For Puno you need a summer dress and a fur coat,' she told Inge. 'On the sunny pavements you carry your coat, but as soon as you cross the street into the shade you must put it on immediately. That is Puno.' We laughed then at what seemed an amusing exaggeration, but we found that her warning was justified; there must have been a temperature difference of more than thirty degrees between the sunlight and the shade. Except for two or three hours round about noon, most of the Punans went about wrapped to the ears in ponchos and overcoats.

Weiss talked in that autobiographical manner which one so often encounters among expatriates, who seem anxious to reconstruct the past with every new acquaintance. He had left Switzerland, he told us, as an act of defiance, to show his father that he could do something better than carry on the family business.

'For a long time after I got here, I thought it was I who had been the fool,' he said. 'Only my pride made me stay. It was very hard at first to get the kind of work I wanted. Peru is different from North America, you know. A white man can't take a

manual job and hope to live it down. But at last I got some administrative work at a hacienda, and then I went into Lima and became
an accountant. Now I have the laugh over my family, because I
earn more than any of them.'

Gradually, as our talk became more general, the attitudes which
lay behind his action of the previous evening began to emerge. He
was an ardent defender of the existing order in Peru, and particularly of the foreign companies that controlled its economic life.
'Perhaps they do make a great profit out of the country,' he argued.
'What does that matter? They bring in money which the Peruvians
would never earn for themselves. You cannot imagine how inefficient a native business man can be.'

He did not even try to deny our arguments that the foreign
companies took advantage of the situation of the Indians. 'Of
course they do, and the Peruvians do the same. Where there is
plenty of unskilled labour, people will buy it cheaply. That is the
situation, and it is unrealistic to imagine that you can change it
straight away.'

It seemed ironical to hear a Swiss being more colonial than the
colonialists, but Weiss went a good deal further in his conservatism, for he was also the first open defender of Odria's dictatorship whom we had encountered. 'Do not believe all you hear
people say about Odria's dictatorship,' he remarked. 'Odria was
hard, and he did some unpleasant things, but he was only acting
as every dictator in Peru has done. You cannot apply Swiss or
English standards to a country like this. It needs a strong ruler,
and Odria was strong. For eight years he gave the country internal
peace and he kept the currency stable. That is something to be
grateful for.'

I was exasperated by these statements, and we argued somewhat acrimoniously over them, yet I am sure that Weiss said
openly what many of the foreigners who made their living in Peru
really felt but would have expressed in a more veiled manner.

Weiss eventually left us to go back to his wife, and we did not
see them again; I believe they gave up in despair the idea of a
mountain honeymoon and flew back to Arequipa the next day.
After he had gone we went on to the market, as we always did in

Peruvian towns, where the pattern of trading reveals so much of the lives and the fortunes of the people.

Puno is the main commercial centre of the Peruvian half of the Titicaca basin, a region whose Indian population is close to a million, and thus, though the market is never so spectacular as that of Huancayo, in prosperous seasons it is large and well-attended by peasants from the lake islands of the Sun and the Moon and from the villages of the altiplano. But we saw it as the starved shadow of its normal self. The covered market, which provided mostly for the needs of the townspeople, was still fairly busy; the outside market of the peasants had almost passed out of existence in the last few months. A few cholo merchants waited for customers beside the cheap soap and shoddy cotton goods they had brought over the border from La Paz; there were some weavers with dull brown ponchos, a man with little armadillo-shell mandolins like those we had seen the conchero dancers strumming 3,000 miles away in the Mexican highlands, a potter with earthenware cooking stoves of a type used on the shores of Titicaca for at least a thousand years. But the great cobbled area where in better days the farmers would lay out the produce of their terraces and islands was deserted, except for about a dozen women with miserable piles of shrunken potatoes which they were trying to sell at famine prices. Two trades alone seemed to flourish. The butchers had plenty of cheap meat for sale, since the peasants had been forced to get rid of their cattle at almost any price rather than see them starve on the dusty pastures. And the coca women sat complacently within the little bivouacs of reed mats that protected them from the wind; famine did not harm their trade, for, as every Andean Indian knows, coca stays the pangs of hunger far more cheaply than food.

The empty market represented to us more effectively than anything else the chronic insecurity of life on the altiplano, a life always marginal and so acutely dependent on seasonal irregularities that when, in December 1955, the summer rains failed to fall —they did not materialize for more than a year afterwards—the effects were disastrous. The potato crop was a fifth its normal size, and more than half the pastures were destroyed. By the time we reached Puno, three-quarters of the Indians in the region were in urgent need of food, and that food the Peruvian government—despite all General Odria's boasts of having made the country's economy healthy and efficient—would have been powerless to provide if the American government had not sent 100,000 tons of grain as an immediate relief measure.

Disasters of this kind have recurred periodically in the Andes throughout the last 400 years, and they emphasize, more than anything else, how much was lost to the Indians of the Sierra when the complicated economic system of the Incas was destroyed. The Andean region has always been susceptible to droughts, and one cannot blame General Odria's administration or any other Peruvian government for such natural failures. What one can condemn is an outlook so much concerned with private profit and so little concerned with public welfare that the caprices of climate are never anticipated and always result in mass distress of a kind which the history of the Incas shows can be averted by intelligent planning.

The Inca state had, to be sure, its own shortcomings; the individual enjoyed little freedom in carrying out his daily life, and few modern Europeans or Americans would have been any happier in the constricted atmosphere of the Empire of the Four Directions[1] than in Stalin's Russia. But, unlike modern Communists, the Incas were not wholly contemptuous of the individual's rights; they were not totalitarians so much as feudalists—feudalists in the best sense of the word, recognizing a carefully defined reciprocity of obligations between the protector and the protected. This reciprocity entered so deeply into their system that, if a man stole because of hunger, punishment was accorded not to him, but to the official whose negligence had been responsible for the thief's need.

Thus Inca economy was based on the notion that every man, woman or child within the realm, whether healthy or infirm, had the right to a subsistence which, if modest, was also sufficient and regular. The lands of each commune were divided in such a way

[1] The Incas called their realm Tahuantinsuyu, which is usually translated as The Empire of the Four Directions.

that every family could feed itself in normal times; when that had been assured, a proportion of the remaining land was allotted to the Inca and a similar proportion to the Sun God. The crops from these latter lands, kept in great storehouses, were used partly to support the Inca's court and to feed his armies, and partly to maintain the official religious cults, but whatever was not needed for these purposes would be kept as a kind of insurance fund against some natural disaster, such as flood, drought or earthquake. The Incas recognized that the Sierra was a poor land, and their system was based on the rational organization of its poverty.

Nowadays the Sierra is intrinsically no poorer than it was in the early sixteenth century, and it supports a population no larger—and possibly smaller—than that over which the Incas ruled. But its poverty is no longer organized, and the result is a condition of chronic want which every few decades assumes the acute form of famine. Partly this is because in many places the terraces built before the Conquest have fallen into disuse, so that the area of cultivated land has shrunk considerably, and partly it is because whatever extra the land gives in good years is no longer put aside for bad times, but is devoted to the profit of the landowners. Over the four centuries of white rule, there has been no provision for disaster like that instituted by the Incas, and the Indians are never free from the threat of starvation; modern independent Peru is in this respect no better than the Peru of the Viceroys, and it is hardly surprising that now the Indians are suspicious even of the gifts of white men. One ironical result of the American relief, which undoubtedly did more than anything else to break the famine, was an increase in anti-Americanism among the peasants, many of whom believed a rumour that the free food was meant to fatten trusting Indians so that their bodies might be boiled down to provide grease for road-building machinery.

The divisions that exist in Peruvian society were emphasized by the Independence Day celebrations which we watched later in the morning in the Plaza outside the cathedral. Banners jostled over the heads of the crowd as the patriotic procession formed in the streets leading to the square. The Guardia Civil whistled and shouted and herded the spectators, and the balcony of the Municipia was garlanded with flags and politicians—swarthy, anonymous-looking men in dark suits and sun-glasses.

The ceremony began with one of the politicians reading an interminable speech from long sheets of paper like galley proofs, stringing on wordy festoons the resonant abstractions of the day—Liberty, Unity, the Fatherland—and evoking the shades of Bolivar and San Martin, and the blood shed for freedom on the fields of Ayacucho and Junin, to support the last grand peroration on the theme of Brotherhood, on the sinking of differences, on the need to work together to preserve the achievements of the mighty Liberators, the Fathers of Independence.

It was one of those virtuoso displays of oratory in which the South American creole delights, a deft juggling of accepted phrases in a pattern almost as set as that of a classic Welsh poem. I wondered how much of it had any meaning for the group of Indian women who stood silently beside us; their hair was dressed, like that of certain Central African tribes, in scores of tiny plaits. Who, to them, were Bolivar and San Martin? And what could they make of this mouthing about Brotherhood by a man whose white skin aroused in them nothing but the distrustful memories of past injustice?

Yet, in its context, the young man's speech was a great deal more than an empty collection of phrases. Compromise was its keynote, and it suggested that in whatever esoteric circles governed the country's destiny some kind of political accord had been reached. The new President had been inaugurated in Lima that morning; the interim of suspense was over, and a couple of days later we were to hear that Odria had discreetly caught a plane to the United States. The procession, which began to wind its halting way around the square after the oration had ended, carefully underlined the fragile unity between the various forces in that half of Peruvian society which belongs approximately to the twentieth century.

A group of mantillaed ladies, august as Roman matrons, carried an enormous national flag before a float decorated with Incaic symbols on which a handsome white-skinned girl posed as the emblem of Peru. A red-faced priest in shovel hat and soutane,

like a figure from an anti-clerical cartoon, danced backwards before a band of khaki-clad boys, blowing angrily on a cornet as he
conducted the music with his free hand. Behind the band the
municipal officials paraded their republican finery of cocked hats
and red sashes, and then—to the tune of a whisper of assurance
rippling through the crowd—came the naval officers from Lake
Titicaca, the army colonels with their guard of dull-eyed Indian
conscripts, the paunchy, corrupt-faced customs officers; they
would not have been there, everyone knew, if the generals had not
made their peace with the new President. Finally, under their
emblematic banners, the syndicates marched, the uniformed
railwaymen and the ice-cream sellers in white jackets, the bakers
and their fat chola wives in Epsom bowlers and new silk shawls,
the artisans—squat men in blue serge suits who, if it had not been
for their flat Mongol faces, might have been Welsh miners going
to May Day in the Rhondda—and, last of all, the building
workers, marching like the delegates of poverty in their ragged,
cleanly washed working clothes.

Everyone was there—everyone except the Indian farmers who
make up nine-tenths of the population of this region; if the procession symbolized a unity, it was that of literate Peruvians, resolved, for the time being at least, to avoid the costly follies of
civil dissension. The Indians expressed themselves by absence, or
at best by the curiosity which is aroused in them by any spectacle.
And, though the activities connected with the state festival lasted
for the next two days, the Indians still took almost no part in
them. The townspeople organized bicycle races through the
narrow streets, and a Dufyish little regatta out on the lake where
boys paddled balsas and all the ships were hung with coloured
paper flags, but, to our personal disappointment, there were
neither the devil dances nor the bull-throwing games with which
the Aymara celebrate their own fiestas.

This almost complete detachment of the Indian from the functions of the state is one of the significant factors in Peruvian political life, and illustrates how deeply the country is still split by
the racial distrust bred over the centuries. The Catholic Church,
thanks to its frequent defence of the Indians against the Spaniards,

gained at least a qualified loyalty, so that both Aymaras and Quechuas celebrate its festivals in their own half-pagan way. But, since the disappearance of the Incas, the Peruvian state has never been able to win even that ambiguous degree of support. To the Indian, from the days of Pizarro, government has represented the interests of conquering aliens, and because of this he sees no reason to co-operate with it; indeed, his chief desire is to avoid as best he can the obligations it seeks to impose on him—conscription and taxes, road work and the census.

Many white Peruvians are inclined to see in this abstentionism a sign of the unworthiness of the Indian for a democratic society. In fact, however, within their own communities, both the Aymara and the Quechua carry on a great deal of practical democracy in their methods of regulating the division of community lands. Moreover, the white criticism of Indian political indifference rings rather falsely when one remembers how little anything other than indifference has been expected of the Indians in the past. Even today the simple device of an electoral law which makes literacy a prerequisite for voting has effectively disenfranchised the Indians to such an extent that, even in those regions where they form a large majority of the population, political control still rests firmly in the hands of the creoles and the educated cholos.

There are signs that Peruvian governments are now becoming anxious about the situation and, fearing the effects of the radical propaganda that seeps over the frontier from Bolivia into the villages of the Peruvian altiplano, are trying to bring the Indians into political life; in some regions, I was told by a local missionary, encouragement is carried so far that the mere ability to sign one's name is regarded as sufficient qualification for voting. Up to the present, however, this kind of action has done little to change the habits of centuries, and the average Indian in the Andes remains no more interested in the government that reigns in the distant and alien city of Lima than he is in the political affairs of Monaco or Greenland.

6

The most extreme of all the Andean Indians in their withdrawal from the modern world are the last members of a dwindling race called the Urus, who once occupied a great region between Lake Titicaca and the Pacific, and who still speak an ancient language completely different in structure and vocabulary from either Quechua or Aymara. Crowded out of their territories by more energetic races, the Urus declined in numbers and today they are almost extinct; their survivors have retreated to a last foothold among the very waters of Lake Titicaca, where they live, on the so-called 'floating islands', a precarious but almost totally independent life.

We went to one of the Uru settlements on our second day in Puno, sharing the hire of a motor-boat with two girls from New York whom we had met in the hotel. Out on the open lake the sunlight became more intense, and the colours deepened, so that the tan of the hills now had a curious purple bloom, as if they were covered with heather, and the deep waters were indigo. After some time the golden horizon of reed beds came into sight and, as we approached the shallows, the lake was populated with an extraordinary variety of birds which found shelter and food among the vegetation there.[1]

Here we saw the first of the Urus, fishing from their balsas, those golden boats made out of reeds which have been the characteristic craft of Lake Titicaca since very ancient times. Despite its flimsiness of appearance the balsa, which is also called el caballito—the little horse—represents a practical solution to the problem of navigating a great lake on whose shores no trees grow naturally, for it is buoyant, easy to manage, and quick to make,

[1] I am not well enough versed in South American ornithology to identify exactly all the species we saw, but they included varieties of gulls, cormorants, herons, egrets, bitterns, divers and ducks, as well as several kinds of waders.

while it costs nothing except the fisherman's labour. The totora reeds from which it is made are bound into four cigar-shaped bundles. The two larger are tied together to form the hull of the boat, and the two smaller are attached to serve as gunwales. The whole boat, including a sail of reeds raised on a wooden pole, is made in about two days, and it lasts for two or three months until it becomes waterlogged; then the fisherman merely gathers another pile of reeds and makes himself a new balsa. Until recently these boats were, apart from the steamers belonging to the Southern Railway, the only craft sailing on Lake Titicaca, and at one time a large type was made for transport purposes which held as many as forty people. Now these cumbersome vessels have been replaced by wooden boats fitted with outboard motors, and only the small caballito is still used; it is so economical that it will probably remain for many decades the craft of the poor fishermen of Titicaca.

As we glided past them, the Urus were casting their nets on the edge of the thick tangle of underwater weeds that grew in the shallows, and occasionally one of them would dart his spear and bring it up with a fish struggling and glittering on the end. They watched us with apparent apathy, until one of the American girls aimed her camera at them. Then they quickly pulled their shapeless felt hats over their faces, lay down in their boats and remained hidden until we were well out of snapshot range. The cholo pilot of the launch was very amused, but I am not sure whether he was laughing at the girl's disappointment or at the action of the fishermen, whom he seemed to despise. 'They are very ignorant people,' he explained to us. 'They do not like to be photographed. They think you will make sorcery with their pictures. But do not be sad, señorita. You will find when we get to their island that a little present will soon make them forget about sorcery.'

We penetrated the winding canals that had been cut into the reed beds. The totoras were bright green at the waterline and graduated to a golden yellow at the tips; they were seven or eight feet high, and completely cut off our view of anything outside the narrow water lanes. Small black birds with yellow shoulders flew screeching over our heads, and at one point some Indians were cutting the reeds and tying them together into a raft to be floated away. We turned a corner and came into sight of what looked like a piece of level ground on the edge of the canal, dotted with small huts and with piles of cut reeds like great corn stooks.

It was one of the floating islands. Some children watched as the pilot drove the nose of the launch on the edge of the trampled reeds and threw out a plank for us to cross. We all hesitated for a moment; the place looked as small and private as a farmyard. 'Do not worry, señores,' said the pilot, who was evidently used to such qualms on the part of the people he carried. 'Nobody will say anything.' He made us feel like Victorian slummers, but curiosity egged us on, and we stepped down on the quaking imitation of dry land. At the first two steps my shoes were filled with water; after that the platform became more firm, though one always felt a slight undulation. The 'island', explained the pilot, had been made artificially by piling the reeds layer on layer until they projected a few inches above the water. As the reeds rotted and settled, more would be piled on top, and many of the Uru islands, despite their temporary appearance, were decades old.

We went over to the huts, which were flimsy structures, four or five feet high, made out of rough mats tied to frameworks of sticks. The men were out fishing, and the only people on the island were an old couple, two young women and the children who had watched us. The old man sat with his back to us, looking over the waterway in senile boredom; the old woman was mashing some barley grains on a large flat stone with another stone which she rolled backwards and forwards. All of them, young and old, were dressed in ragged, filthy garments; the children were half-naked and looked, like their elders, as if they had not been washed since birth. Apart from the old woman's quern, the only possessions I could see were a few fire-blackened pots; three or four lean black pigs wandered over the island, snuffling in and out of the huts, and a few small fish, of a species which the Indians call succha, were drying in the sun.

One sensed a mild yet inactive resentment on the part of the older people, but the children followed us about like puppies attaching themselves to strangers. The American girls wanted to take photographs, and Inge went up to the old woman, who alone had returned our greetings, and asked her permission. I do not know whether she understood the question or whether the money Inge handed her spoke for itself; at any rate she took it and muttered an incomprehensible sentence which we took to mean assent. The girls themselves had brought pocketfuls of sweets, which they handed to the children as they hopped energetically about with their cameras, eyeing and clicking with a lack of inhibition which I found both enviable and embarrassing. The sweets were wrapped and the children turned them over and bit at them in mystification, until the smallest girl finally gave a great howl of frustration. Then, since none of them understood the Spanish which any of us spoke, we had to go through an elaborate dumb show of demonstration. The children seemed to enjoy the miming even more than the sweets and with them at least we established a bond of mutual amusement.

The Urus were by far the poorest and dirtiest people we saw in Peru. And, if tradition is to be believed, poverty and filth have always been their characteristics. When the Incas subdued them, says an old legend which is still current in Puno, they recognized these attributes of their new subjects by imposing a strange tribute—the annual presentation at Cuzco of a hollow totora reed filled completely with lice. The legend does not tell what use was made of the lice once they had been received. Certainly, whether or not this curious story is true, the Urus seem to have escaped the rigid work laws which the Incas imposed wherever they could, and liberty is still the reward of their marginal existence. But it is a liberty bought by renouncing almost everything that comes from beyond the lake, which itself satisfies the greater part of the Uru's needs. From the totora reeds he makes his boats, his houses, his ropes, his nets, the mats that form his only furniture and the very semblance of land on which he dwells. It is his only fuel, and its pith and roots contribute to his diet; he even makes tiny farms in the middle of the lake by spreading thin layers of soil over parts of the floating islands and planting potatoes which nourish themselves by plunging their roots into the sodden mass of reeds below. Apart from the reeds, the lake sustains the Uru with fish and wildfowl, which are not only his food, but also his sole means of exchange; he barters dried fish and ducks with the Aymaras of the lakeshore for earthenware pots and cloth and grain to brew chicha for feasts.

Looked at from outside, through our eyes of intruders, it seemed a horrifyingly miserable existence. Cold and damp and dirt, a limited and precarious diet, and the monotony of daily living which is the curse of all restricted communities—these were only the obvious disadvantages of living in the Uru manner. Yet the impulse to get away from the demands of a regulated life evidently has its appeal to primitive as well as to civilized people, and, impatient as one may become of the hearty cult of the open spaces, there is no doubt that the wide skies and vast waters of a lake like Titicaca give a genuine sense of unconfinement and escape. Such feelings are doubtless the rewards of Uru life, and it is significant that, now the Urus themselves are dwindling away, their manner of living is being continued by groups of Aymara and Quechua who flee to the reed beds as a refuge from the tax collector and the conscription officer, and find the casual, individualistic life of the lake so much more appealing than the closed systems of the village communities that they adopt it as their own. The process is not much different from that which produces the English diddikai, the man who becomes so attracted by the life of the gypsies that he gives up the predictable securities of the good citizen's existence and takes gladly to the hardships and compensating freedoms of the hedgerows.

7

On our third day in Puno a great wind blew along the lake, whipping through the town all the dust it had swept up from the parched fields of the altiplano. People went through the streets head-down against the blast, their mouths muffled in scarves or ponchos, and some Bolivians who had driven in from La Paz told us that dust storms had held them up for hours as they came around the shore of the lake.

Most of the day we took the wind as an excuse to sit before the big fire of eucalyptus logs that had been built in the hotel lounge; we were, in fact, feeling a little frayed from travelling, for both of us had contracted new colds since arriving in Puno, and we had also been burnt painfully by the deceptively powerful sun during our trip on the lake. We talked with two art historians from Florida—Bob and Barbara Ebersole—who had been touring in the Sierra on some American university project of investigating the present condition of native craftsmanship in the Andes. Tramping to out-of-the-way villages, interviewing weavers and potters with the help of local teachers who acted as interpreters, they had come to much the same conclusion as we had reached from touring the markets. The crafts of Peru were moribund, and a few more years of Bolivian cotton goods and Lima enamel ware would make it as pointless to search for good craftsman's work in Peru as on Miami Beach.

In the afternoon Señorita R. came to take us on a visit to the Maryknoll Fathers. Señorita R., whom we had met through a series of introductions initiated by Dr. Schaale from Arequipa, was a young woman from Puno who had studied fine arts for four years in a Californian university, had spent two years working in Lima, and then, for family reasons, had returned to her native town. Intelligent, attractive, dressed with a kind of cosmopolitan good taste, and yearning for the sophistications of New Orleans and San Francisco, she looked and clearly felt very much out of the swim in this chill eddy of provincial life. She was shocked by the narrowness of a social atmosphere that had seemed natural in her youth, and her very desire for something less mentally restricting made her feel isolated among the people she had known since childhood.

But what she found most frustrating was the difficulty of making any use of the training she had brought back from the United States. She had tried teaching, in the primitive Andean schools where there were neither blackboards nor any other kind of equipment, but it was not the material difficulties that had defeated her so much as the attitude of her fellow teachers, many of whom resented new ideas and were concerned with little more than getting through the curriculum in the quickest and easiest way. And she had attempted to arouse in her fellow townsmen some sense of the historical importance of Puno, some idea of the need to preserve the monuments of the past and to collect the dying traditions of colonial days, but, more often than not, they imagined she was merely trying to show off the knowledge and ideas she had acquired abroad. She was clearly disappointed and unhappy, and her feelings emerged in a strain of cynicism about Peruvian life—as compared with European or North American life—which ran all the time through her remarks. But it was a cynicism of the kind that emerges from frustrated love. Peru angered her because it was not as good as it might be, and she was really expressing another aspect of that impatience with conservative and obscurantist habits of life and thought which we had already encountered in Robles and D., and which was to me one of the best omens for the future of Peru.

We saw Señorita R. two or three times during our stay in Puno, and to her we were indebted for much of the background knowledge we gained of the Titicaca region. But, like most of her fellow creoles, she had only a very limited contact with the Indians, and it was she who suggested that we should visit the Maryknoll Fathers, an American order of Catholic missionaries whose members have been working for many years among the Indians on the shores of Lake Titicaca.

The Fathers occupied an old colonial convent behind the cathedral. Within the cloister was one of the few green gardens we saw in Puno and crabbed roses bloomed there, out of the wind. Father Donelly, the superior of the order, received us in his study, a large, functional room with card files and worn leather chairs and a single large crucifix hanging on its bare walls; without the crucifix it would have looked more like an old-fashioned doctor's consulting room than a priest's sanctum. The afternoon was bitterly cold, and all the time we were there I coughed, hacking and spluttering into my handkerchief, and wondering whether, in politeness, I should not leave. But Father Donelly did not seem to be disturbed, and twice, when I apologized and made a tentative suggestion of departing, he almost brusquely waved aside my protestations and continued with the explanations which he so obviously enjoyed.

He gave the impression of being a genial and tolerant man, and certainly he talked of the Indians with more charity and genuine understanding than any other white man we met in Peru. 'They are God's children', he said, 'and it may be that God has more need of them than he has of us. You will hear stories of how bad they are, and how hard to trust, but you must remember that there are always two sides to such tales. They find us hard to trust as well, and it is because they are suspicious that they are so difficult to know. But once you do know them you realize that they are a simple people, very kind, very generous towards their unfortunate fellows, and very conscious of honour. Honour is most important to them.'

Father Donelly went on to tell us, as an example of the attitude of Indians who know they are being trusted, the story of a Puno priest who had become interested in the co-operative experiments of the Jesuits at Antigonish in Nova Scotia. He decided to imitate them by starting a credit union among his Indian parishioners. The white people in Puno told him that the Indians were thieves by nature and that he would only bring trouble on himself, but he went ahead and set up his union; more than that, he arranged for it to be run democratically by the members, keeping only an advisory function for himself. At this point the creoles decided that he was crazy and talked of calling in the bishop. But the priest was proved right, for the credit union gained a very large membership, and those Indians who borrowed from it astonished even the priest himself by the punctiliousness with which they made their repayments.

From this point we went on to talk of the hard Indian life, of the sicknesses that carry off half the children before adolescence, of the illiteracy that results from the virtual non-existence of schools in many large areas of the Sierra, and of the drunkenness and coca addiction which we had heard were particularly common among the Aymara.

Father Donelly shook his head over this as sadly as if he were admitting some sin in the family. 'It is true,' he said. 'All you are told about it is true. Alcohol and coca are parts of their lives, and you will hear of the most terrible orgies in which everybody, the old people and children as well, take part. And yet, when you see the lives they live, you realize that you dare not—you have not the right—to stand in judgment. You cannot conceive unless you have stayed in an Indian village the abysmal monotony of their lives, even when there is enough to eat. There is no comfort in their houses, they have nothing to distract their minds, they have not even the power to sit and read a newspaper to pass the time, and they drink out of sheer boredom and despair. How can we, who have never been tempted in such ways, presume to condemn them? As for coca, I'm not at all convinced that it does so much harm as many people say. It certainly isn't habit forming; you'll find that Indians who go down to live in Lima very soon cease to worry about coca. And in some circumstances it can be a good thing, for it makes a man less sensitive to hunger and exhaustion. You will sometimes see a small, frail Indian carrying a load of 120 pounds for miles on end without becoming tired so long as he has a few pinches of coca to chew. And if you deny him the relief of coca, how can you justify giving another man an anaesthetic to relieve a different kind of pain? It isn't easy to tell the point when something that has been given by God for man's benefit ceases to be a good and turns into an evil. Often we have to leave the decision to God himself.'

I could not help comparing the compassion that irradiated his point of view with the kind of intolerance so many Protestants would have shown on such a question. But I found even more impressive the fact that, though he knew we were not fellow Catholics, Father Donelly did not attempt to represent his Indians as fully converted Christians; on the contrary he admitted frankly that there was a great deal of paganism in their religion. The great Gods of the Incas seemed indeed to have been forgotten; no Indian now worshipped Viracocha or Pachacamac. But the local spirits, the lesser but more ancient deities who governed the fields and the elements and the mountains—they had lived on. An Indian would attend mass, and then go out of the church and throw chicha on the ground to appease the earth spirits. Even the curanderos, the most devoted guardians of pagan lore, would sometimes try to trick the priests into blessing their magical remedies in order to increase their power.

Some of the ancient customs had vanished, Father Donelly remarked; one rarely heard, for instance, of infanticide. But others, particularly those concerning marriage, were as much alive as ever, despite all the efforts of Church and civil authorities to discourage them. Among the Aymara, for instance, a kind of trial marriage was still practised similar to that of Inca times. A man would take a fancy to a girl of twelve or thirteen, and her parents would agree that she should go and live with him. In a year or so, if she did not suit him, he could return her, and she would go back into circulation on the marriage market, without any apparent loss in value. There was also a tendency towards furtive polygamy, and an Indian who was a little more prosperous than the rest might keep two or three women on the sly as extra wives or concubines.

But of the old customs that still lingered, the worst was that of selling one's children into bondage. Children sold in this way are called yanaconas; the custom had its obscure origin in Inca times, but it persisted into the colonial era, when an Indian would sell his child as a servant, and the child would have to stay, without payment, until he had worked off whatever his father had received; often this meant that he was tricked into remaining a virtual slave for the rest of his life. Now, Father Donelly remarked, this kind of arrangement was illegal, but he and his fellow priests had no doubt at all that the existing famine had brought about a revival of the custom, and that many Indian families had sold their children into servitude during the last few months merely to buy enough to keep themselves alive. How it was done or who bought the children he could not tell, for on such matters even the priests did not have the confidence of the peasants.

Yet the Indians who carried out the trial marriages and sold their children still claimed to be Christians. In their minds the two religions seemed to have set up house together, and, though the pagan concepts were slow in disappearing, the Christian also held their own. Even in remote villages, where a priest had not been for a decade, Father Donelly had found the elders still carrying on baptism; often they would repeat the formulas with strange deformations, and sometimes they would replace water by chicha or even, perhaps in the hope of adding some new magic to the ceremony, by Coca-Cola, but still in their own dim way they were recognizing their membership of the Church.

It was to dissipating the obstinate remnants of paganism, to bringing the Indians back to a purer Catholicism, that Father Donelly devoted his days. To me there seemed a disturbing division between the breadth of his sympathies and the narrowness of the function which he and his fellow missionaries had set themselves. Here, in an environment of appalling material distress, was a community of Christian priests engaged, undoubtedly with great devotion, in the consciously limited task of trying to provide enough priests in a region which, for some reason nobody could clearly explain, had become almost priestless at the end of the nineteenth century. Today, among the million people in the province of Puno, there were twenty-eight priests, not counting the members of the various missionary orders who operated there.

'Our function is the propagation of Catholic doctrine—nothing more,' said Father Donelly, carefully defining his position. 'It isn't merely a matter of ourselves going out into the villages. We do that, but, after all, we are still foreigners, and what we want are native priests. We are training lay catechists to fill the gaps temporarily, and we have our own seminary. But it needs a real dedication to make a man content to spend his life in one of those Indian villages, and we shall think ourselves lucky if ten out of the fifty boys we have in the seminary today go through with it and become ordained. We ourselves shall stay on until there are enough native priests to take our places, and then we shall depart, wherever the Church orders us. Perhaps to Timbuctoo. Perhaps to Alaska.'

I found all this hard to understand in the context of my own Protestant upbringing. My respect for organized religions has always tended to run in proportion to their deeds, and here, it seemed to me, there was scope enough for any sect to justify itself in this way. Literally hundreds of thousands of people needed

176

education, medical attention, agricultural advice, even food itself
—and the Maryknoll Fathers were giving them more priests and
more masses!

'Ah, you must not think we ignore those other needs,' Father
Donelly replied, after I had expressed my point of view. 'They are
in our minds always, and we do what we can. But we must render
unto God the things that are God's. Our duty as priests is first to
the souls of the Indians, and only afterwards to their bodies. We
did try to run schools for a while, but we found that it divided
our energies, and there were others who could do it better, so we
abandoned the effort.'

The difference between our attitudes was so obvious and so profound that it would have been superfluous and ungracious to argue
further. Father Donelly's sincerity was evident, and now, in retrospect, I think that, in order to preserve the logical purity of his
viewpoint, he was perhaps minimizing the practical acts of good
which he and his fellows performed, for I have since heard that,
after we left Peru, the Maryknoll Fathers were very active in
distributing the food which was sent from abroad to assist the
victims of the Andean drought.

8

The day's journey from Puno to Cuzco was long and leisurely.
The train crossed the flat fields of the altiplano, sauntered up the
valley which climbs out of the Titicaca basin to the pass of La
Raya, and then followed the Vilcanota down to Cuzco. Nowhere
did the altitude fall below 11,000 feet, and only at the top of the
pass did it rise above 14,000 feet, so that the general character of
the landscape did not differ greatly from that to which we had
already become accustomed on other roads and railways through
the Sierra. There were the terraced farms, the ichu pastures, the
red or grey crags towering up beyond the grassy slopes as we penetrated deeply into the valleys, and, at the highest points, the white

peaks gleaming at the ends of the quebrados that brought snow-water falling in thin cascades down to the rivers.

Yet within this almost familiar frame of landscape we passed through valleys and villages which had preserved, perhaps more strongly than anywhere else in Peru, the atmosphere of the Sierra as it existed under the Spaniards, with its curious mingling of Indian and Iberian influences, varying in nature from settlement to settlement. It was, indeed, the kind of day's travelling in which one became immersed in the crowded pattern of personal contacts and of detailed observations, and I think this quality can best be given by reproducing some of the notes which I jotted in my diary during the course of the journey.

* * *

July 30th. Leave Puno at 7 a.m. On the train a priest, a Dutch Sulpician, talks to us. He has heard of our visit to Father D. Why, he asks, did we not come to see his Order's school for 250 Indian children outside Puno? I am annoyed that Father D. did not tell us of this, and suspect rivalry between the two Orders. The Dutch priest comments on the coldness of the weather, and says that two weeks ago in Puno the temperature was 10 degrees below zero (this was well within the Tropics). August will be a bad month, he prophesies. Every August many children die from respiratory diseases, and this year of drought it will be worse than ever. From Puno we travel beside the lake; long stretches of dried, cracked mud show that the water has receded far this year. Ice fringes the beaches; blue herons and white egrets stand among the rotting balsas in the shallows, still and Chinese.

Juliaca, 29 miles from Puno. Here we change trains. A small boy in khaki drill school uniform asks so eagerly to be our porter that I let him carry the lighter case and take the heavier myself. Afterwards he is discontented with his payment of two soles for one case, and pointing to the case I have carried, claims payment for that as well, but laughs when I refuse with mock-Latin gestures of protest. He wins; he gets another sol. We share a table in the

Pullman with a curious group—a young creole couple and a florid, Taurian priest, who speaks Iberian Spanish (the shortage of priests of which Father D. told us is not evident when one travels). The wife sits opposite to us beside the priest, and talks to him, animatedly. The husband sits on the seat behind, his back to them, and occasionally the wife passes him some crumb of conversation through the crack between her seat and that of the priest. The priest reads *La Nouvelle Revue Française*, the woman a book on the Upanishads, but as *hors-d'œuvres* they buy from the news peddler a pile of cheap film magazines, as sexily illustrated as any in the United States, and read them with appetite, the priest taking first turn, passing them on to the woman, who finally tosses them back into her husband's lap.

Calapuja, 43 miles from Puno. A curious region of little pointed hills, tiny lagoons, sheep pastures; haciendas with white-washed quadrangular enclosures out of which rise tiled towers of small chapels. The village stands beside a slowly-running river where bare-legged men are fording with pack mules, loaded with sacks striped brown and white like Moroccan blankets. Here the Indian fishermen come with rainbow trout as big as salmon, which they sell to the cooks on the train.[1]

Laro, 53 miles from Puno. Valley country, with hills closing in, haciendas giving way to peasant farms. We are in Quechua territory once more. The women and many of the men wear high-crowned straw hats with narrow brims. The cylinders of the hats are almost completely covered with elaborate geometrical embroidery in red, blue and green threads; the designs are clearly pre-Spanish and resemble those on some early Inca pottery.

Pucara, 64 miles from Puno. An ancient tradition of craftsmanship. The people of P. have been producing pottery for at least 1,500 years, since the time of Tiahuanaco. The station is two miles from

[1] The rainbow trout, introduced into Lake Titicaca and its rivers after World War I, has thriven in the cold waters to such an extent that specimens weighing 30 lb. are not uncommon.

the town, whose redstone campaniles are visible in the distance, but the Indians have set up a trainside market. There are potters with animal figures and glazed vessels that imitate pre-Columbian forms. The latter are degenerate, probably made with an eye to the Lima tourist shops where one sees them for sale. The animal figures are roughly finished but vigorous, particularly the bulls, which are often large (a foot high) and have a fine air of ponderous strength. One wonders how non-utilitarian pottery of this kind came into existence; it is common in Peru (at Ayacucho the potters make miniature churches), yet there are no mantelpieces in Indian houses for it to rest like Staffordshire cats in English cottages. It may derive from the pagan custom of burying effigy pots with the dead to carry over into the other world the images of this life, though this was more prevalent in northern Peru than in the Sierra. Here the purpose of the effigy ceramics may well be magical; around Huancayo we saw animal figures placed on the roofs of stables and cowsheds. As well as pottery the peasants at Pucara are selling lean sheep's carcasses, split open and cleaned—witnesses of the famine, which no amount of sympathetic magic has averted.

Ayaviri, 85 miles from Puno. Once a great Inca centre, with a palace, a Sun Temple and rich storehouses—now a nondescript market village where the train stops for Indian morning dinner. Ayaviri women wear a curious hat with a rectangular brim curving upward over brow and nape; from fore and aft hangs a curtain of embroidered cloth, level with the wearer's eyes. The effect is hieratic, as if one entered a town populated by priestesses of some obscure Oriental cult. One of the dusty streets of adobe houses in A. is called Avenida Tupac Amaru, in memory of the Inca pretender of 1780. Here, evidently, the ideals of the past have not died completely, though it is significant that rebellion is *remembered* rather than practised; since Tupac Amaru no leader has united the Indians.

Santa Rosa, 110 miles from Puno. Hills covered with green-gold grass, greenish crags—too far to see whether their colouring is from copper or lichen—and tiny whirlwinds twisting the dust into spirals up and down the parched valley. Icefields glitter on the ridges behind the tin-roofed town. As the train leaves Santa R., an Indian jumps on to the steps of the Pullman carriage and settles down on the little platform outside the door. Through the glass we see the half-breed conductor stand shouting over the man, threatening, insulting. The Indian squats there, unanswering. He is put off at the next halt. At lunchtime (chupe of prawns, rainbow trout, tough beef from the dry ranges) we enter the pass of La Raya. Snow peaks multiply, frozen waterfalls on crags, dolomitic pinnacles. In the high valley are large green marshes well-fed by springs, inhabited by wild geese and blue-black ibis-like birds.

Aguas Calientes, 104 miles from Cuzco. The Valley of the Vilcanota. Geysers of bubbling mud gurgle grossly among rocks with thin stratifications like fossilized millefeuilles. The passengers rush excitedly to our side of the carriage to look at them. The priest, finding NRF heavy going and becoming conversational, assures us that the mud at Aguas Calientes is effective for many sicknesses. There is, however, no sign of its being used.

Marangani, 94 miles from Cuzco. Countryside rich in colour and cultivation in comparison with the Titicaca altiplano. This cannot merely be a question of altitude, since M. is less than 500 feet lower than Puno; perhaps it is the warmer air drifting up from the jungle, which begins 150 miles down the Vilcanota. Here the fresh green fields make vivid geometrical patterns on the red ferruginous hillsides. Double-towered churches stand on small pectoral hills, and on a wooded cliff a fortress-like monastery. From the roofs of new houses project tall poles quivering with ribbons. It is ploughing season, and in one hamlet the ploughmen race, ribbons on their whips and on the collars of their mules; women, in orange skirts, work also in the fields, bunches of green leaves tucked into their hatbands. Note the variation in seasonal feeling of Andean valleys. Jauja, with harvest, seemed autumnal; Puno seemed wintry; Marangani has the festive air of spring.

Sicuani, 87 miles from Cuzco. Largest town since Puno. Reawakening commercialism. Indian hawkers sell objects of llama and alpaca skin—gloves, slippers, foot-muffs, rugs with frightful pictorial patterns (School of Interlaken, c. 1880) made from sewing together fur of different-coloured animals. Also naturalistic metal figurines of llamas, cast and then filed down roughly to give a 'hand-made' finish. 'They are not silver,' a girl shouts in warning when we look at them. 'They are amarillo.' Amarillo (literally *yellow*) is an alloy like German silver. Beyond Sicuani villages proliferate, and the golden colour of the hills, like that of stubble, gives an appearance of richness. A deceptive appearance, the priest tells us. 'It is merely the colour of the dying grass. If you had come this way last year you would have seen the whole valley filled with green, but now only the fields by the river are fertile. It will take many years for the pastures on the hills to recover.' He speaks in French, telling us that he is a Spanish Basque. Have we travelled in Spain? No? 'Then you must go as soon as you can. Go to the Pyrenees. They are different from the Andes, but even more beautiful.' We talk about the American famine aid. 'It helps,' he says. 'But there is not enough to go round, and those who need it most do not get it because they are the inarticulate Indians from the most backward villages. The people who benefit are, as always, the craftiest and the cleverest—les plus politiques et les plus habiles.'

Casha, 70 miles from Cuzco. Here we see the first Inca remains—a high adobe wall standing in the fields like a row of gigantic teeth among which time has made its gaps; ragged-looking, like most adobe ruins, but massively impressive. The remnant of the Temple of Viracocha, father of the Inca Gods. This wall alone, says the priest, is a hundred metres long and fifteen high, and the original temple was probably even longer and higher. 'Viracocha was the God of the waters,' he remarks, 'like the Mexican Quetzalcoatl.' He is wrong in this, but I cannot say whether from ignorance or from a reluctance to acknowledge the presence in the Inca pantheon of a creator god like his own.

Quiquijana, 40 miles from Cuzco. The most beautiful village I have yet seen in the Andes, almost completely colonial in appearance and probably in its life. Q. lines the top of a shallow canyon where the Vilcanota splashes whitely over sharp boulders; across the canyon a Spanish bridge leaps in two perfect arches; beyond it, red adobe houses glow within orchards of blossoming apple. The tiled roof of the church sags and is green with grass; over the porch hangs a carved wooden balcony, and around the door are painted curious blue arabesques which seem to have been kept bright by generations of worshippers. Next to the church a large mansion with arcades of red stone, an upper story covered with pink stucco, a balcony of green gingerbread; an atmosphere of deliquescent gaiety. The men wear orange and vermilion ponchos, belted at the waist so that they look like Inca tunics, with wide black pantaloons which reach a little below the knee, sandals of leather strips and round coolie hats, black above, vermilion below.

Near Cuzco. To the sound of a cantina wireless, Indian women are dancing beside the railway, babies swinging rhythmically on their backs. The creole woman sitting beside the priest giggles and speaks to us for the first time. With a moue of contempt, 'I think they must be drunk.'

9

Arriving in Cuzco one felt immediately—and for the first time in Peru—the swirl of the tourist current which flows down each vacation season from the United States and weaves its erratic course over the surface of Latin America. It is true that, in comparison with the many thousands who swarm over Mexico and the Caribbean, a relatively small number of American tourists actually get as far as Peru, but most of those who do follow a narrow and dutiful route. A couple of days for Lima, a couple for Cuzco, and then they are off, flying south for Santiago and Buenos Aires, busily swallowing a continent in fifteen days of carefully packaged self-improvement. The exceptions who wander freely, like the girls we met in Puno, are few indeed.

In cosmopolitan Lima one hardly notices the tourists except in the two largest hotels or around the gift shops near the Plaza San Martin. But in Cuzco, a provincial city no larger than Shrewsbury, one can neither avoid them nor remain impervious to the corruption of manners their presence has induced. Indeed, one plunges immediately into an atmosphere of hustling and rather cynical money-making which seems all the more unpleasant because one contrasts it inevitably with the disinterested courtesy one encounters almost invariably in other parts of Peru.

The process began almost before the train had drawn to a halt, for the taxi-drivers immediately came running into the Pullman coach to tout for custom. 'You go to the Government Hotel? Yes, mister?' shouted the man who came towards us; he grabbed at our luggage without waiting for an answer. We had already been warned in Puno—and later by the Basque priest—that our chances of getting a room in the Government Hotel were slight if we had not wired for a reservation at least a week beforehand, so I laid my hand on the cases and asked the taxi-driver whether there was in fact any accommodation to be found there. 'Sure, mister! Plenty rooms today!' he bawled cheerfully, and set off with our bags. He packed two other passengers in to get a double fare, and then drove off through the ill-lit outer roads—for night had fallen by now—and into the arcaded streets of the city.

We soon found that he had misled us. 'You have no reservations?' asked the German reception clerk. 'Then I can give you no room.' A moment later he admitted that there were unreserved rooms, but these had to be kept for the people who would be arriving on the plane in a few minutes. The inference in terms of the comparative spending powers of plane-travellers and train-travellers was obvious. He spoke with a kind of calculated insolence, letting his eyes wander deliberately over our worn suitcases and the dirty raincoats we carried over our arms, and when I asked whether he could give us any advice about a possible alternative he merely shrugged his shoulders and turned back to his register. Annoyed at his manner and my own powerlessness, I blustered a little, but this merely relieved my feelings; it did not get us a room.

Fortunately the kindness of Dr. Schaale of Arequipa followed us even into this unfriendly environment, for he had given us a letter to a young Cuzcan who ran a travel agency in the hotel arcade, Señor Americo Luna. Luna was sympathetic with our predicament, 'You should have written before,' he remarked, clicking his tongue at the thought of our improvidence. 'Nobody comes to Cuzco without booking in advance. Now you have only one chance to get a reasonably good room. You must get to the Hotel Continental before the other people who will be turned away from the Government Hotel. Wait—I will send my man with you. He'll fix things up.'

And so, accompanied by Señor Luna's half-breed clerk, we rode back in another taxi over the very roads by which we had come, and eventually reached the railway station. The Hotel Continental was in fact the old Railway Hotel, renamed for the tourist trade. The taxi drove into the station yard, and we entered from the platform, picking our way between barrows loaded with parcels. We were lucky, and got the last room; the grey-haired houseboy, true to the Cuzco spirit, held out his hand for a tip before he unlocked the door.

The Hotel Continental belied its name; the nostalgia of the British railwaymen who built it before the First World War seemed to have lingered permanently, and it was like a parody of a station hotel in some Midland provincial town—the same desolate lounge with sad potted trees and sagging sofas and greasy antimacassars, the same cold dining-room with putty-coloured walls and heavy varnished sideboards, the same insinuating smell of coal-smoke and the same clank of buffers to wake one at five in the morning. It was managed by a haggard Hungarian woman who had come to Peru by way of hotels in the Thames Valley; she was fighting a tired, desperate battle against the inertia of the Indian boys—'How I would like to run some place where you did not have to say to the servants, "Take a bath—you smell!" ' she would cry—but it seemed to be a losing battle if one could judge by the dust lying thickly on the floors of the rooms.

At the Continental, on the town's edge, we lived in a grimy island of the railway age quite different in character from Cuzco itself, where all the cultures from the days of Manco Capac to those of the Pan-Demonian Airways are mingled together like the interlocking ages of Rome.

Dominated by the towers of its twenty-odd churches, Cuzco first impresses one as a town of the Spanish conquest. But very soon one realizes that the Spaniards never really destroyed the old Indian capital; instead they built it so intimately into the fabric of their new city that it is often hard to decide where the work of the Incas ends and where that of the Conquerors begins. Here, more than anywhere else in Peru, the two cultures grow together, and, as Madariaga once remarked, 'the most symbolical city of the New World may well be Cuzco, an Incaic Babylon on the cyclopean walls of which the Spaniards built a Salamanca.'

Indian Cuzco, as the Spaniards found it, was perhaps not the most beautiful city of the ancient Americas, for the functional sobriety of its architecture can hardly have made it comparable with the graceful cities of the Maya and the Zapotec in Mexico and Guatemala. But it was a rich and populous metropolis whose planning showed a conception of civic engineering at least as advanced as that of contemporary cities in Europe.

Despite much that has been written rather loosely about its extreme antiquity, Cuzco was still a relatively young city when de Soto and his companions, sent there by Pizarro to superintend the gathering of the treasure for Atahuallpa's ransom, first saw it in the richness of its gold and silver decorations. There had been, indeed, ancient settlements in the region long before Cuzco itself was built, but even the Incas did not claim any particularly great age for their capital, though this may have been because their concepts of time were not so strongly developed as our own. If one accepts Manco Capac as a historical figure, all the traditions agree in placing at approximately A.D. 1100 the date when this heir of the Sun God founded Cuzco. But, the small and doubtless relatively primitive settlement that existed during the following three centuries was neither large nor splendid enough to be the capital of the great empire which was established when Pachacuti began his wars of conquest in 1438, less than a century before the arrival of Pizarro; the new imperial Cuzco was built during that incomplete century in the intervals of war and with the aid of the conquered peoples.

The very name of Cuzco suggests one of the functions of the new city; it means, in Quechua, the Navel, or the Centre, and Cuzco was in fact the pivot of an empire whose administration was even more centralized than that of Rome. There the sons of the conquered chiefs and the Gods of the conquered peoples lived as hostages, and there the civil service of the whole Empire of the Four Directions was concentrated. The Incas had no writing, and, consequently, no recorded literature, but they investigated certain aspects of mathematics as deeply as the Maya and the Hindus (they discovered zero, for instance) and their passion for statistics made their records so complex that, even if the story that not a single pair of sandals could leave the public stores without its absence being discovered is probably apocryphal, it symbolizes a concern for accuracy which undoubtedly had a great deal to do with the success of the Incas as administrators and engineers. But besides being a great administrative centre, Cuzco was also the religious hub of the empire. It was the home of the deities, in both their supernatural and their human forms, for the Inca, like Pharaoh, was God as well as King, the living avatar of the Sun. And thus the priests in the temples and the statisticians who kept and read the knotted strings in the record offices were servants of two aspects of the same theocratic power.

Within this imperial and sacred Rome of the Andes, the rulers sought, not merely to govern their empire well, but also to demonstrate their own greatness, like that later Sun King who showed his splendour in the building of Versailles. Indeed, in one way Cuzco was a whole collection of miniature Versailles, since each Inca built his own palace, as splendidly as he could afford, and after death occupied it as he had done in life, sitting mummified on his golden stool and emerging to join his ancestors and his descendants in the great plaza of Huacay-Pata (the Square of Joy) whenever a public ceremony demanded the visible presence of tradition.

Around the palaces and the temples of Indian Cuzco stretched the twelve wards of painted adobe houses in which the common people lived. Inca Cuzco seems, in fact, to have been considerably more populous than the present city; it was a well-planned community with wide plazas, streets arranged in rectangular patterns, canalized rivers, reservoirs, a drainage system, and conduits to preserve the cleanliness of the water that ran down the middle of the streets.

Now it is no longer easy to visualize the appearance of the Cuzco of the Incas, though one is always conscious of its presence, for the same plazas and many of the same streets serve Cuzcans today as they served their predecessors, and here and there a fragment of the ancient city has been left almost intact, such as the Callejon de Loreto, a lane lined by high walls of massive stones, broken by trapezoid doorways and laid so accurately that when one sees them the hackneyed claim that a knife cannot pass between the uncemented joints of Inca masonry no longer seems an exaggeration.

But such purely pre-Conquest streets are rare in Cuzco. More often one encounters some surprising blending of the Indian and the Spanish, some seventeenth-century house with elegant miradors and airy Moorish arches raised on a foundation built before the Conquest. For the Incas constructed with such formidable solidity that the Spaniards soon gave up the attempt to demolish all their buildings, and today the work of the conquered people often survives more sturdily than that of the conquerors. When the most recent earthquake shook Cuzco in 1950 it was among the Spanish buildings that the destruction was greatest; the pre-Conquest walls remained undisturbed. One of the most striking examples was the old Coricancha, the Sun Temple where the famous gold and silver discs representing the heavenly bodies used to blaze on the plated walls. The Spaniards pulled down the upper part of the temple and built on its foundation walls their own Church of Santo Domingo. When we went to see this composite building we found that the Spanish structure had been so shattered by the earthquake that it was unsafe to enter. But below its cracked walls and shattered columns the great curved bulwark of black Inca stones remained solid and unstirring. Not a block had shifted, not a crack opened; it looked as smooth and as un-troubled by time as it must have done on the day the pagan builders completed it.

The many churches of Cuzco—which make it the most archi-tecturally complete of all the colonial towns of Peru—date mostly from that century, after the great earthquake of 1650, which pro-duced the best artistic work of the Spanish period. We did not see them all; indeed, with some experience of the depressing effects of too much church-visiting, we picked what we imagined would be the two most interesting, and left it at that.

The Jesuit Church of La Compañia stood in the Plaza Principal —the Inca Square of Joy—next to the city's tiny university, which is housed in the old Jesuit convent. La Compañia was built on the site of an old Inca palace called the Serpent Enclosure, which be-longed in life and in death to Huayna Capac, the father of Atahuallpa; in the street beside the church we saw the carefully bonded Inca wall acting as a solid foundation and, rising raggedly above it, the shoddy masonry which one finds so often behind the façades of even the best of Peruvian colonial churches. From the front, however, La Compañia was a magnificent building, but in quite a different style from its counterpart in Arequipa. Here was none of the lyrical simplicity with which the Arequipa Indians had worked out in stone the relationship between the two religions they were trying to reconcile in their hearts. The great complicated portal, designed by a Spanish architect, was in the Churrigueresque style which spread all over Latin America—both Spanish and Portuguese, during the eighteenth century. It is a style which I admire greatly, but in neither La Compañia nor in any other of the Cuzco churches was it handled with as much subtlety as in the Mexican buildings in the same manner.

The interior of La Compañia had the same air of sophisticated competence as the façade; there was ingenuity rather than spirit in the curious altar pieces with the elaborately curved doors which gave privacy to the saints whenever they did not happen to be available for devotion. The one really appealing feature of La Compañia was the series of paintings which documented, with eccentricity, the life of Ignatius Loyola and his family. Some of these were among the best Indian work we saw in Cuzco, and I was particularly attracted by one which portrayed the wedding of Loyola's brother. The stiff, brilliantly coloured little figures of Spanish ladies and grandees, their clothes painted with an almost surrealist intensity of detail, posed like sleepwalkers across the canvas, and the dreamlike quality of the whole painting doubtless reflected the state of mind of the artist, for whom the Spain in which this event had taken place, far away and years ago, was indeed a world that he could construct only through the fancies of an untravelled mind. Another painting symbolized the role of the Jesuits in the Counter-Revolution; Loyola, holding aloft an open copy of the Spiritual Exercises, stood in triumph over a group of Moslems in enormous turbans who cowered on the ground in an agony of shame. To make sure of recognition, the artist had labelled the Moslems; they were Wycliffe, Luther, Calvin, Melanchthon and Huss.

The cathedral, which stood across the Plaza from La Compañia, on the site of the Palace of Viracocha Inca, father of the conqueror Pachacuti, had much more of the Indian-Spanish flavour that is really typical of Cuzco. The pillared portico, with its heavy baroque sobriety, harmonized well with the massiveness of the Inca walls, and inside the cathedral the interplay of Spanish and Indian themes impressed one constantly. Even the high altar was half-pagan, for the plating of dull silver that covered it had been beaten into rayed suns like miniatures of those which hung in the Temple of Coricancha.

Again the best paintings were the Cuzco primitives. There were several of those girlish virgins, full of colour and stiff vitality, which showed this school at its best, but some of the other pictures expressed more strangely the efforts of the half-educated Indian painters to realize in terms of art the unfamiliar world of Christian mythology. One painter had chosen Joseph and Mary for his subject; he showed them lying in bed of a morning like any other married couple, with the clothes drawn up to their chins, Joseph's beard spreading out over the sheets, and a startled look of awakening on their faces; in Arequipa we had heard a rumour that a priest with Jansenist leanings was agitating to have the painting removed because of the reflections it might cast on the Virgin's morals, but fortunately it was still there, with its simple man's view of the private lives of the holy.

The cathedral is the most popular shrine in the Cuzco region—and perhaps in the whole Sierra—because of the miraculous image of El Señor de los Temblores, the Lord of the Earthquakes, a crucified Christ, brown with the candle smoke of centuries, who is said not only to have power over earthquakes but also to weep and to sweat as if he himself were undergoing the agonies of the hundreds of unfortunate people who bring their supplications each day to his altar. To the Quechua Indians of the region the Lord of the Earthquakes has become a substitute for the lost Gods of the past, and they are his most devoted worshippers.

A great effulgence of candles at the end of a dark aisle marked the shrine of this powerful Christ, and as we went up to it we saw an Indian and his young son approaching in their red belted ponchos and black pantaloons, with their cropped heads bared and bowed. Both had a hungry look, but nevertheless they had bought a couple of thin candles, and now they lit them and shyly joined the line of devotees who knelt before the altar. It was getting late; the other petitioners left one after the other, but the two Indians remained, praying with a look of concentrated misery. One imagined the thoughts running in their heads. Would El Señor make the rains fall at last? Would a candle in the cathedral be any better than the chicha spilt to the rain spirits last Sunday? Would they have to kill their cow? Could El Señor not help?

And then, before their candles were even half consumed, the half-breed sacristans began to stamp down the church, shouting like publicans at closing time and jostling down towards the main door the people who still lingered. One of them ran up to the altar of the Lord of the Earthquakes and, with that familiarity which the servants of religion so often allow themselves in the presence of deity, flapped at the candles with great swipes of his trilby hat. Out, with the last swish, went the candles of the two Indians, still less than half-consumed, and now the sacristan was standing over them, urging them to get up, shouting phrases about Time to timeless people. The father rose and even his stolid face had the look of a man who has suffered some incomprehensible defeat. He did not try to protest, and he and the boy went off quietly down the church and out into the Plaza. For him El Señor had spoken. In the minds of Andean Indians the relationship between man and the Gods is a matter of contracts based on gifts. This Indian's gift had been rejected by the servant of the miraculous image, and so there was nothing he could expect in return.

10

Pierre Gris described himself as an artist-traveller; he was a tall fair Belgian with a bristly moustache and a monocle lodged over one of his glittering grey eyes. Up and down the corridors of the Continental he would strut in the baggy breeches and concertina boots of an Argentinian gaucho, the red-and-white woven sash of a Peruvian peasant, the tartan shirt of a Canadian logger, telling one of his adventures in a staccato and hyperbolic English.

He and his wife, who looked as colourless beside him as a female bird, were engaged on the curious venture of travelling every road in South America along which it was possible to drive their car and trailer. 'Ab-so-lutely original enterprise, old man! Never been done before. U-nique experience!' Now they had already been four years on the road, making a living by selling paintings; a year disappeared in Patagonia alone. 'Ah! Pa-ta-go-nia! Must go there, old man! Ab-so-lutely marvellous country. Farms—oh, millions of acres, hundreds of miles apart! Un-believable hospitality! Dying of thirst for human faces! Ranchers beg you to stay for weeks—months! Fantastic chaps!'

Pierre was caught in Cuzco because of the curious improvidence that had made him start on his Homeric journey with a Belgian car of rare and ancient make. 'Marvellous car, old man! Stands up to anything, li-te-rally anything—desert, snow, bogs, corduroy roads—good as a jeep any day! Only trouble—can't get parts except in Brussels! Every time one of 'em breaks, have to wait until a new one comes by sea! Stuck for two months in Chile—nine weeks in Lima—now waiting again—six weeks at least to go! No trouble! Marvellous opportunity in fact—painting—photograph-ing! The human side of life! That's what I want to get down on film, old man! The human side of South American life! Nothing like humanity! Fascinating!'

Gris, like many another person in Cuzco, was convinced that the ground beneath the city was thick with Inca gold, and not entirely unhopeful that he might find a clue to some of it. It was he who first told us the pleasant tale, which we heard several times afterwards, of the boy who—two or three years ago—went to play in an underground passage below one of the old Indian fortresses in the hills. He lost his way, disappeared for three days, and then emerged in the cellar of an ancient house in Cuzco, carrying in his hand a golden ear of maize which he said he had found in a great cave stacked with treasure. Unfortunately he did not re-member his way well enough to take anyone back to the cave and this made me most disinclined to credit the story—nobody could say what had happened to the material evidence, the golden ear itself.

But, though several people, both natives and visitors, talked to us about the story, none shared our scepticism, and this anxiety to believe the marvellous was one of the characteristics of Cuzco. Many people there lived in a world of recurring legends, haunted by the dream of gold, and sustained by a rhapsodical worship of the past that was manifested all around them in the black walls of the Incas and the palaces of those colonial days when Cuzco was the centre of the civil wars between the Conquerors and withstood the besieging hordes of Tupac Amaru.

Just how heady the dreams of the past can become I did not realize until I picked up a curious booklet called *The Touris't Guide Book of Cuzco*. It was compiled a decade or so ago, not by some callow copy-writer, but by a group of local scholars—doctors, engineers, an art historian—for the use of both English- and Spanish-speaking visitors. To convey the kind of intoxication that came over these serious-minded men as soon as they began to write of the history of their own city, I need only quote a passage from the introduction; the English, I hope it will be evident, is that of the authors of *The Touris't Guide*:

'Imperial Cuzco. . . . Thou art the eldest among the ancient cities, coming forth with thy brow laden with a crown of exploits and glory upon the earth. How many other cities as old and majestic as thyself have given in to the furious attacks of time, falling down to the last stone, while you have defied the onslaught of numberless centuries which have fallen stricken to death against thy walls. You have maintained the bulwarks of your epic poems upright in spite of all the tempests. Thou hast survived, Manco Ccapacc's Cuzco and Tupacc Amaru's. Thy ancient eyes are the nests of Andine condors and are lighted by the wing strokes of imperial eagles; they have seen how the never ending flocks of swallows have flown from the highest belfries of time, to sleep the sleep of many centuries in the shade of thy flags. Life itself seems to stop its course before thy huge blocks of granite, the issue of thy bronze-like Incas.

'Some think that you no longer live O Cuzco of my elders. There are some who think that you are but the aching shadow of the past. That is not true. We, your sons, who proudly bear you in our hearts alive with the fiery flood of your blood do know well that the beating of your heart is still latent under the embers of the years.

'Your squares, palaces, all of the cyclopean fortresses standing guard upon your millenarian sleep, remind us of the days of your greatness and brilliancy. Even thy narrow and steep alleys through which the Spanish conquerors thundered on their horses, tell loudly of the marvel of thy better days.

'The world traveller, impenitent, romantic and ever scene-loving hunter with a better understanding of the charm and enchantment of old cities, comes from all over the world, seeking within thy ancient walls, the witchery escaping mayhap the grasp of thine own sons. Thus, the adventurous heart, seeking new experiences worthy of his risks, converges through his everlasting steps, to thy source of beauty, the Mecca of the sight-seer.

'The never-satisfied tourist, ever departing, may have crossed all the oceans, anchored in all ports and lived in the most beautiful and tumultuous cities, but his adventure loving soul, his tenacity in discovering new places and solving new misteries, will invariably lead his steps to thy gates and having seen you, he will never forget thy charm. He may then proceed filling his eyes with new scenery and his heart with new adventure but during his never ending travels through the world, your remembrance, pinned unto his soul, will forever be his most astounding life exploit.'

II

On our second day we hired a car to take us to some of the Inca ruins outside Cuzco. The driver was an almost pure Quechua Indian, a dark, compact, humorous little man, dressed in black like a sexton—even his shirt was black. He drove us out through the Plaza Principal and up a hilly street called the Calle Sueco—the Swedish Street. 'When I was young,' he said, 'it was called Calle Sucio—the dirty street. It was a very truthful name. But since that time we have to consider what the tourists will think. So we changed the spelling, but the dirt is still there.'

Out on the hills we looked down on Cuzco with its companiles, and then the road twisted and the city fell out of sight; we were among dry slopes, covered with aromatic plants and rock-roses, like those of Provence. A few men hoed in potato patches and once we met a train of llamas on their way to Cuzco with firewood. Otherwise the hills were deserted, and yet the broken stone walls which one saw at almost every turning of the road suggested that all this area must have been well-populated in the days of the Incas.

It did not take long to reach Colcampata, which local legend identifies as the Palace of Manco Capac. All that remains is a double terraced wall a hundred yards long and broken by trapezoid niches which the driver insisted were used for walling up criminals. Archaeologists, more prosaic than local patriots, believe that Colcampata was actually built many centuries after Manco Capac and may have been nothing more romantic than a large granary.

The next two sites we visited were, like Colcampata, of little more than archaeological interest. Puca Pucara was a castle of red stone guarding a shallow pass through the hills; it was well-planned, with turrets and curtain walls, concealed entrances and underground passages, and it must have been an efficient fortress in the pre-Spanish days when the favourite weapons of Indian warfare were the sling and the star-headed mace. At Tambo Machay, about five miles from Cuzco, the remains of a terraced building clung to the slopes of a small, green valley. A trickle of water still ran down the carved channels from terrace to terrace, and filled a series of rectangular basins which Cuzcans call the Baths of the Incas. Some archaeologists suggest that the building may actually have been a temple devoted to a water deity, but if this is the case all signs of its religious uses must have been very thoroughly eliminated by the Catholic priests.

All the time, even when discussing buildings in Peru which were certainly in use as recently as five centuries ago, one has to talk in these provisional terms of May-Have-Been. Definite history sweeps into Peru with Pizarro who, himself as illiterate as the Incas, brought the scribes and the chroniclers in his train. Before that time all is vagueness, a mist of hearsay and oral tradition, in which only a few dates, a few names, stand out like rare signposts. And thus, because their functions were never clearly recorded, there is no definite knowledge of the purposes which more than a small proportion of the Inca buildings in Cuzco served before the Conquest. For the rest, one has, however unwillingly, to use the language of caution and conjecture.

What impressed me most about buildings like Colcampata, Puca Pucara and Tambo Machay was their obvious practicality. They were as efficiently constructed as a Norman castle or a Roman bastion, and the resemblance was appropriate since they also were the products of a military caste concerned primarily with such matters as durability, defensibility, storage space and water supplies, a caste which valued good workmanship and efficiency more than originality and charm. One admired the rational planning of these structures, the neat masonry, the cleverness with which the lack of the arch had been circumvented. But the more one looked at them the more one became conscious of the monotony of the long façades and the lack of colour or carving to break the neat networks of the joints between the stones. Such building seemed the work of masons and engineers rather than of architects, for it was precisely the imaginative element in architecture, the element of beauty beyond usefulness, that the Incas so often lacked—so often, but not always, as Kkenko and Sacsahuaman showed.

At Kkenko we left the car on a farm road and walked downhill through a eucalyptus grove to a natural amphitheatre which looked out towards the white pinnacles of Salcantay, far beyond the valley of Cuzco. A low, semicircular wall of large stone blocks defined the shape of the amphitheatre; at regular intervals stones had been left out of the top course, creating a series of seats which faced across the intervening stretch of turf towards a menhir-like natural stone, about twelve feet high, surrounded by a low circular platform of masonry. On the slope below the menhir a cluster of large rocks had evidently been thrown together by some natural convulsion; we climbed down into the deep clefts among them, and there, in a dim recess where the daylight hardly reached, we came upon an altar cut in steps out of the whitish rock.

Kkenko struck one's imagination in a way none of the solid, practical, rectangular buildings had done. There was drama in the circle of seats facing the great phallic stone and mystery in the altar hidden away in the underground shadows. They evoked, not the thought of military men building themselves sanitary palaces and practical storehouses, but that of the devotees of some mystery gathering for a sacred drama whose final act—like that of Eleusis—would take place in the intimate, sacrificial darkness of the cave below. Pierre Gris had claimed that Kkenko was the centre of a fertility cult, and that here the girls of Cuzco came to be initiated and to pray to the menhir stone that they might be saved from sterility. It was not impossible; the phallic rock, the womb-like cave—everything might be fitted to the theory. But, once again, nobody knew for certain.

From Kkenko the car bumped on over rough field tracks and

past the latticed towers of the radio telephone station to the megalithic stronghold of Sacsahuaman. The authors of *The Touris't Guide* remarked of Sacsahuaman that 'it marvels and amazes the most skeptical and unbeliever', and certainly, though I was prepared to see something unusual, I did not expect anything so immediately impressive as the structure which towered above us when we drove into the flattened grassy valley that led up to the walls of the fortress.

Sacsahuaman consists of three terraced Cyclopean walls, protecting the face of a hill naturally impregnable from behind. The walls—and one has to resort to statistics in order to give a full idea of the magnitude of Sacsahuaman—are 600 yards long and 60 feet high, built in a saw-tooth line of salient and retiring angles, so that at no point could an enemy attempt to scale the fortress without being subject to the flanking fire of the formidable Inca slingmen. Nor could an attacker armed with anything less than dynamite hope to breach these massive defences, for the stones that compose them are among the greatest megaliths ever used in masonry. The largest is 27 feet high, 14 feet broad and 12 feet thick, and has been estimated to weigh upwards of 200 tons. Yet these enormous masses of stone, all polygonal in shape, are cut in such a way that their irregular forms fit together just as accurately as the carefully squared blocks in the foundation walls of the Temple of the Sun.

Sacsahuaman was completed by men with no iron tools and with only the simplest of mechanical devices, and for centuries other men have been wondering how they did it. The early Spaniards, who admitted that nothing even the Romans built could compare with Sacsahuaman, refused to believe that it was the unaided work of men, and thought that demons must have had a hand in its construction. A later Spanish writer, Zapata, suggested in the eighteenth century that, though the fortress might indeed be of human construction, the Indians must have discovered some process, now lost, by which they could soften and mould the great stones into the appropriate shapes. Even nineteenth-century archaeologists found it hard to believe that any known race could have built such a structure, and so they attributed it, not to the

Incas, but to some earlier 'megalithic empire', back in a conveniently distant corner of pre-history.

But in fact nothing less than the elaborate centralized organization of the Inca realm at its peak of power could have embarked on such a project, and modern scholars are now agreed that the fortress represents the master work of the great public engineers of the fifteenth century. Victor von Hagen, who examined the evidence critically, suggests in his *Realm of the Incas* that it was started about 1440, not long after Pachacuti began his campaigns of conquest, and that construction took seventy years and employed round about 30,000 men, recruited by the mita system of forced labour. The stones seem to have been dragged to the site by teams of men using wooden rollers (presumably brought from the montaña since few trees grew around Cuzco until the eucalyptus was introduced a few decades ago), and to have been placed into position by a complex system of levers and earth ramps. The final shaping and fitting, other archaeologists have suggested, may have been done, after a rough cutting to size, by rubbing the stones against each other, with sand and water between their edges. Again it is largely conjecture, but whatever the methods used to assemble these gigantic walls, their patterns of vast polygonal surfaces have an extraordinary beauty which, combined with the massiveness of the fortress as a whole, make Sacsahuaman by far the most dramatic building in Peru.

The purpose for which it was constructed takes one back into the realm of May-Have-Been. It may have been a fortress to protect Cuzco from the invasion of jungle tribes; it may have been a refuge to which all the people from the city could withdraw in the event of danger. There is only one recorded instance of its use as a defensive structure, and that dates from after the Spanish Conquest. At first, demoralized by the death of Atahuallpa, the warriors of Sacsahuaman put up no resistance to the invaders, but later, when Manco Inca rose in 1536 to re-establish the Empire of the Four Directions, the Indians seized the fortress and used it as a base from which to harry the Spanish garrison of Cuzco. The Conquerors finally captured it in a violent battle during which Juan Pizarro was killed by a Quechua slinger and the Inca general

Cahuide jumped to death from the now-demolished central tower rather than face the ignominy of capture and execution.

Apart from its military function, Sacsahuaman is known to have played one important role in the ritual life of Inca Peru. From one of its gates, once each year, a prince of the royal house would emerge fully-armed to initiate the ceremonial driving of sickness out of the streets of Cuzco and to start on their ways the runners who would chase the evil spirits down the long roads to the far boundaries of the Empire of the Four Directions.[1]

As we were about to leave Sacsahuaman a young Quechua woman came driving her llamas with sharp cries into the meadow below the walls; she halted them in one of the defensive angles, and began to adjust their straps. The bizarre and graceful animals and the woman in her full skirts and coolie hat, grouped under the vast stones, seemed too good a picture to be missed, and Inge raised her camera and snapped it immediately. The woman saw her and came running over, complaining loudly and incomprehensibly in mingled Quechua and Spanish. I had never seen a Sierra Indian become so animated. 'She says,' explained the taxi driver, who was himself bi-lingual, 'that when you took a picture of her llamas you took something that belonged to her. Give her fifty centavos, señora. It will be enough.' Unfortunately we had nothing smaller than a note for fifty soles, and our funds were now becoming too tight for indiscriminate generosity. We tried to give her cigarettes, but most of the Andean Indians, despite their addiction to coca and alcohol, have no use for tobacco, and she refused with something very near to disdain. Finally we managed to borrow a sol from the driver, who was much amused by our embarrassment, and the woman went off, still shouting, to rejoin her llamas. From that time we were more cautious than ever about taking photographs in which Indians might appear. But the eventual irony of this incident came when we had the film developed and found that the shot over which so much had been made did not even come out.

[1] This ceremony is described more fully by M. Louis Baudin in *La Vie Quotidienne au Temps des Derniers Incas* (Paris, 1955), who based his account on that of Garsilaso de la Vega, himself a descendant of an Inca princess.

12

A discovery made in 1911 changed the nature of Peruvian archaeology. Every important Inca site known up to then had been violated in some way by the Spaniards, but in that year the American archaeologist Hiram Bingham, touring the jungle valley of the Urubamba, seventy miles north-west of Cuzco, heard from the local Indians of a group of ruins on a neighbouring mountain. Expecting to find merely the remains of some small village or tambo, he followed his guide through the thick tropical growth and high on the ridge came upon a whole deserted city which he christened Machu Picchu—the Great Peak—after the mountain on whose slopes it stood.

At first we thought of visiting Machu Picchu on our own, but we found that if we went on the slow daily train which winds its way along the Urubamba it would be impossible to return the same day, and that to stay overnight would be difficult, since the only likely sleeping place near Machu Picchu was the small inn at the ruins, which was booked for weeks in advance. The only alternative was to join one of the tours that go once or twice a week by railcar from Cuzco and return the same evening, and this we rather reluctantly decided to do.

We left in the morning darkness, members of a party of about twenty sightseers—half American, half Peruvian—accompanied by a young Cuzcan who acted as guide. The journey to Machu Picchu took about three hours, first over typical Sierra grassland, and then down a long, eroded gorge that descended to the elaborately terraced and canalized banks of the Urubamba. Soon, hanging in a great cleft on the eastern side of the valley, the yellowish-grey walls of the stronghold of Ollontaytambo came into sight, resembling one of the Tibetan monasteries that cling like nests to the slopes of the Himalayas.

Ollontaytambo was a great citadel even before the rise of the

Incas, who destroyed the early fort, massacred its garrison, and later built their own castle there as part of the defence line against the forest tribes. But the fortress is famous chiefly because it was the setting for a tragi-comedy in the Quechua language, entitled *Ollontay*, which was long believed to be an authentic Inca drama. According to the romantic plot, the hero Ollontay was a general commanding the fortress who fell in love with the daughter of the Inca Topa Yupanqui; she returned his love, but when their relationship was discovered both were threatened with death for their blasphemous defiance of the sacredness of rank. In the end, however, they were forgiven, and married with the Inca's imperial blessing.

Having been accepted for more than a century after its 'discovery' as a genuine indigenous play—and having been acted as such in places as far away as Buenos Aires—*Ollontay* was eventually exposed as an example of Peruvian Ossianism, confected in the years just before Tupac Amaru's rebellion in 1780, when pro-Inca feeling was strong in the Cuzco region. The author, thought to have been a cholo named Antonio Valdez from the obscure mountain town of Tinta, obviously knew a great deal of Peruvian history, but in form and sentiment his play was influenced by contemporary Spanish sentimental drama. Nowadays it is recognized that, though the Incas almost certainly had some kind of orally transmitted ritualistic drama, this was not concerned with themes of amorous tragedy; the idea of romantic love came into the Andes as an import from Europe.

After Ollontaytambo the jungle began, and here, if the Incas built at all, their works must long have been submerged by the dense undergrowth. In the sunlight, the forest trees and bushes were at the height of their flowering, with red as the dominant colour, and among them the Urubamba swept, green and lucid, over white stones which the water had sculptured into beautiful curved forms.

At last we stopped at a platform in the middle of the forest; it bore the name of Machu Picchu. A settlement of unpainted shacks like chicken houses straggled for a hundred yards or so on each side of the railway line, which acted as the main street, and in front of them Indian women dozed beside piles of oranges and plantains, waiting, with an evident lack of any feeling that Time is Money, for the customers whose arrival seemed, to say the least, doubtful. Even this ragged village was, in jungle terms, a centre of civilization, for behind the platform stretched a little dead plaza where a lean donkey slept on the bare earth in front of more chicken houses, a little larger than the rest, labelled Municipia, Guardia Civil and Correos. We prepared to get off, but the guide stopped us. It was only a village of railway workers which had sprung up since the line was built. We had to go on for another mile to reach the end of the road that climbed the mountain to the real Machu Picchu.

Here the valley had deepened and narrowed, so that the forested slopes rose sharply from each bank of the Urubamba. A small bus waited beside the railway, and when we had all got in the driver started quickly towards the narrow bridge across the river. A jolt, a tearing screech, and the bus shuddered to a halt; it had run into one of the girders and half its plywood side was ripped away. The driver and the guide took half an hour to patch it up by banging nails with stones, while we leant over the bridge and watched the great morpho butterflies, iridescent blue and bigger than a man's palm, that fluttered over the water towards the flowering bushes on the edge of the forest. Incongruously, the voices of two Brooklyn girls tore the quietness of the jungle morning with a harsh chatter about dates and professors and last term's rushes.

The next time we made the bridge with an inch to spare and went climbing up the zigzag of sharp hairpin bends which constitutes the road to Machu Picchu. Soon the vistas widened to reveal a land of steep sugar-loaf peaks, covered to their summits in green. It was on the col between two of these peaks that Machu Picchu had been built, almost invisible from below; not until we turned the last bend of the zigzag did it come into sight, a labyrinth of soft grey walls rising like a pyramid to the high natural platforms, dominating the col, on which the largest buildings stood.

From the stark little hotel which had been built on the edge of the city we set off on foot, threading our way in single file through the one tortuous gateway in the ramparts, and clambered upward over the terraces and along the steep llama roads between the ruined houses on the higher levels. After the thin air of Cuzco, the dense humid atmosphere of the montaña made effort exhausting, and soon we were sweating and puffing our way up the paths and cursing at the mosquitoes that came out of the thick grass on the terraces to bite savagely at our legs. A quiver of demoralization ran through the party when a geologist who had climbed in curiosity to a higher part of the hill came hurrying back to say that he had disturbed a snake. 'Undoubtedly a fer-de-lance!' declared the guide with relish. 'Look out, ladies and gentlemen—these mountains are full of them!' We took his warning as a joke, but afterwards, re-reading Bingham's account of his discovery of Machu Picchu, we were reminded that the fer-de-lance constituted a serious danger while he and his men were clearing the ruins of vegetation; undoubtedly there must be many snakes of this vicious species left in the forests that still lap up to the edge of Machu Picchu.

Eventually we reached the highest point of the town, where the sacred dial stone called the Hitching Post of the Sun cast its sharp noon shadow among the temples. From the watch platforms we looked down over the grey contours of the city and the green cliffs of the mountains plunging into the valleys where tea plantations looked like small tiles of jade set in the dark verdure of the forest. The view was dominated by the precipitous cone of Machu Picchu's sister mountain, Huayna Picchu; along the knife-edge ridge that joined the two peaks a path ran as precariously as a tightrope to a nest of Inca terraces on the very tip of Huayna Picchu, where a watch post had been built that could only have been reached by climbers of skill and nerve.

The most immediately impressive aspect of Machu Picchu was undoubtedly its setting, and this tended to divert one's attention at first from the city's interest as a kind of Inca Pompeii, preserved by the jungle instead of by lava. It was in fact a carefully arranged community, protected by ramparts and ditches guarding the gentler slopes and by watchtowers hanging like swallows' nests on the more precipitous sides. Within this protecting circle life could be self-sufficient; there were terraces large enough to feed several

hundred people, an elaborate water system which was still func-
tioning when Bingham discovered the city, and a residential area
arranged according to industries.

The small gabled houses of trimmed stone were very similar to
the huts a group of present-day Indians had built on the edge of
the ruins. The comforts they provided must have been Spartan,
for they had no fireplaces, and the raised stone platforms that
served as beds seem to have been the only furniture; the life of the
ordinary subjects of the Inca, like that of modern Andean Indians,
was lived mostly out of doors, with the houses serving merely as
refuges from bad weather and from the dreaded night air.

It was on the upper levels of the city, approached by wide stone
stairways, that the larger mansions stood, and here also, nearest to
the sky, was the Sun Temple, with its curved walls like the Coricancha in Cuzco. But the Gods in Machu Picchu were not all
worshipped in the light, for there, as at Kkenko, an altar lay in a
dark cavern where the sacrifices were made out of sight of the sun.

A great deal of the fascination which Machu Picchu evokes is,
of course, due to the aura of mystery that has been woven around
it since its discovery. As the city was never known to the Spaniards
and cannot be clearly identified in any of the chronicles—like that of
Garcilaso de la Vega—derived from Inca sources, archeologists have
had to resort to their imaginations in order to explain its purpose
and origin, and in the last half century they have built an impressive
body of conjecture on a very thin foundation of established fact.

Hiram Bingham, in the pride of discovery, put forward two
challenging claims on behalf of his newly found city. First he
pointed out that one of its mansions had three large openings or
'windows'; this building he promptly identified with the place of
three openings called Tambo Toccu—the Inn of the Dawn—
from which, according to one of the many legends explaining the
origin of the Inca dynasty, Manco Capac started his wanderings
to found the Empire of the Four Directions.[1] If one accepts this

---

[1] This story of the origin of the Incas seems incompatible with that which
identified Lake Titicaca as the birthplace of the Inca dynasty. It is impossible
now to tell whether the inconsistency is due to the Incas themselves or to the
chroniclers who recorded their legends after the Conquest.

identification, Machu Picchu must be regarded as the mother city of the Incas. But Bingham wanted his city to embrace the whole of Inca history, to be the last as well as the first centre of the dynasty, and so he claimed that Machu Picchu was also the mysterious Vitcos which was the capital of the mountain principality where Manco Inca and his descendants ruled for four decades after they had escaped from the Spanish conquerors. For neither of these claims could Bingham offer any conclusive proof, but merely by making them he invested Machu Picchu with the air of mystery that has drawn more attention to it than to any other Inca town except Cuzco.

Bingham's first claim—that Machu Picchu was one of the earliest Inca centres—seems doubtful in view of the lack of archaeological evidence suggesting a long occupation. On the other hand, since the city was never found by the Spaniards but contained Spanish objects—such as beads—which suggest occupation after the Conquest, it may very well have been part of Manco Inca's refuge domain. At the same time, recent finds in the montaña have rather diminished the importance which Machu Picchu assumed in the eyes of archeologists when it was first discovered. An expedition in the early 1940's found five other fortress cities on the mountaintops overlooking the Urubamba, running in a line from Machu Picchu towards Cuzco, connected by a stone-paved road and standing about ten miles apart. Our guide told us that he had tramped along the ridge through the whole chain, and he remarked that, though none of them was as large as Machu Picchu, they were all self-contained, walled cities of the same type, with agricultural terraces, industrial quarters, temples and storehouses. Thus Machu Picchu seems to have been not an isolated stronghold in an otherwise empty jungle, but the last citadel in a line of defence works oriented towards Cuzco, and doubtless intended, like Ollontaytambo, for protection against the forest tribes. Yet this defensive function at the height of the Inca power does not lessen the possibility that in the end, when Cuzco became Spanish, these outlying cities may have been the refuge of the Inca princes, in much the same way as the mountain fortresses of Snowden sheltered the last princes of Britain.

Even here, however, archaeology throws in a last joker. When Bingham cleared the hillsides around Machu Picchu he found 173 graves which at first he imagined would be those of warriors. Instead, all but a few of them were the tombs of women. And this discovery brings in the further possibility that Machu Picchu may have been, for at least part of its life, an isolated convent in which the religious vestals known as the Virgins of the Sun sought refuge from the Spanish invaders.

One's knowledge of Machu Picchu is unlikely to go very much beyond conjectures of this kind, since the lack of writing among the Incas robs one for ever of the chance of finding the conveniently revealing inscription which brings all things into place.

As we were returning to Cuzco the guide came and sat beside us in the railcar. At Machu Picchu we had developed a considerable respect for him, since his knowledge of Peruvian archaeology was obviously thorough, and he had a professional honesty which made him distinguish very scrupulously between fact, legend and conjecture.

He pulled a small metal object out of his pocket and handed it to me. It was a chunky, stiff-limbed silver figurine of a woman, about two inches high. 'Real Inca,' he said. It had the look of a genuine piece, but simple objects of this kind can be so easily cast that we did not feel sure enough—or find the figure in itself attractive enough—to pay the rather high price he asked.

Later, as we talked, I asked him whether such objects in precious metals were often discovered. 'Not as often as you are told,' he replied. Inge then mentioned the stories of hidden hoards of Inca gold. 'Many people believe them,' he said. 'I will tell you one example. Last year, when I had finished taking a party around Machu Picchu, I counted them up as they got on the bus. One man was missing. He was a Costa Rican. The driver and I went back, called, looked everywhere. Nothing to be seen of the Costa Rican. Next day we organized a search with the Guardia, but nobody found a trace of the man, and we thought that he must have been bitten by a fer-de-lance or that he had fallen in one of the quebrados. Then, four days afterwards, he walked into a village along the river. And what a state he was in! Clothes torn to bits with thorns—nearly dead with hunger! But he said he had found a city full of temples covered with gold, and he wanted the people of the village to go back with him.'

'Did they go?' I asked, while the guide paused for effect.

'No. They live here. They know the mountains. They know there are no golden cities any more. They went with him to the Guardia instead, and the Guardia sent him back to Costa Rica, and the Costa Ricans put him in the casa de locos. He was mad, señores.'

PART IV

Realms of the Desert

I

The day after we went to Machu Picchu was our last in Cuzco. The manageress at the Continental told us that our room would be needed the next day for members of a convocation of priests, and though Señor Luna, the travel agent, talked without conviction of other hotels with English arboreal names, we decided that what we had not already seen in Cuzco would add little to our understanding of the Incas and that in any case it was time we set off to visit the Mochica and Chimu sites of Northern Peru.

But it seemed almost as difficult to leave Cuzco as it was to stay there. The planes to Lima were booked up for at least two weeks ahead, and we did not want to spend three days returning by way of Arequipa. There remained one possibility—to take the route via Ayacucho and Huancayo which we had once thought of following in the reverse direction. Señor Luna, with whom we discussed it, was no more encouraging than Señor Merida had been on our first day in the Sierra. In all his time as a travel agent in Cuzco nobody had asked him about it before. But he believed there was some kind of camioneta that went to Abancay, the next town beyond Cuzco, and he would try to get seats for us. Beyond Abancay our only chance would be the trucks going up with produce from the Apurimac valley to the Sierra: we would be lucky if we reached Huancayo in three days.

To me the situation seemed contrived by fate for the purpose of forcing us along the route we had talked of so lightly a few weeks ago, and I accepted it with a mixture of resignation and curiosity; I knew it would not be comfortable, but I hoped it would be interesting. Inge, however, was not so easily inclined to bow to a sense of destiny. 'Let's have another try at the plane office,' she said. 'It's no use,' I commented. 'I'm going to try in any case,' she insisted. 'I still think we'll get something.' To my surprise she was right; there had been two cancellations ten minutes before, and we could go to Lima on the next morning's flight. I had to admit that I was relieved by a stroke of apparent good fortune which made it pedantic to insist on preferring the trucks on the Ayacucho road; I too was tiring of the rigours of mountain travel.

We spent the rest of our last day trying to buy some specimens of Cuzco weaving, which was by far the best modern craftsmen's work we had yet seen in Peru. But there was little to be had, and most of that was expensive, largely because the Indian weavers are reluctant to sell their best pieces to white people. Tourist shops were selling red and orange ponchos, like those worn by the peasants, for 450 soles (about nine pounds), which was far more than an Indian would have paid, and also more than we could spare out of our remaining funds. In the end we found a small piece of material in the market which was of the same weave as that used in the better ponchos. It was a child's manta, and it had a rich red ground with wide stripes in multi-coloured geometrical patterns. Later we bought a red and green sash decorated with cubistic figures of men and llamas; everything else we would have liked was priced for fuller wallets than ours.

By the time we had reached Lima the next day we wondered just how much more fortunate we had been to fly over the mountains than to cross them by road, for plane travel within Peru bore no resemblance to the well-fed and air-conditioned ease in which we had flown down on the Canadian Pacific plane from Vancouver to Lima. Except for a few lines to small points in the jungle which are run by the Army, the internal air services of Peru are the monopoly of a large American-controlled company. One result of the lack of competition is that almost all the planes are antiquated and unpressurized. In crossing the Andes there are inevitably great and rapid changes in altitude, and though in the plane by which we travelled oxygen tubes were provided, on which the passengers sat suckling as if they had suddenly been relegated to a state of infantile dependence on some mechanical foster-mother, these by no means countered the effects of the extremely quick changes in atmospheric pressure.

First the plane rose fairly slowly from Cuzco at 11,500 feet to its maximum height of 20,000 feet; here we were on a level with the white peaks of the Nudo de Salcantay, the knot of mountains to the north-west of the city. The flight continued over the dense jungle of the Apurimac valley, and across a great expanse of snowless uplands, dotted with many small lakes and scantily settled, which lay in the Sierra provinces of Ayacucho and Huancavelica. Then, having crossed the ridge of the Cordillera Occidentale at 19,000 feet, the plane began to descend so quickly that it reached the sea-level of the Lima airport in less than half an hour. It was during this descent that the lack of pressurization made itself felt. Our ears and temples started to ache violently, and the pain ran searing into the jaws and neck; our hearing almost vanished, though enough remained to hear the homespun voice of the American captain performing his ironic public relations ritual of hoping that we had enjoyed a pleasant journey as we reached the ground with heads that felt as if they had swollen into hydrocephalic monstrosities.

By the next day I had recovered; Inge, on the other hand, was still deaf in one ear, from which the pain spread over the whole side of her face, and when we went to pick up our mail at the C.P.A. office Norman Sanderson suggested that she should go to the Anglo-American clinic. This establishment is run for the benefit of English-speaking residents and dollar-carrying tourists, but its staff is Peruvian, because of a curious gnat-straining provision of Peruvian law, which allows thousands of foreign engineers, hacienda managers, railway officials, etc., to work in the country, but no foreign doctors. Neither of the two physicians who examined Inge spoke any English, but eventually, after some difficulty in explaining symptoms, one of them diagnosed an infection aggravated by the rapid increase of pressure during the descent of the plane. He gave Inge some ear-drops and antibiotic tablets, and eventually the infection disappeared, though for at least ten days, and often with great intensity, the pain returned whenever the damp winds blew in from the sea.

The doctor also warned Inge against any further flight in an unpressurized plane, and this caused a radical change in our plans. We had intended to round off our journey with a trip to Iquitos, the Peruvian port of the Amazons. Since I had to be back in Vancouver by mid-September for the beginning of the University year, we did not have the time to go by road from Lima to Pucallpa on the Marañon (three days each way) and then wait until one of the cargo boats (which travel without regular schedules) might be going downriver to Iquitos; such a journey could not take less than three weeks and might easily run into five. Flight was the only way to reach Iquitos quickly enough to spend any reasonable time there, and since the planes to Iquitos were of the same type as that on which we had flown from Cuzco, we had to abandon the project. We did so very reluctantly; my desire to see Iquitos has been, if anything, increased by this frustration, and I play with the idea of reaching it eventually as the goal of a journey up the Amazons from the Atlantic.

This, however, did not affect our plans to visit Trujillo, and we arranged to make our way north after two days of relaxation in which we hoped that Inge's ear would make some progress towards recovery. It was our third visit to Lima, and by now the city had acquired a certain bloom of familiarity which concealed the aspects that had distressed us most on our first arrival. Indeed, by a subtle shifting of values, it now represented the height of civilization, a link with the known, a place for resuming established human contacts. There were bookshops, and cafés, and places where people began to recognize us—the Austrian porter in the Crillon, the waiters in the Viennese coffee shop where the journalists gathered, and Señor Alvarez, the antique dealer, blandly demonstrating how to play on a prehistoric jaguar-bone flute and explaining his theories of the messages conveyed in patterns of chili peppers on the pottery of the southern desert. In the neo-classical gloom of the cathedral, we even ran into people we had last seen many miles away among the mountains, for there, contemplating Pizarro's ornate tomb, we found the Ebersoles with whom we had talked on a dusty afternoon in Puno.

That evening we had dinner with them and they entertained us with accounts of their experiences on earlier searches for native crafts in countries as distant as Costa Rica and Nepal. Reluctantly, since I know they intend to write of their adventures, I suppress the temptation to recount what they told us. For reasons of this kind, one's fellow writers, though they may turn out to be fascinating companions—as the Ebersoles certainly were—are often in retrospect the most frustrating of people to meet upon one's travels; there is so much one could say about them that professional loyalty forbids.

We woke the next morning to what in Lima is a miracle—sunshine in August. The grey sullen buildings had come to life, the streets were full of girls in summer dresses and men who had shed their usual solemnity of manner with their dark formal jackets. We too felt exhilarated and thought it would be the right day to take a trip out of Lima to the sea coast and Callao. In the Plaza San Martin we bargained with the taxi drivers and found one who was willing to take us for a reasonable price. Anxious to show his city to the greatest advantage, he insisted on taking us through Miraflores, the most affluent of all Lima suburbs, past the white stucco mansions with their sub-tropical gardens, past the brand-new supermarkets and the pseudo-Parisian couturiers' salons, until, as we reached the shore at Magdalena, the display of wealth ebbed like a spent wave. We had expected that the richest houses would be nearest to the sea, but only a few isolated villas and open-air restaurants crowned the sandy clifftops, and northwards in the direction of Callao the market gardens alternated with stretches of bare dune.

Almost without a warning our brief spell of summer ended. Low clouds drove in from the sea, shutting out the sun, which we were never again to see in Lima, and the mist all but obscured the bleak offshore islands, the penal islands where Odria's critics shuddered in their monotonous isolation. It was a dismal shore.

Callao, however, was a more pleasant town than we had expected, with a modesty of aspect that hardly suggested its long history of tragedy and destruction. For few places can have been more persistently beaten by ill-fortune than Callao. In the sixteenth century, when the Spaniards imagined that the Pacific was their private sea, Drake sailed up the South American coast and took advantage of the town's lack of defences to burn and loot. When fortifications were built against human enemies, it was Nature that turned hostile. Earthquake after earthquake shook Callao, and then, in

1746, the sea broke loose, lifted the ships in the bay over the town walls, and destroyed the city and all its people; after the tidal wave had receded only the massive gateways of the town remained. With the nineteenth century human destructiveness returned; during the war of Independence in the 1820's Callao was bombarded by loyalists and liberators alike; in 1866 it was shelled by the Spanish fleet in a last effort of the Bourbons to regain a footing on South American soil; in the 1880's it was stormed by the Chileans during the war over the phosphate deserts; a dozen revolutions since then have left their marks upon its walls.

From such experiences the people of Callao learnt to build their streets wide, to lessen the risks of falling masonry and to leave plenty of room for a quick escape, and the result was a town of airy boulevards along which women sat on open balconies, calling to each other and watching the sailors and the mulatto girls strolling around the stalls under the dense-foliaged ficus trees. The scene was gaudy, plebeian and just a little theatrical, like the setting for a musical comedy on the randy life of the Southern Seas. Around the harbour, with its freighters at anchor in grey water and little wooden ships lying half-completed in the boat-builders' stocks, the land span out into a fragile isthmus, at the end of which, like a tiny Gibraltar, the town of La Punta clustered on its few acres of peninsula. A miniature casino, a truncated pier, a few white-painted boarding houses, and the tall waves hammering on the beach; it was Lima's nearest approach to a seaside resort.

We drove back into Lima by the Avenida Colonial, the old Viceregal highway connecting the port and the capital. Along this main road the two cities were approaching each other like cautious armies, casting out their skirmishing screens of villas and petrol stations, and following them up with the solid ranks of small factories and of large new housing estates, built mostly for the increasingly powerful lower middle class whose support every modern political leader in Peru seeks to enlist. There was still a green no-man's-land where oxen dragged their wooden ploughs across the fields of maize, but it was clear that in a year or two Callao and Lima would be united, and a single great metropolis would radiate from the Plaza San Martin down to the sea. The small-town atmosphere which one still felt in parts of Lima belonged to a receding past, and it was not difficult to foresee the time when it would become a metropolis on the scale of Rio de Janeiro and Mexico City.

2

The last drunkards were shouting their way home and the first workers were already waiting at the bus stops, when the Trujillo collectivo drove across the Rimac and through the dark slum streets of northern Lima towards the Pan-American highway. It was half-past four, we had slept only three hours the night before, and I felt desperately tired and tried to doze a little while the darkness lasted. But I was too cold and hungry to be very successful, and soon I began to talk to an invisible passenger in the back seat who had spoken to us in English while we were getting on to the collectivo outside our hotel. By this time a glimmering of light had already begun to appear—enough to show that we were travelling along the edge of some kind of immense dune; on the right a steep slope spilt its sand down over the verge of the road, and on the left the ground fell away into the darkness and the mist.

'Pity we do not go here in daylight,' said the man in the back seat. Neither his high-pitched voice nor his accent was Peruvian. 'It is very remarkable,' he continued. 'Steep—steep cliffs and sea, many metres down. Very spectacular. Muy pintoresco.' He paused, and then added, almost diffidently. 'When I see, I think of La Grande Corniche.'

I caught the hint of regret in his voice, and asked him when he had been in France.

'Very long time ago. I was young man then.'

As we travelled on he told me how he had come from England to Peru twenty years ago; it was thirty years since he had seen his native Nicosia. And as the light strengthened his features became definite, the rather handsome, hawk-like features, dark-skinned against greying hair, that one sometimes sees on ageing men of the Levant. Later, when we returned from the north in daylight, I looked down at the spot to which he had drawn my attention. The masses of greyish sand cascading towards the cliffs had nothing in common with the humanized wildness of the Côte d'Azur; only the sea, hundreds of feet below, reflecting the sunlight like a burnished shield, reminded me of the complex vistas of the Grande Corniche.

The desert, which remained with us all the way to Trujillo, was much softer in outline than that to the south of Lima, because here the constant sea wind had submerged the harsh edges of the rocks under the shifting sands. But, except in the valleys, it was as barren as ever, so barren that I still remember as something extraordinary in this plantless waste the sight of a large bush that grew, completely isolated, in a hollow by the roadside where its roots had evidently been able to strike down to some buried trace of moisture.

Yet here I did not feel the same depressing boredom as I had experienced on the way to Arequipa. No doubt, this was partly because I was getting used to the desert, recognizing more surely the beauty of its smooth-blown forms and burn-out colourings. But it was also due to the fact that the desert itself had much greater variation, for valleys were more frequent, and there were many more fishermen using the beaches close to the road.

A hundred miles north of Lima we stopped for breakfast at a small town called Barranca. The restaurant was the usual grimy collectivo-drivers' pull-up. When we asked the waitress to bring us eggs, she shook her head. 'No hay huevos,' she said laconically. Could we have ham sandwiches, then? 'No hay jamon.' Finally, she explained that all she could give us was chicharron. 'Chicharron is fried skin of pig,' explained the gentleman from Nicosia, who sat at the next table. 'Very good, I eat it.' Since there was no alternative, we overcame our initial doubts, and ate the rolls stuffed with chicharron which the waitress brought us; they were crisp, savoury and excellent.

At intervals, all the way through the desert from daybreak until we reached Trujillo, we saw the adobe mounds—the huacas—of the ancient peoples. The most important of these was the great citadel of Paramonga on the estuary of the Rio Fortaleza, not far north of Barranca. Until the Inca invasion of the 1470's, Paramonga was the southernmost stronghold of the kingdom of Chimu. Its vast adobe ruins still squatted massively on the hillside to the east of the road; in the desert climate disintegration had been slow, and one could detect the outlines of the individual mud bricks in the high brown walls that squared off the curves of the hill and jutted in bastions from each corner of the great rectangle of receding terraces. Paramonga was the pivot of an elaborate defensive system by which the Chimu sought to protect their kingdom from the hostile peoples to the south and particularly from the Incas; eastward from it, up the Fortaleza valley, a long line of fortifications—which later we were to have the opportunity of seeing more closely—ran as far as the natural barriers of the Cordillera Negra. But when invasion actually came, Paramonga and its great wall played as passive a role as the Maginot line in France; the Incas, like the Nazis, by-passed the enemy's main defences and attacked through the lightly guarded mountains to the north-east.

Beyond Paramonga the wide delta of the Fortaleza was dense with sugar-cane, planted in enormous fields stretching from the hills down to the edge of the river. It was one of the large foreign estates, belonging to the American firm of Grace, which controls almost a third of Peru's sugar production, and the elaborate system of irrigation ditches that criss-crossed the land suggested a greater efficiency than that of the rather roughly cultivated sugar haciendas we had seen in the mountains near Huanuco. Many of the fields were burnt and black, like woods of saplings after a forest fire, and at first I imagined that this had been due to accident, or perhaps even to sabotage, since guards were riding on horseback along the great alleys that divided the fields. But the Nicosian explained that this was not the case; the canefields were fired deliberately before harvesting in order to get rid of the weeds and the lower leaves of the canes; the charred sticks that were left preserved their sugar unharmed.

As we passed the last fields of the valley, the Nicosian pointed excitedly towards the sea and exclaimed, 'Is my hacienda.' I looked, and saw only the sand and a little dune grass sucking up the fugitive moisture on the edge of the desert. When the Nicosian explained that he had bought the land for a mile along the road and would start work on it next year, I wondered for a moment whether the story was not merely the product of some whimsical flight of humour. But the enthusiasm with which he told us how he intended to develop vegetable growing was too authentic to be doubted. He went on to remark that most of the desert land along the coast was good soil; given water and fertilizer it would bear crops and build up humus, as the Indians of the past had shown by cultivating many regions which now were only desert. He had schemes for getting both water and fertilizer. First, he had been careful to buy his land next to the irrigation outflow of the big estate; what water they did not use would be enough for him. As for the fertilizer, he pointed to a white wall on the far side of his land; beyond it lay a government preserve for guano birds. If only he could entice the birds to skip the wall, his problem would be solved. 'But how do I get them? That is the question.'

I admitted that I could think of nothing better than fish. 'Aha, fish! That is the solution,' said the Nicosian, as if I had presented him with some extraordinary revelation. 'Now,' he mused, his eyes suddenly lighting into humour, 'what I must do is combine the farming with the fishing. Catch anchovies, put them on land. Gulls find anchovies, and do business for me.' He returned with a cackle of laughter from the heights of fantasy. 'But I think that too complicated process, no?'

The northern section of the Pan-American highway was in excellent condition, and, despite one short stop for repairs, the collectivo made good time. At mid-morning we were already passing through the fishing port of Chimbote, more than 250 miles north of Lima, where we planned to stop on our return southward. At half-past eleven we crossed the last hill and saw the vast green triangle of land that nurtured the Mochica and the Chimu civilizations, rimmed on two sides by the shadowy hills, and on the third by the surf-laced blue of the Pacific. To the west the little seaport of Salaverry shone in the sunlight, white and deceptively inviting, beside a bay spattered with coloured fishing boats. To the north, blurred still by its ten miles of distance, Trujillo floated in the broad valley like a brown and white island on an aquamarine lake. 'You are early, Maestro!' shouted the Nicosian, addressing the driver by the title given in courtesy to Peruvian chauffeurs; the Maestro silently put his foot on the gas, sped down the long hill past the great yellow piles of the Mochica pyramids and drew up outside the Government Hotel in the Plaza de Armas at a few minutes to twelve. It was the only occasion in Peru on which we reached a destination before the scheduled time.

3

Trujillo is the oldest of the cities built by the Spanish conquerors of Peru, founded by Pizarro early in 1535, and named after the town in distant Estremadura where he had passed his youth as a despised swineherd. Remembering his proud and resentful character, one is tempted to imagine that he did this less in affectionate memory than for the satisfaction he must have derived from the existence of a Trujillo in which he was the ruler and not the servant.

Today Trujillo is still one of the three important cities of Peru, as indisputably the capital of the North as Arequipa is that of the South, and the rivalry between the two towns is one of the major factors in Peruvian national life. Both are creole cities, Spanish in spirit, but, while Arequipa reflects all that is conservative in the Spanish heritage, Trujillo embodies the rebellious strain which is equally alive in the Iberian character. If, by accepted convention, the generals start their military uprisings in Arequipa, there is just as strong a tradition which makes Trujillo the centre of popular revolution.

Peruvian independence was first proclaimed there in 1820, long before military adventurers like San Martin and Bolivar appeared to claim the laurels of Liberators, and ever since then the Trujillans have been ready to fight—in the streets if need be—for a rebellious cause. Haya de la Torre, founder of the Aprista movement, was a native of the city, and during the 1930's, in its first idealistic upsurge, APRA drew most of its support from Trujillo and the province of Libertad which adjoins it. In 1932, unaided by the rest of Peru, the people of Trujillo and the peasants of Libertad rose against the tyrannical dictatorship of Sanchez Cerro. It was the last important popular rebellion in Peru, put down with a cruelty exceptional in a country which had hitherto been celebrated in Latin America for the bloodlessness of its civil wars.

The Trujillans, as we discovered, had not forgotten the tragedy of 1932, or the long period of military vindictiveness that followed it, and they looked forward much more eagerly than people in the rest of Peru to some kind of improvement now that a general was no longer President. Even the houseboy who looked after our room in the hotel lingered over his bed-making to talk politics and to tell us that for a working man like himself any government that gave a little more freedom was better than what he called El Gobierno Malo—The Bad Government.

Trujillo had the air of a well-cared-for city, and the regular patterns of its streets were broken by paved plazas before the colonial churches and by many unexpected corners of public gardens with green lawns and jacaranda trees. Its feeling of openness was increased by the character of the patrician houses—vast, low mansions that revealed, as one looked through their escutcheoned arches, long vistas of doorways opening from patio to patio like the receding perspectives of double mirrors. It was a city in which one was always conscious of greenness—for many of the streets were planted with large old ficus trees surrounded by circles of whitewashed stones—and of the sky, which each day went through the same series of changes. Mornings were always overcast by a thin veil of bluish-white cloud, but by lunchtime the veering wind had cleared the sky, and the sunny afternoon prolonged itself into a soft golden afterglow that persisted longer than is usual in the tropics; night brought a slight chilling of the air, but nothing like the sharp cold of the Sierra.

John Harriman of the British Council had given us a letter of introduction to the manager of a small, British-operated railway that ran between Trujillo and the sugar-growing valleys of the hinterland, and on our first morning we walked down to the station on the edge of the town. Mr. Ramsay, the manager, had spent almost all his working life on the railways of Ecuador and Peru, and he had the patient, easily courteous manner which Darwin many years ago noted as an acquired characteristic of British business men who live long enough in the atmosphere of South American trading. He admitted that he himself could tell us very little about the historical and archaeological questions in which we were interested. The man we should see was Colonel M., one of the most important hacendados of the region, who was much interested in local history. Mr. Ramsay took up the phone, failed to connect with the Colonel, and suggested that we might take a turn with him around the railway yards while we waited for the line to clear.

'You should get on well in Trujillo,' he said, as we strolled along the platform. 'There's a tradition of liking the British here, mixed up with Canning and the part we played in the War of Independence. But I must say that things aren't so easy as they used to be before the war. Then the British had a really big hand in trade, but now the Americans come down with their give-away programmes, Point Four and so on, and they use them as a lever to get trade for their own companies. But you'll find that people in Trujillo still like us more than they like the Americans. The American can't help being a hustler, and that doesn't go down well with South Americans. Even when they're in trade they like to keep up the pretence that they're gentlemen playing at business, and they expect to be treated as such.'

By this time we had reached the station yard, where Mr. Ramsay conscientiously pointed out the bits of antiquity at his command —the piece of seventeenth-century rampart that stood on the edge of the sidings, the old Spanish well that was still being used to water the locomotives. But it was with a great deal more pride that he took us into the sheds and showed us the Peruvian fitters working on a new locomotive that had been sent in parts from England and was being assembled in the Trujillo yard. 'They're good mechanics, you know,' he commented. 'They have a real aptitude for machinery, and if you give them a chance and a bit of training, they'll do work as good as any locomotive fitter in England.'

Walking back, he talked of the railway he managed. It was a small line—its total length, including branches, was little more than a hundred miles—but it served a rich country and paid its way by bringing raw sugar down from the haciendas and mineral ores from the small mines in the foothills. 'Here's one thing you should think of,' he laughed, 'next time you drop a lump of sugar in your coffee. You see those tank wagons?' A line of extremely grimy vehicles was standing in the siding to which he pointed. 'They belong to the sugar companies,' he explained. 'They are sent down full of molasses, and they go back filled with crude oil for use in the mill on the hacienda. It's done regularly, and the wagons are never cleaned out between the oil and the sugar. But I'm told that it doesn't do much harm to either of them.'

By now we were back at the office and Mr. Ramsay went in to see whether he could now get through to Colonel M. He came out five minutes later. 'Colonel M. is down with 'flu,' he reported. 'Otherwise he'd have been glad to see you. But he's fixing up for a man he employs, a kind of journalist named Manuel, to show you around. Manuel knows all there is to know about Trujillo. Chan Chan, Moche—anything you want to see. . . . He'll be around at your hotel some time this afternoon.'

We went back to the hotel, ate an excellent lunch—for the Government Hotel in Trujillo rivalled that of Arequipa in the good quality of its cooking—and settled down to wait in our room for Señor Manuel. The siesta hour drew to an end, and in the lounge somebody began to give piano lessons. All the afternoon tortured melodies of Czerny and Tchaikovsky came stuttering up the landings, while Inge nursed her aching ear with a hot-water bottle and I impatiently dipped into Herodotus and kept looking out of the window at the peasants who came into town riding on donkeys which carried curious cylindrical panniers made of hardened cowhide.

Each time a man in a suit came across the Plaza towards the

hotel I would watch him carefully in the hope that he might be Señor Manuel; each time I was disappointed. We had no description of Manuel, and to pass the time we compared the images of him that were forming in our minds. Inge imagined him as young, emaciated, a little melancholy, like Philip II in his youth. I saw him as fat, round-faced, untidy and middle-aged, with dog's eyes and a shifty smile. Finally, after most of the afternoon had passed, I went down to the reception desk to see whether he might at least have left a message; I noticed a discreet smirk on the face of the clerk when I mentioned his name, and it was then that I began to suspect that we would not have the chance to decide whose image was nearest to the real Señor Manuel.

By the evening we gave up waiting, exasperated by the thought that, with so much to be seen, we had wasted the best part of a day lounging in a hotel room. To assuage our frustration we went to a picture house on the edge of the town; it was a relaxing experience, not because of the shoddy Hollywood melodrama of pursuit and murder, but for the uninhibited and infectious responses of the audience, who laughed at every amorous gesture and howled in the best tradition of the popular theatre whenever a villain was beaten up. It made one realize how much the use of sound in films has turned audiences into silent spectators instead of vociferous participants, for the Peruvians, who almost always see undubbed foreign language films whose speech they cannot understand, are still, to all intents and purposes, in the same stage as the spectators of the so-called silent films in those distant days when one joined in shouting down the enemies of Pearl White.

It was half-past eleven when we left the picture house, and we expected, after our experience of the Sierra towns, to find that the city had long gone to sleep. In fact, the streets were alive with people, the newsboys were shouting the final edition of the local newspaper, and all the cafés were busy and ablaze with light. Trujillo was one of the few cities in Peru with a street life that kept going until the early hours of the morning. The first night we stayed until one o'clock on the narrow terrace of one of the cafés, which was run, like most in Trujillo, by Italian immigrants. We watched the groups of students who drifted arm in arm along the street, singing or arguing, and the swifts that flew black against the moonlit sky and swooped screaming between the upper storeys of the buildings. But most of all we became interested in the activities of the shoeblacks who were still busily scuttling about the feet of the people sitting on the terraces.

Most of the boys were young—between eight and twelve—and about a dozen of them worked the cafés of the main street. There was also a boy of fifteen or sixteen who did no work himself, but evidently operated a kind of protection racket, arbitrating between the smaller boys in their squabbles over territory, and occasionally pocketing small pieces of money in tribute. On one occasion, instead of acting as a peacemaker, he encouraged two of the boys to fight, and then, when their attention was concentrated on each other's flailing fists, he quickly slipped his hand into the brush box which one of them had left on the pavement, extracted a note for five soles which he slipped into his pocket, and then blandly stepped forward and declared the fight at an end. Evidently the gentlemanly business relations of which Mr. Ramsay had talked did not penetrate to all layers of Trujillo life.

4

The next morning, when we told him of our fruitless afternoon of waiting, Mr. Ramsay shook his head in sad amusement. 'Manuel must have sold an article,' he commented. 'He always goes on a binge when he does, and if the article was a long one we may have to wait a week before he turns up. I'm sorry about it all, but I'll find you someone more reliable.' Within a few minutes he had kept his promise by ringing up Professor Uceda of the University of Trujillo, whom we met shortly afterwards at the Peruvian-North American Institute.

Professor Uceda, a mineralogist and a devoted Americanophile, was a brisk man of a type more common in northern Peru than in the rather languid south. He showed an immediate interest in our travels, delivered a condensed impromptu lecture on the climate and topography of northern Peru, and then sent one of his student assistants to take us on a tour of the University and particularly to introduce us to the archaeologists who were working there.

After San Marco in Lima, the University of Trujillo, with its 1,500 students, is the most important educational institution in Peru, yet we found that its activities were crammed into a small group of buildings covering much less than a city block. It was also clear that funds as well as space were lacking, for the inadequately large lecture rooms needed plastering and the furniture looked as if it had served since Bolivar founded the University in 1824. The library was small and restricted mostly to works in Spanish, while the laboratories were less well-equipped than those in many an English secondary school.

Material inadequacies of this kind are part of the background of all university life in Peru, but the students there have also to reckon with a peculiar system of honorary professorships. A professor will be a practising lawyer, doctor or engineer, who lectures at the University not for the very nominal salary,[1] but for the help which the prestige of a chair may give to his career. The result is obvious. Unless a professor is dedicated to teaching, his career will come first and as his practice grows he will tend to cut his own lectures.

A system of this kind is obviously inadequate to provide the kind of specialized training in the sciences which will be increasingly necessary as Peru becomes more industrialized and seeks greater independence from foreign technicians. On the other hand, it can sometimes produce unexpectedly good results in the humanities, where the individuality of the teacher comes more into play.

Certainly one of the most vital sections of the University of Trujillo was the Department of Archaeology, partly because of the personality of its director, Professor José Eulogio Garrido, an internationally recognized authority on Peruvian antiquities, and partly because of the enormous research facilities provided by the presence of so many unexplored monuments in the Trujillo region.

[1] This amounts to about 400 soles (eight pounds) per month, far less than the salary of a teacher in one of the exclusive private schools in Lima.

The archaeologists had established their own musuem within the University buildings. When we arrived, Professor Garrido was busy with a team of photographers, but he called his assistant and asked him to look after us. The assistant's name was Pedro Puerta; he was a slight, dark, sympathetic man in his early twenties. 'The last writer I had the honour of taking through our museum was an Englishman,' he told us. 'His name was Arnold Toynbee.'

The pleasant little museum through which we followed in Toynbee's steps was more of a workshop than a place of exhibition; tables were spread with fragments of vases in the process of re-assembly, and with exhibits waiting to be labelled, while, except for a few cases where exceptional pieces were shown, the museum's stock stood on high stacks of open shelves, loaded with thousands of ceramic vessels taken from the tombs of northern Peru, mostly of the Mochica[1] and Chimu cultures.

The first of these flourished about the beginning of the Christian era, and had its religious and possibly also its political centre near the present village of Moche, a few miles south-west of Trujillo. The vast adobe temples and massive aqueducts built by the Mochica suggest that they were engineers of considerable ability, while they maintained an extensive military road system[2] over which, anticipating the Incas, they operated services of post runners. They were accomplished surgeons, and, if the theories of some archaeologists are correct, they may even have invented—alone among the ancient Peruvian peoples—a rudimentary form of writing by which messages were scratched on coloured beans which the runners carried in their pouches. But, for posterity at least, the most interesting achievement of the Mochicas is the

[1] Modern archaeologists tend to call this the Moche culture, but, since I shall have reason to mention the modern village of Moche, I retain the older title of Mochica for the ancient civilization in order to avoid confusion. Both titles are arbitrary, since no one knows what the people who founded the culture actually called themselves.

[2] In 1957, Professor Garrido and Señor Puerta discovered an extensive system of Mochica fortifications along the Santa River, almost 100 miles south of Moche, and this would seem to confirm that the people of this culture were military conquerors, extending their rule far beyond their native region.

elaborate record of their way of living that was created by their potters.

The Mochica pots—which Puerta explained were called *huacos* by the modern Peruvians—were made specifically as grave furniture, intended to hold food and chicha for the dead, and also to allow them to carry into the world of shadows at least a few images of the life they had left behind. There were two types of these funereal vessels—those moulded into portrait or effigy form, and those on whose rounded surfaces linear designs had been painted.

Generally speaking, the effigy pots were realistic in their approach, and some of them reached such a degree of exact representation that one could distinguish, for instance, between the expressions of sleep and of blindness. Many captured the character of a face with psychological subtlety, others pursued the exaggeration of features almost to the point of caricature, and a few declined into a coarse expressionism that reminded one of a third-rate Toby jug. On rare occasions some artist would break away dramatically from the realistic convention; one remarkable effigy vessel represented pain by a distortion as deliberate and stylized as that of a West African carving; the face had been reduced to a flat mask drained of personality, the eyes to straight, unseeing slits, and the mouth to a rectangular hole that seemed to echo with agony.

But it was the pots with painted designs that presented, with great fluidity of line and expression, the most detailed record of Mochica life. Across their surfaces the postmen ran through cactus deserts, the chiefs held court under thatched awnings, the warriors bashed each other with star-headed maces, the fishermen rode their reed boats through the surf, and the ordinary people carried on their domestic lives in cane huts no different in any perceptible way from those we had seen as we travelled beside the beaches of the Pan-American highway.

The most pleasing of these painted pots were those which represented scenes of natural life—the underwater inhabitants of the rivers and the sea, the birds of the cane brakes and the foxes that came down out of the hills; these had a sensitive feeling for living forms that reminded one of the Egyptian paintings of animals and birds in the period of Akhnaton. Almost certainly they expressed something more than a simple love of nature, for the Mochicas represented their religious beliefs in a zoomorphic manner, and many of their vessels showed conflicts between half-human and half-animal beings resembling the Gods of Egypt. There was a crab-god and a fish-god, and also a double-headed serpent deity which we found particularly interesting because it bore a close resemblance to figures we had seen represented on the inner walls of the pyramid at Cholula in Mexico and on the memorial poles of the Kwakiutl Indians in British Columbia. Like the recurrence of the jaguar deity, which appears both in Mexico and ancient Peru, the incidence of a special kind of snake-cult at places spread over thousands of miles suggests that there may have existed a common religion in the ancient Americas which antedated all the individual cultures at present known to us.

But the strongest impression one gained from looking at these hundreds of specimens of Mochica pottery was that of a people who, whatever their beliefs may have been, were possessed of a delight in the visible world that gave their work a power of direct communication over the centuries not unlike that which one experiences on seeing for the first time the paintings of a neolithic cavern. The corporate personality of a vanished people seemed to emerge in them, and in the end I felt that I understood the Mochicas—despite the fact that they have no known history and their very name is an invention of modern scholars—far more than the Chimu, even though the latter belonged to the one pre-Inca civilization about which we have a certain amount of historical information.

The Chimu, in fact, had no really characteristic art which embodied their civilization in the same way as ceramics embodied that of the Mochica, or textiles that of the race of Paracas. Their culture, which centred around Chan Chan and emerged about the time of the Norman Conquest, seems to have been linked by traditions of craftsmanship with that of the Mochica, since the Chimu also made effigy vessels for their tombs. They, however, worked mostly in a black ware whose deadness of appearance was not wholly due to its lack of colour; spontaneity had been refined away by excessive stylization and by the invention of mass production processes. The ceramics of the Chimu no longer represented a vital interest in life; they were merely a conventional tribute to the dead.

Puerta spent almost the whole afternoon with us, explaining patiently, and making sure that we missed nothing of interest. Then, when we had reached the last room, he said, casually, 'Tomorrow, if you have nothing else to do, I could go with you to Chan Chan and Moche.' Naturally we were pleased, and accepted immediately, but, since Puerta had mentioned that he sometimes acted as a professional guide, we asked to employ him in that capacity. 'No, no,' he replied emphatically, 'we are friends. Besides, I shall gain too, for I shall have a whole day in which to practise my English.'

As we were about to leave, a stocky, copper-faced young man came into the museum. Puerta shook hands with him, and brought him over to meet us. 'This is my friend Miguel,' he said. 'He is a descendant of the Mochicas.' There was, indeed, a resemblance between Miguel's round, rather thick features and many of the faces on the portrait pots we had been handling a short while before.

Miguel, it appeared, was a fisherman. 'But only in the winter,' he explained. 'When the summer rains come and the floods lay bare the clay in the river beds, I become a potter.'

'But he is no ordinary potter,' Puerta remarked; bursting into laughter. 'He is the kind of potter of whom all travellers should beware. He is a reproducer of huacos.'

Miguel went on, without self-consciousness, to explain his trade. He would use an original vessel taken from a tomb, make a mould from it, and then cast a dozen or so facsimiles. He employed the same materials, the same firing techniques, the same method of polishing as the Chimu themselves, and he claimed with some pride that even an expert would find it hard to tell the difference between one of his pots and a real huaco.

Puerta agreed that this was the case. 'That is why,' he warned us, 'if you get a chance to buy ceramics, you should always choose

the painted ones, which are very much more difficult to reproduce.'
When the time came we followed his advice.

5

The ancient peoples of the Peruvian coast always built their towns and cemeteries away from the green fields of the valleys, and so, to reach the ruined Chimu capital of Chan Chan, we had to travel several miles northward into the desert. Two miles out of Trujillo we came to a village of white cubical houses which clustered around an ornate mansion in the unexpected style of the French Second Empire. This, Puerta remarked, was Manciche. 'There is something here which I would like you to see before we go on to Chan Chan.' He directed the driver of the car down a lane that led past the village church, through white-flowered yam-fields, to a terraced adobe structure that stood on the edge of the dunes.

'This is called the Huaca Esmeralda,' Puerta explained, as we walked towards it. 'It may be one of the royal tombs of the Chimu.' He went on to recount a local legend which claimed that the bodies of the last of the Chimu kings, nominally converted to Christianity, were buried in the church of Manciche and then taken secretly by their pagan followers to the Huaca Esmeralda. But since the tomb had been opened long ago by the huaqueros (grave robbers) in search of gold masks and ornaments, there was no chance of telling who might have been buried there.

What survived of the Huaca consisted of a stepped platform whose highest level was reached by a ceremonial ramp. The walls of the platform carried characteristic Chimu relief decorations, consisting of stylized birds and animal figures, repeated as in a block print, and alternating with geometrical arabesques; they resembled closely the patterns used by the Chimu weavers. The walls had been built of adobe blocks, plastered with a layer of mud, into which the designs were cut; the slight variations between repeated motifs ruled out the possibility of their having been stamped. Though now the reliefs had reverted to their natural mud tint, originally they had been coloured, and the effect must have been barbarically splendid as the whole building shone out multi-chromatically against the tan of the surrounding dunes.

Inge remarked on the sharpness with which these patterns in mud, even though they had lost their colouring, had survived so many centuries of existence. 'It's a matter of climate,' Puerta replied. 'No frost, and no rain. The only enemy they have, apart from man, is El Niño.' El Niño—the child! We were puzzled at first until Puerta explained that El Niño was the warm current that flows around the coast of Ecuador and meets the Humboldt Current at Tumbes, near to the northern edge of Peru. Occasionally El Niño, pushing like an angry child, forced its way southward, and then the life of the desert was disturbed by the unexpected and not altogether welcome gift of abundant rain. 'The last time El Niño arrived,' Puerta went on, 'was in 1925. It rained for three days. Trujillo was flooded, the crops were washed away, and the fishermen starved because the fish went to cooler waters. You'll see some of El Niño's work when we get to Chan Chan.'

After we had left Manciche the desert opened out towards the mist-scarved hills, and two or three miles farther on we entered Chan Chan. The eroded ruins reared up on every side of us, and at first we felt bewildered by this maze of time-bitten walls which sprawled over eight square miles of desert between the foothills and the coastal dunes. For Chan Chan was the largest of all the ancient cities of Peru, and larger than any modern city in the country except Lima; at the height of the kingdom of Chimu it sheltered a quarter of a million people, who lived from the produce of the rich sea and the irrigated lands of the Trujillo oasis.

Its origins can be seen only indistinctly in the haze of prehistory, but it was probably built between eight and nine centuries ago; all the evidence suggests that its life had the luxury and colour of an oriental capital; even after defeat the princes of Chimu remained exotic beings as, turbanned and tinkling with great nose-ornaments of gold and precious stones, they lived their exile among the grey walls of Cuzco.

The end of Chan Chan is known more certainly than its beginning, for old men who remembered it were still alive when the Spaniards came. It was in the early 1470's that Topa Inca Yupanqui, son of Pachacuti, led the Inca armies down from the Cordillera Occidentale and cut the aqueducts that led to the desert city. As the water sank in the great reservoirs, the king of Chimu talked of leading out his armies to a last trial of power with the invaders, but his counsellors, remembering that the Incas massacred those who resisted too fiercely, but dealt gently with those who surrendered, argued against him. The realm of Chimu disappeared without a struggle. Deprived of its chieftains and its water supply, Chan Chan died quickly, and by the time the Spaniards marched through it, sixty years afterwards, it had already become a city of ghosts and of legends.

Without a guide one would have been lost in Chan Chan's deserted complexity, but Puerta knew every path and courtyard, and when the car had driven as far as it could go, he marched ahead down the narrow lanes among the ruins and led us through the crumbling gateways from one enclosure to the next. Above us, ochre-yellow against the blue sky, the walls towered like the ramparts of some Saharan metropolis; El Niño had bitten deeply into them, washing away almost half their height in the disastrous three days of 1925, but still the remnants stood more than thirty feet above the ground. The foundations were made of boulders; the walls themselves—several feet thick at the base and tapering towards the top—were built of tamped earth and gravel, reinforced by canes whose tops still projected from the ragged summits.

In the whole deserted city there was not a tourist or a guardian to be seen, and the only human being was a boy who came unexpectedly galloping down one of the dead streets on a white horse and disappeared in the direction of the sea. But the very completeness of the desertion created an extraordinary atmosphere. Spring was beginning, whatever spring comes to the desert in normal years; the few carob trees in the empty courtyards were clouded with the pale green of opening leaflets, and often the wind would carry the fragrance of a creeping mimosa that blossomed over the heaps of rubble. Groups of bunting-like birds, pale as ghost-moths, flew in silent and dipping flight before us, and once a red-breasted falcon darted low over our heads. The only animate sound was the crying of the gulls over the dunes on the seaward side.

These scanty manifestations of life took on a peculiar intensity of suggestion in the emptiness of the metropolis whose own life had once been so active and so rich. Walking through the ten double-walled barrios, cities within a city, into which Chan Chan was divided, it was possible to envisage fairly concretely how the people had lived, divided into self-contained clans, yet drawn together by their needs, of which the great pit of the central reservoir, where the bulrushes still rustled in the damp bottom, seemed the most evocative symbol, since its exhaustion had meant the death of their common life.

Chan Chan's history did not end with the Chimu; the empty city has its tragic place in modern Peruvian history. As we were walking out of the ruins Puerta pointed to a plain wooden cross that had been erected in a stretch of open sand near the main road. 'You have heard of the revolution we had in Trujillo in 1932?' he asked. 'Well, that cross commemorates the rebels who died when the generals took their revenge. They brought them out to Chan Chan in trucks, shot them among the ruins and left their bodies to the vultures. More than a thousand men were murdered here. Sometimes people still find their bones.' He was silent for a moment. 'An uncle of mine was one of the men who was shot,' he added. 'I was named Pedro in memory of him. Among our people they say that if you are named after a man who dies violently you have bad fortune all your life. But up to now I have had no reason to complain about my luck.'

Over lunch in Trujillo we discussed the lack of any kind of adequate protection for the monuments we had seen during the morning. It would clearly have been impossible to save the many miles of Chan Chan's walls from further rain damage, but something could at least have been done to preserve the comparatively small areas of fragile relief work which we had seen both there and at the Huaca Esmeralda. In fact, the only effort at protection was an ineffectual cane awning over one of the carved walls in Chan Chan; the rest had been left open to any harm that the weather or human vandalism might do. This neglect, we gathered, was due mostly to the fact that the government in Lima had so far been insufficiently interested in the sites of northern Peru to spend any money on their conservation.

In the afternoon we started off for Moche in order to visit the temples of the Sun and the Moon, the most important remaining monuments of the Mochica culture. Moche itself was a nondescript Indian village in the middle of the rich alluvial land south of Trujillo. Outside the doors of the square adobe houses, scattered beside the narrow lanes along which we drove, stood clusters of thick earthenware vessels with pointed ends thrust into the ground; they were at least four feet high, and resembled Greek wine jars. 'Chicha jars!' Puerta remarked. 'People live well around Moche. You remember my friend Miguel? He and his family live here, and sometimes they invite me to a real Mochica meal. We start with seviche—that is raw fish pickled in lemon juice—and then we go on to stuffed guinea-pig and potatoes and plenty of fresh chicha. It's a traditional meal that people around here have eaten for centuries.' Visiting Moche farms to taste the chicha seemed to be a favourite occupation of people from Trujillo, for a man in town clothes staggered and shouted blindly out of one of the cottages almost under the wheels of our car. 'You see, the chicha of Moche is very good,' Puerta commented.

As we wound along the lanes the yellow masses of the temples of the Sun and Moon grew larger and more distinct against their background of shifting dunes and arid hills. Finally the car dipped through a grove of willow trees, forded a shallow stream, and emerged in the harsh sunlight of the desert where the two Huacas squatted, like vast faceless sphinxes under the eroded slopes of the Cerro Blanco, the White Hill.

Both of these adobe temples had the shapeless grandeur which any large structure assumes when the weather and the centuries have worked upon it long enough. The front of the Huaca of the Sun was a great cracked escarpment of mud bricks, out of whose crevices the martins fluttered and glided over the sugar fields towards Moche. The rains had cut deep channels and brought the rubble down in heaps on every side of the Huaca, but it remained a vast, forlorn monument of human dedication. Industrious archaeologists have measured it—250 yards long, 100 wide, and almost 50 yards high to the top layer of the stepped pyramid— and have estimated the number of its bricks at more than 130 million.

These figures, if they do nothing else, convey some idea of the tribute which the Mochica farmers and fishermen and potters who built the Huaca were willing to pay to their Gods—Gods who are now as nameless as their worshippers, for the titles given to the two temples, though they are traditional, have no backing of archaeological evidence. Yet to what other deities than the heavenly bodies could these temples, oriented so obviously towards the sky, have been erected? Hardly to the crab-gods and the fish-gods of the Mochica potters, and the only alternative to accepting the Huacas as survivals of Sun and Moon worship lies in the possibility that here also there might have existed a cult of that creator God who appeared in the Sierra under the name of Viracocha and on the southern coast under the name of Pachacamac.

The Huaca of the Moon was much smaller than its neighbour— barely a quarter of its volume—but still large enough to be impressive, and Puerta suggested that we should climb it to look at the frescoed rooms on the top platform. We walked over soft sand full of red potsherds to the base of the Huaca, and up a gulley half-clogged with fallen adobe bricks.

The frescoed rooms were actually small chambers so filled with rubble that it was hard to see very much of the paintings, but what were visible had kept an intensity of colour—mainly reds and blues—which gave an idea of the oppressively garish effect these geometrically decorated rooms must originally have produced. No similar chambers have up to now been discovered in the Huaca of the Sun, but there seems reason to believe that an altar—possibly surrounded by a now-vanished building—stood on its highest platform.

As we climbed down from the Huaca of the Moon and started back across the desert to the waiting car, a series of piercing yells echoed from the Cerro Blanco behind us. We looked around, saw no sign of movement among the white boulders, but the shouts continued as we walked away—'Gringo! Gringo! Gringo!'

6

The following day we travelled southward to Chimbote. From there we planned to return to Lima by way of El Callejon de Huaylas—the Alley of Huaylas—an enclosed Andean valley between the Cordillera Negra and the Cordillera Blanca about which, during the last few weeks, we had heard a great deal of vague and slightly sensational talk. Weiss in Puno had mentioned it first. 'You should go there. It's just like Switzerland,' he remarked. After that several other people talked of the valley, and all of them said, 'It's just like Switzerland'. We found, however, that none of them had been to the Callejon de Huaylas and that only Weiss knew Switzerland, so that this comparison really told us nothing. However, as the weeks went on we picked up a few facts about the Callejon de Huaylas—that it was a centre from which alpinists tackled the high peaks of the Cordillera Blanca, that geographically it ranked among the high valleys of the Andes next to those of Cuzco and Jauja, that from the north one could reach it only by means of a light railway from Chimbote to a mountain village called Huallanca.

In Chimbote we found that the next train to Huallanca did not leave until Monday, two days ahead. We did not regret this, since the air was soft and warm, there was a good Swiss-owned hotel on the beach, and the town itself turned out to be the only example we found in Peru of a community in the acute stage of transition from a primitive to an industrial way of life, a community whose raw chaos was emphasized by the contrasting beauty of its setting.

For the bay of Chimbote was closed in like a calm inland sea by a dark-pinnacled headland and a line of whale-backed islands whose slopes were white with a perpetual snow of guano. A very thin haze gave a muted dazzle to the light over the water and softened every colour; the wide, long curve of the beach was grey-yellow and even the sea was pale and northern. As we walked beside it, watching the black squadrons of porpoises rolling and leaping northward up the bay, Inge remarked how much it reminded her of the shores of the Baltic in East Prussia where she had once spent a holiday in childhood.

Until 1940 all that stood beside the Bay of Chimbote was a malaria-infested village and a pier from which the minerals brought down on the railway were carried by lighter to the tramp steamers moored out in deep water. The earnings from fishing were scanty, and the men often eked them out by turning huaqueros and roaming through the desert with long iron probes to find the tombs buried under the sands.

Yet for many years the possibilities of Chimbote as a naturally sheltered harbour had been recognized; in particular, the village had attracted the roving eye of Honest Henry Meiggs, who built the railway to Huallanca and pegged out on the dunes behind the beach the streets of a whole industrial city. He died too soon to start building it, and his plans lay unrealized until the early 1940's, when the Peruvian Government formed an organization called the Santa Corporation, devoted to developing Chimbote and the valley behind it. The Corporation drained the fever marshes and malaria vanished. Industry made its first appearance in the form of small fish-canning factories and fertilizer plants. Late in the 1940's the hotel was built, and venturesome people from Lima began to drive northward for the unfamiliar experience of a seaside holiday.

In 1955 the last stage of Chimbote's metamorphosis began when a French engineering syndicate started work on a steel mill. It was the first steel mill in Peru, and it meant that Chimbote had changed in little more than a decade from a disease-ridden village of fishermen's hovels into a pioneer centre of heavy industry—and also a chaotic working-class settlement which showed in a desolating way what can happen when the Industrial Revolution creates its bridgeheads in a hitherto unindustrialized country. Every week, attracted by the promise of work, hundreds of people had trooped in from the coast and the Sierra, farmers ruined by drought, hacienda hands seeking something better than starvation wages, until in a year or so the population of Chimbote had swollen to twenty times its pre-war size, and the village had become, hardly a town, but rather a conglomeration of people resembling nothing so much as a large refugee encampment.

A district called the Barrio de Acero—the Steel Quarter, was the centre of this encampment. We travelled through it on our way into Chimbote and later wandered on foot along the rough lanes of sand where its inhabitants—thousands of them—were living in shacks and shelters made out of rush mats, canes, flattened petrol tins, cardboard, any material that was easy to get and cost next to nothing. The normal facilities of urban life were non-existent; there was no electricity, no sewage system, no water other than that provided by the vendors who wandered shouting through the lanes with their old oil-drums lashed on to mule carts. The garbage lay in fly-infested heaps behind the houses, the vultures hopped about as tamely as chickens; and the stench of excrement mingled with the reek that floated up from the fish-rendering plants on the quays. In one corner of the Barrio a mad woman with matted hair dragging over her face sat nodding and moaning on the ground, and a crew of ragged children danced around her, screeching, 'Loca! Loca!' and pelting her with rubbish. In another street an old Indian, begging for the centavos of the poor, played his eerie Sierra tunes of the Pan's pipes which the Andean llama herds have been using for a score of centuries.

The piper's presence was symbolic, for the Barrio was a gathering of people trying to live primitively in an unprimitive environment. They were men and women who had never inhabited anything better than cane or adobe hovels, had never enjoyed piped water or electric light, had never disposed of their garbage in any organized way, people for whom the vulture was the natural scavenger and the earth the natural receiver of excrement. But circumstances which are only moderately unhealthy in a group of huts at the end of a fishing beach or a remote holding in the Sierra, become lethal when they are multiplied on an urban scale, and one of the most formidable problems facing a country like

Peru, as it becomes more urban and more industrialized, is that of educating primitive rural people in the sanitary disciplines of urban life. There was little in the Barrio de Acero to indicate that this education had begun, or to suggest that much was being done to help its inhabitants to obtain better living conditions.

The Barrio de Acero ended at the shabby, boomtown main street of Chimbote, where girls in black trousers lingered in the doorways and bottles shone like jewels in the windows of the endless saloons and the houses were made of corrugated iron which the sea air had rotted in a few years until it looked like a lace of rust. And beyond this street, in the little isolated domain of the hotel, with its garden patios and its private beach, visitors less curious than ourselves could doubtless remain reasonably unaware of the slum half a mile away.

Indeed, there were times in the hotel when one could feel worlds away from any part of Peru, for most of its guests were French—either connected with the steel plant or attracted from Lima by the presence of their compatriots—and at evening in the bar, when the dark-skinned waiters padded softly around the tables and the sound of Gallic voices rose high over any other language, a nostalgic Frenchman might easily imagine himself, if not in France, at least in some French tropical colony.

Abroad, the French seem to serry their ranks even more tightly than at home, and in the Chimbote Hotel they gathered in private circles from which the alien—and the Peruvian—was sharply excluded. We did, however, talk—or rather listen—to one Frenchwoman, an Ancient Marineress who buttonholed us in the bar and settled down to a session of confidential revelation while we steadily got drunk on Martinis. She was an elderly and rather handsome woman in the gaunt, hollow-eyed French blonde style, and, as she told us in a gin-cracked voice of grievance, she had been in Peru for twenty years. 'Nom de Dieu! Quelles années perdues! Je ne veux pas vieillir au bout du monde!' Yet there she was, condemned by the obstinacy of her husband—she waved her hand towards a complacent fat man at one of the other tables—who owned a business in Lima and would not depart. A frightful man, she insisted, grasping and above all vain. 'Do you know why

he will never—I tell you, never—return to France? Do you know?'
She gesticulated wildly and we cautiously lifted our drinks from
the table. 'It is because if he walks from the Plaza San Martin to
the Plaza de Armas in Lima twenty people, twenty useless ridicu-
lous people of no importance whatsoever, will want to shake him
by the hand. Il se croit un homme célèbre!—un-homme-célèbre!
But if he goes back to Bordeaux, not a single person will even
recognize him. Ha! Mon mari est épris de la gloire! Qu'est-ce-que
la gloire au Pérou?' She knocked back her fourth Martini with a
vindictive gulp. 'You play bridge? No? Then I must find someone
who does.' She went off unsteadily and hovered over the card
tables, predatory and desperate.

7

Even the lives of the fishermen in Chimbote had been changed
by the arrival of industry. Ten years ago they went out in fragile
sailing boats; now they all had sturdy, wide-beamed power boats,
and had become to all intents and purposes the employees of the
canneries and the fertilizer factories.

The Swiss owner of the hotel, Herr N., offered to take us out
to one of the larger canneries, a few miles up the coast. 'I'm going
there in any case,' he said. 'I've a farm of sorts up the Santa
valley, and I go every Saturday to see how things are getting on. So
I'll drop you at the plant. The manager is a friend of mine, and
he'll be glad to show you around.' We set off in his half-ton
truck, with a couple of houseboys in the back, keeping a tight
hold on the tubs of pig-swill for the farm.

The cannery, like all industrial plants in Peru, was heavily
fenced with barbed wire, and when we arrived an armed guard
telephoned to the office and kept us waiting outside the gate until
the manager—a young blond Hungarian—came out to meet us.
As we went in with him, he apologized for not having very much
to show us. 'Until the tuna run we are more or less on holiday,' he

explained. 'But come down to the wharf, and we can see what's going on.'

At the wharf a fishing boat had just come in with a load of anchovies; its hold was filled with a silvery soup of small fishes which were being sucked up by a large pump and dumped on the conveyor belt that would take them through the automatic processes of the fertilizer plant. 'I'm afraid we don't respect anchovies here as much as in Europe,' the manager remarked. 'There's no ready market for them as food, so we extract their oil and turn the rest into fertilizer.'

The gunwales of the boat, and the side of the wharf as well, were lined with pelicans, one of which would occasionally drop into the hold with a clumsy clatter of wings and pouch a few fish from the pile. Nobody disturbed the birds, and they in turn were so tame that they would only waddle out of one's path at the last moment and with evident reluctance. They too had prospered from the expansion of the fishing industry; we gathered that since the canneries had opened many pelicans had adapted themselves to the situation by giving up fishing altogether and by spending their time waiting, like people in food queues, for the fishing boats to arrive at the wharves. They were tolerated as useful scavengers.

We left the wharf and went back through the plant, where the manager explained in detail the various processes that went on automatically until, in the choking stench of the roasting room, the fertilizer eventually emerged as a fine grey powder; it was exported mostly to the United States, since few farmers in Peru itself could afford to buy it. Afterwards he invited us to go over to his bungalow, and there we sat on the veranda looking out over the neat yellow bay, with its ragged fringe of palm trees and banana groves, and the white guano islands dazzling in the rich sunlight of the late afternoon.

I had been less interested in the technicalities of the fish-plant—which I do not imagine were much different from the technicalities of fish-plants in Aberdeen or Alaska—than in the conditions under which people worked there, and, after we had chatted for a while around such standard Peruvian conversational gambits as the efficacy of Indian medicines and the inefficiency of

Indian servants, I asked the manager if he would tell me something about the earnings of the people he employed.

He did so more willingly than I had expected, and the facts he repeated seem worth reproducing since they give some insight into the economic situation of working men in Peru. Most of the workers in the plant were seasonal; now thirty men were employed, but at the height of the tuna season there might be 500 casual workers, all of whom had to find other ways of living when the canning came to an end. The wages paid in the factory were based on the official national minimum wage for industrial workers—10 soles a day for men (less than 4s.) and 4.80 for women (less than 2s.). The slow workers never earned more than this, but the quick ones benefited from a system of piecework calculation, and some of the women fish cleaners earned as much as 12 soles (4s. 6d.) a day, while a skilled machinist could reach 40 soles (round about 15s.); very few workers, however, came into the last category.

These rates of pay, the manager remarked, were probably higher than the average for Peruvian industry, since most employers did their best to pay no more than the national minimum, and yet industrial rates in general were far higher than anything paid on the haciendas. He himself had worked for a time in the administration office of a large sugar estate, and there he had seen men earning as little as 2 soles (9d.) and women 1.60 soles (7d.) for a day of much harder work than was expected in the canning factory. It was true that the hacienda workers were given some kind of shelter and a certain amount of maize and potatoes, but their standard of living remained far below that of workers in industry.

When one considers that the cost of living in Peru is in many items equal to that of countries like England, it is easy to see what wages of this kind mean in terms of daily life. Nearly all a Peruvian worker's earnings are spent on food and cheap clothing. He usually lives in a decrepit and insanitary hovel, he smokes little, and he gets drunk periodically on chicha and cheap raw spirits. To him the modest comforts of an English working man's home would be luxury, and the life of an American factory worker a dream of impossible wealth.

Thus, in Peru, manual work and poverty are almost inseparable, and the closing of the economic gap between social classes that is taking place in other countries has hardly begun. This is due partly to the low level of Peruvian production, partly to the tenacity with which class barriers are maintained. But in both of these directions there is a possibility of fairly quick changes. Peru is already becoming modernized, and a rapid industrial and agricultural expansion, like that which has taken place in Brazil, may well begin during the next few years. At the same time, I noticed among the younger educated generation a tendency to loosen the ideas of caste associated with manual work, a tendency even towards a certain feeling of guilt because of social advantage. These circumstances between them may result in the gradual lessening of the great disparity between the living conditions of various classes which still causes one so much distress in a country like Peru.

8

The Monday on which we went to the Callejon de Huaylas started badly. We both felt unwell, and dragged ourselves unwillingly from bed for another dawn departure. Then, as we were following the boy who was pushing our handcart load of luggage to the station I realized that we had forgotten a parcel of huacos from the local graves which we had managed to buy the day before, and I had to run back to the hotel to collect them. And when we got on the train we found that our seats had been sold twice over, and became involved in a wrangle with the conductor who, though we had arrived first, seemed inclined to favour the other claimants, one of whom happened to be a captain in the army. We sat tight, doggedly pretended to misunderstand almost everything that was said to us, smiled benevolently at our rivals, and in the end exasperated them so much that they left us in peace.

It took almost seven hours for the train to travel the 86 miles from Chimbote to Huallanca, an average of less than 13 miles an hour, and the country we traversed hardly merited such a leisurely progress. Despite the occasional golden brilliance of the stubble rice paddies, the general tone of the lower Santa valley was the mud-grey of the bare irrigated fields. Mud tinged the strong turbid flow of the Santa, stained the poor clothing of the peons who worked in gangs across the wide fields of the haciendas, and coloured the adobe walls of their huts.

A new desolation began when we entered the hills, which at this point consisted of some kind of friable shale and had the appearance of a series of heaps of debris left over from the workings of some titanic quarry. The whole landscape looked on the edge of collapse. Indeed, in places it was collapsing, for at one canyon the conductor went systematically through the train, lowering every window and closing all the wooden shutters; almost immediately the rocks dislodged by the passing of the train began to clatter on the iron roof of the carriage.

The waste of stone through which we travelled was by no means deserted. Occasionally the wires of an aerial trolley spanned the river to the gallery of some small colliery opening into a cliffside, and there must have been a good deal of prospecting in the remoter parts of the range, since at most of the stations up the valley miners waited with pack-horses to pick up their supplies. The villages occurred only when there was a shelf of land on which irrigation became possible and orchards could be grown; our progression from the hot lowlands towards the mountains with their cold nights was marked by the change in the species of fruit which the Indian peddlers thrust up towards the windows of the carriage. We started off in the morning with red bananas, went on to green oranges, and progressed through locust beans and sweet lemons to the large avocados that were grown in some of the higher villages. By the end of the journey I had become morbidly fascinated by the gluttony of a peasant woman who sat facing me like a gigantic Mochica effigy, her dark and rather malignant face framed by a vivid pink headscarf. At each station she would buy a store of fruit and of little tamales wrapped in maize leaves, and with slow, mechanical persistence she munched the morning away.

By noon the sun blazed in the narrow gorges and the heat reflected from the rocks beat stiflingly through the open windows of the slowly moving train. The wooden benches felt harder and harder; to the stench of sweat and oranges, already pungent, was added that of the blocked latrine from which, whenever the train lurched around a curve, a little tide of urine would flow under the suitcases piled in the gangway (it was only later that we realized one of ours was in the bottom layer). When Huallanca came into sight—a ragged line of sheds and shacks hugging the bottom of a steep mountainside—we both felt nauseated and exhausted, and would gladly have given up travelling for the day.

But Huallanca, we realized quickly enough, was not the kind of place to do so. It had sprung up originally at the railhead to serve the small mines in the mountains, and had expanded, since work began on the power station to serve the Chimbote steel mill, into a primitive construction camp. The train ran down the only street, which was lined with Chinese stores and cantinas crowded with Indians in miners' helmets. The village was crawling with Civil Guards, and it had a feeling of violence which I had sensed nowhere else in Peru. In any case, there was nothing nearer to a hotel than the doss houses over the cantinas, and we did not seem to have any choice but to go on the sixty miles up the Callejon to Monterrey, where N. had booked a room for us in what he claimed was a reasonably good hotel.

In the station yard the passengers who had left the train were milling around a dozen trucks and buses, and we had no idea which of them went to Monterrey. A workman with whom we had exchanged one or two remarks on the train noticed our bewilderment; he immediately hoisted one of our cases on to his shoulder, pushed a way to the right bus and, after quickly shaking hands, disappeared into the crowd.

The bus climbed slowly away from Huallanca into the Cañon del Pato—the Gorge of the Duck—through which the Rio Santa penetrates the western ridge of the Andes. The original wildness of the canyon had evidently been somewhat tamed by the engineers who were building dams and power stations there to harness the cataracts over which the water leapt down from the high valley above, but the rough concrete bastions they had built were not entirely out of keeping with the starkness of the bare cliffs above them, and the road that had been constructed as a by-product of the power scheme was the most daringly engineered mountain highway on which we travelled in the Andes; it coiled all the way along rock faces so sheer that in fourteen miles we ran through forty tunnels.

Beyond the last tunnel we entered the Callejon de Huaylas. A landscape in the grandest of romantic manners it certainly was— equal, in its own way, to anything we had seen before in the Alps or have since seen in the Pyrenees, but resembling either of these great ranges as little as they resemble each other. But if it was not 'just like Switzerland', the Callejon de Huaylas was nearer than anything I had yet seen in Peru to the combination of luxuriance and starkness, of the tropical and the alpine, which had consti-tuted my preconceived idea of Andean scenery.

Much of the valley's spectacular quality derived from the con-trast between the two ranges that held it like a long green trough within their grip. To the west the sombre, saw-toothed line of the Cordillera Negra, the Black Mountains; to the east the grey rock-faces and the plunging snowfields and glaciers of the Cordillera Blanca, the White Mountains. The rain-bearing winds from the Pacific overleap the Cordillera Negra, leaving its summits per-petually bare, and release their moisture on the higher peaks and ridges of the Cordillera Blanca, where the Peruvian Andes reach nearest to the sky. Huascaran, the greatest mountain of them all, rises like a double-headed pyramid more than 22,000 feet above the sea, and more than 13,000 feet above the town of Yungay which nestles below it on the floor of the valley. And for a hundred miles beyond Huascaran the great white peaks follow each other in glittering procession.

Between the stark extremities of darkness and light, by which the opposing mountains seem to assert in their very forms some Zoroasterian conflict of elemental forces, the Callejon itself runs in temperate softness, blander in its colouring, more pastoral in the variation of its landscape, than any other of the valleys in the Sierra. It is a country of wooded hillsides, green fields of young wheat, neat farms bounded by hedges of agave, and small white-washed towns in the lees of the great mountains.

These towns—Yungay, and Caras, and Carhuas—were Spanish in feeling, with their flowery, palm-shaded plazas and their tidiness of aspect. But the adobe villages were wholly Indian, and the peasants, whose dark ponchos enveloped them almost to the ankles and whose round hats of home-made felt were decorated with coloured ribbons, had a rough-bearded bravado that reminded us much more of Mexican peasants than of people we had seen in other parts of Peru.

Festivity was in the air as we drove up the valley. Groups of musicians were travelling in trucks with their bellied harps and big llama-skin drums, and the dark chicha dens in the villages were packed with tipsy men and women. I asked the driver if a fiesta were in progress. 'Si, si, señor, the fiesta of Assumption.' 'But that is the day after tomorrow,' I remarked. 'That is true,' he laughed, 'but here fiestas never last just a day. We like to enjoy ourselves for two, for three days, maybe even longer.' And almost immediately he gave a practical demonstration by shouting out, as we drove into Caras, 'Hay chicha!' and stopping the bus outside one of the taverns. 'The chicha here is very good, very healthy,' he assured us as he jumped down, followed by most of the passengers. But by this time we felt much too queasy for experimentation. The procedure was repeated three or four times before we reached Monterrey, but the reflexes of Peruvian drivers seem to be proof against a good deal of alcohol, and, though our man became very talkative, I saw no diminution in the skill with which he avoided the cattle and the unsteady peasants wandering in the road at twilight.

The one aspect of travelling in the Callejon de Huaylas that we found unpleasant—and for this neither the valley nor its people were to blame—was the exceptional activity of our pet Peruvian bugbears, the Guardia Civil. In the sixty odd miles from Huallanca to Monterrey there were eight police posts, and each time the driver had to present his papers and his list of passengers. It is true that so far as we were concerned the activities of the Guardia went no further, but at one of the posts a truckload of Indians were being forced to get down one by one so that the guards could question them. I never found out the specific reason why the Callejon de Huaylas was policed so much more heavily than other parts of the Sierra, but it was probably connected with the tendency of the peasants towards a rebelliousness that sometimes goes beyond the passive non-co-operation practised by most Andean Indians. In 1885, for instance, the people of the Callejon waged a guerilla war against the Lima authorities which lasted several months and at times left the whole of the valley and its principal towns in the hands of the rebels. In matters of this kind Peruvian governments have long memories.

It was already dark when the bus turned off the main highway and bumped on to an eroded gravel lane. 'Señores, here is Monterrey for you!' announced the driver. At first we saw nothing at all, then a few feeble lights gleamed from the open doorways of Indian houses, and a dog ran barking in front of the bus. What kind of a hotel, we wondered, could exist in this back lane? But at last a small neon sign glinted in the rural night, and the bus drew up before a stuccoed porch where a uniformed houseboy waited to take our luggage.

My relief to get to the end of the day's journey was mingled with a feeling that this arrival at a hotel with liveried flunkeys in the remote Andean countryside was a little too providential, a little too much like an incident in a picaresque novel, like one of Don Quixote's mad visions of the highway. In the pessimism of exhaustion I felt sure that something was bound to go wrong. The manager was waiting at the reception desk, already dressed in the dinner suit in which he would shortly act as head and—as we found later—only waiter. He was a cholo, with the arrogant manner which position sometimes brings to Peruvian half-breeds, and he began immediately by expressing doubts as to whether he could find us a room—such a busy season, and we had arrived so late! Ah, we had wired for reservations? Well, that might make a difference! What was our name? Ooadkuk? He riffled through his notebook. No! No reservation for anyone named Ooadkuk! And so, for five exasperating minutes, the game of a busy hotel continued, until, doubtless deciding that he had impressed us sufficiently, he admitted that he had received a telegram from Chimbote, and offered us the choice of three rooms; later, at dinner, we counted four other guests.

It was time we settled down, for by now we both felt very unwell. This was due partly to hunger—since breakfast we had eaten only oranges—and partly to our extreme tiredness. Now, after six weeks of rough travelling, we found that any long day's journey left us far more exhausted than it would have done during the earlier part of our trip; for the same reason the change of altitude had become more trying and, having escaped any serious mountain sickness at 16,000 feet, I experienced my first severe attack of soroche at the 10,000 feet level of Monterrey, and fainted in the dining-room. Worse than that, the usual tropical disorders, which until recently we had staved off easily with the drugs we carried, had now become more serious, and it was obvious in Monterrey that Inge had contracted a rather violent attack of bacillary dysentery.

There was certainly no question of setting out immediately on the trips we had thought of making into the countryside of the Callejon de Huaylas, and we spent most of the next day in the gardens of the hotel. It was—and this explained its presence in a somnolent pastoral countryside—a spa hotel, with a hot, foul-smelling spring bubbling into a tank and running out to feed a swimming pool and a series of cubicles equipped with thermal hip baths. The water of the spring, if one were to believe a notice displayed in the hotel office, was a kind of mineral panacea, infallible for the cure of such varied ills as rheumatism and neuritis, kidney, liver and heart ailments, digestive and nervous troubles of several kinds, the after-effects of cerebral haemorrhage, and circulatory disturbances. For good measure, it promised relief from sterility.

Peru has many small spas which make equally extravagant claims, but which are situated in corners of the Andes too remote from Lima to enable them to develop into even minor imitations of Bath or Harrogate, and Monterrey was fairly typical of them. The hotel had been built a decade ago, in a fit of speculative enthusiasm, and at the same time a line of stucco villas had sprung up along the lane running down to the main road. Doubtless the place enjoyed its brief flurry of fashion, but the interest had clearly ebbed, the villas were empty, with their windows broken and their gardens of roses and geraniums running to weeds, and the timeless rhythm of Indian life had resumed control. Even the hotel had been invaded by the creeping lassitude of the place; the thermal baths were deserted, the pool was dark green with algae, the deck chairs on the terrace were broken and rotted by the weather.[1]

If we had both been well, I am sure that all this neglect would have had its decrepit charm, particularly as the countryside itself was beautiful enough. But Monterrey was certainly no place to be ill and, since Inge felt no better during the day—and even worse towards the evening—we decided that we should get back to Lima as soon as we could, which meant catching the collectivo at five o'clock the next morning.

The night before our departure was sleepless and anxious, and, to make matters worse, the hotel generating plant broke down, the lights went out and the water supply failed. As a kind of bar-baric accompaniment to this miserable night, we heard the Indians up and down the valley heralding the feast of Assumption. At ten o'clock the people in the cottages near the hotel began to celebrate; they had no musical instruments to accompany their dancing, but the women sang in shrill, metallic voices, and each verse of their half-Oriental songs was followed by a complicated rhythm of hand clappings, which in its turn would end with a cry like a yapping fox. This went on in monotonous repetition until midnight; then the local dancers quietened down, but we could hear the fireworks banging all over the countryside to celebrate the first hour of the day of Assumption.

The next morning we got up at four o'clock. Inge was exhausted, but insisted that she would sooner travel the 250 miles to Lima than stay on at Monterrey. The collectivo picked us up at six o'clock, an hour late; the driver's excuse was that he had not been able to find enough petrol to take us down to the coast. Driving southward into Huaras was like going through the territory of

[1] In fairness I should say that the hotel was taken over in 1957 by a new owner who, I gather, has made it very efficient.

some great medieval pilgrimage, for the whole countryside seemed to be on the move; by horse, by truck, by donkey and on foot, the Indians were converging on Huaras for the fiesta, with flowers and ribbons in their hats, and very often with musical instruments on their backs.

In Huaras we picked up the remaining passengers—a nondescript middle-aged man who looked like a minor functionary, and two women—a mother and her daughter—who got on at a small grocery store and appeared, like many Peruvian shopkeepers, to be of Italian extraction. The girl, who was about nineteen, was very beautiful, with features of classic regularity and a magnificent Mediterranean colouring.

For fifty miles from Huaras the road followed the Rio Santa as it dwindled from a river white with rapids to a thin stream trickling its sluggish way through the upland marshes. And then we turned westward, into the Pass of Conococha which would take us over the Cordillera Negra and down to the Fortaleza valley.

As we were crossing these high moorlands the girl with the classic features began to moan loudly; a moment later her mother shouted, 'Stop, Maestro!' and the girl leant over and vomited loudly out of the window. The rest of us murmured sympathetically, and shortly afterwards we started off again. We had only gone another mile or two when the mother started to moan, the driver braked quickly, and she in turn leant out and vomited—even more copiously than her daughter. A few more miles, it was the daughter's turn again, and so, in a kind of empathic rhythm they continued for the next fifty miles, until at last they could do nothing more than lie moaning weakly across their seats.

Up to this point, despite the gusto of their uninhibited retchings, pity was predominant in our feelings towards them. Then, at midday, half-way down the Fortaleza valley, we came to a village called Chasquitambo, a sweltering little place among the cane brakes and shaly hills which seemed to exist to serve the needs of travellers, for every building was either an eating-house or a petrol station or a shabby little shop. The two women revived immediately at the smell of cooking that hung in the stagnant air of Chasquitambo, headed like bird dogs for the nearest restaurant, gulped down the five courses of the standard Peruvian midday meal, and came back to the collectivo with a bagful of pepinos, a cucumber-like fruit, which they munched loudly as we drove away.

The consequence was inevitable. Two miles on they erupted, simultaneously, showering the floor, the window, the seat before them, and the driver's back with a stinking mixture of prawns, pepinos and rice. The man sitting beside them buried his face in his hands and groaned with disgust. The driver stopped, got out slowly, and looked miserably at his car and at the two women, who lay on the seat wailing as if they were in the final throes. 'Señoras, señoras,' he exclaimed, spreading his hands and speaking in the voice of hurt dignity, 'why did you have to eat so many pepinos?' And with that single reproach, to which they replied by howling into tears, he set about cleaning up himself and the stinking car as best he could with scraps of newspaper.

But by this time the sympathy which the rest of us had felt on the Pass of Conococha had long vanished, and when the women started again a few moments later the man who sat beside them shouted angrily to the driver, 'Put them out, Maestro! Let them travel with the Indians!' 'You see, señoras,' said the driver, still speaking with a kindness which would have been beyond my power, 'you are annoying the other passengers. Wouldn't you like to spend the night in Barranca?' The women replied with inarticulate wails of protest; never did it enter their heads to apologize for the discomfort their feasting at Chasquitambo had caused the rest of us. Eventually, when we reached the smooth main road at Paramonga, they subsided into sleep, and the driver compassionately ignored them as we went through Barranca. When we saw the last of them in Lima, the classic face of the girl, which had aroused such admiration when first I saw her, now provoked only a distaste so profound that for several days afterwards, whenever I saw a girl with the same Italianate looks, I would feel an immediate nausea.

But that journey is connected with other and much more provocative memories. I have already mentioned the line of fortifications that ran up the Fortaleza valley from the Chimu fortress of

Paramonga on the coast. The Fortaleza line has been observed and partly photographed from the air, but up to the present I believe that no ground expedition of archaeologists has investigated it thoroughly. Yet the country was full of suggestions of the presence of ancient peoples. Fragments of walls clung high on the hillsides above the goat pastures that were purple with flowering asters. Caves with wide earth platforms before them opened into the bases of the great basaltic cliffs, and in some of these caves the shepherds of the valley still lived. A face in relief, carved in the manner of the Chimu sculptors, looked down from a smooth limestone crag above the road. Everywhere one saw levelled hilltops, adobe mounds by the roadside, fragments of ancient road, and by the time we had reached the end of the valley our imaginations were stimulated so much that for a long time after we left Peru we still talked about returning one day to explore the tantalizing hilltops that look down upon the Rio Fortaleza.

From Paramonga we returned over the desert road to Lima. In the nine days since we travelled north the waste land had been transfigured by a fragile spring, and long stretches which before had seemed arid and heartless sand were now covered thickly with small, delicate plants whose bright green foliage was studded with mauve cup-like flowers and bright yellow blossoms like celandines. With spring, the nomads had appeared, and in the middle of the new green growth there were encampments where Indians with goats and geese had set up their tents like the Bedouin moving into the ephemeral pastures that spring up in the heart of Arabia when the desert blooms.

Epilogue

When we returned to Lima from the north, it seemed as though our journeys in Peru were at an end. Apart from Iquitos, we had visited all the places whose names and legends had drawn us to the Andes; we had walked in the cities of the Incas and the Chimu; we had seen the white desolation of Huascaran and sailed on the cold expanse of Titicaca; we had travelled beside the green rivers of the jungle and through the long deserts of the coast and over the highest passes of the Sierra. Yet if we had, in this sense at least, finished with Peru, Peru had by no means finished with us. It still had some experiences in store, and not all of them were to be pleasant.

It was now late August, time to think of returning home, but we found that the planes to Mexico City and Canada were so heavily booked that we would not be able to leave for another nine days. Inge had not yet recovered fully, and both of us felt so worn down by our 4,000 miles of roads and railways that we decided the best way to spend the time on our hands would be to retreat to some quiet town where we could rest in the sun.

Tarma seemed the ideal place, since the climate was good, we liked the hotel, and the journey there would give us a last look at the Andes before we left Peru. We stayed one day in Lima to perform various small and necessary chores, and the next morning caught the Tarma collectivo, which we chose because it was quicker than either the train or the bus. We soon regretted this minor economy in time, for the car was old, its springs had been ruined by the mountain roads, and the hours of jolting over the rough gravel highway brought Inge to the verge of physical prostration. Her sickness returned with alarming violence, accompanied by headaches and fever; she went to bed as soon as we reached Tarma and recovered slowly and incompletely, for the infection from which she suffered was of so stubborn a strain that it did not disappear entirely until the end of almost three months of treatment after we had returned to Canada.

Such experiences inevitably help to shape one's recollections of a place and a time. Our last stay in Tarma was virtually dominated by Inge's condition, and the room we had returned to no longer reminded us of the pleasure with which we had once looked out from its windows at the half-pastoral wildness of the valley. We fell, for the time being, into the mood of noticing acutely whatever was alien rather than whatever was sympathetic in our environment; one day, just before our departure, we walked at noon into the market, and Inge suddenly exclaimed, expressing our whole attitude of that time: 'When I hear that music, and smell that smell, and see that white sunlight, I begin to hate Peru!' The music was that of the Sierra, playing interminably on the radios in all the shops, the smell was the biting mixture of urine and aji —a pungent pepper used in all popular Peruvian cooking—which was so constant a part of the Andean background that in normal times one hardly noticed it. As for me, by the time we left Tarma, though I still found the valley as beautiful as ever, I no longer indulged in the fancy that there I might live in tranquil productivity.

We remained in Tarma for five days, until Inge felt well enough to return to Lima. The three days that remained to us in the capital were consumed by a mounting activity. There were unexpected arrangements to be made before we could leave; to give only one example, the control of travellers was so strict that we had to obtain a permit from the Ministry of Foreign Affairs before we could even leave the country. And then, when all such formalities had been completed, we realized that on past visits to Lima we had been too intent on seeking its relaxations and had neglected many of the places which more conscientious travellers would have visited.

So, for certain mornings and afternoons, we crammed in our sightseeing with the zest of nineteenth-century Baedekerites. Below the Church of San Francisco we followed a brown-robed Negro friar through the catacombs, and flocks of tiny moth-like bats fluttered before us as we found our way to the underground galleries where the dismembered skeletons of 12,000 Francisans lay arranged with neat symmetry in their great cylindrical charnel pits. In the Sanctuary of the Virgin of La Merced we found our only Peruvian golden temple; the walls of the chapel where this jewel-laden saint presided as the patron of Peru (and incidentally as a perpetual honorary marshal of the army) were covered from floor to ceiling with thousands of golden ex votos, glittering in the candlelight like a cave in a Cuzcan dream of buried treasure. And, on the edge of the modern slums north of the Rimac, we discovered the graceful imitation Trianon where Lima's favourite heroine, La Perricholi, reigned like a scandalous queen two centuries ago. Michaela Villegas was a half-breed girl from a remote village near Huanuco who became celebrated under her nickname of La Perricholi—the Chola Bitch—as the great South American actress of the eighteenth century. In due course La Perricholi became the mistress of the sexagenarian Viceroy Manuel de Amat, and for sixteen years—until Don Manuel went back to Spain in his mid-seventies to settle down and marry an heiress—she played the great lady of Lima, shocking the Castilian prudery of the older colonists and behaving with such insolence, dash and generosity that she won herself a place, not only in the memory of Lima people, who still gossip about her as if she were a living film actress, but also as a heroine of world literature. Her palace, we found, had been transformed into a military headquarters; a small museum had been created to preserve the surroundings of her extravagant life—her furniture, her bath carved out of a solid lump of marble, and even her golden coach—but the courtyards clanked with the tread of high-booted cavalry officers, and in the formal gardens where Michaela and Don Manuel had walked, the apprentice bandsmen of the army rent the air with a tuneless braying of their cornets among the rioting espaliers and the crumbling belvederes.

But most of all, these last few days were dominated by the generous hospitality of the people we had met during our various passages through Lima. I cannot record all the occasions, but there are two which I remember with particular warmth. One was a lunch with Harry Horn of the Canadian Embassy and his wife at their villa in San Isidro. It was the last of a long series of kind-nesses. Because of his work as Commercial Attaché, Harry Horn had acquired a close knowledge of the Peruvian background, and, since he was an irrepressibly energetic man with a great curiosity about unfamiliar ways of life, he had travelled far and observantly. Ever since our arrival in Peru he had been so ready to inform and advise us on the basis of his own experiences that in retrospect it seems to me our travels owed more to him than to any other person we met in the country. Even on this last occasion his good-humoured hospitality was mingled with the willingness to inform, as he filled in some of the last gaps in my knowledge of the oddities of Peruvian political life.

Señor Alzamora, our host on the second occasion, was one of the great collectors of Peru. Even before we left Canada we had heard of his private gallery of Cuzco primitives, and afterwards, in Lima, we had met his son, Jaime Alzamora, who was then the Assistant Manager of Canadian Pacific Airlines. Jaime knew of our interest in his father's collection, and when we returned to Lima for the last time he invited us to dinner.

Until three years before, Señor Alzamora had lived the ordinary life of a wealthy and cultured Lima lawyer. He had begun buying antiques as investments whose values rose in a world of declining currencies—a Venetian ring, a piece of colonial sculpture, an in-laid box that had once belonged to Marie Antoinette—and then he had discovered, as the odd pieces built up into a collection, that these objects from other times and other worlds which at first he thought of in terms of speculation had a life of their own, a life which began to dominate his. Within a few months he turned from a business man into an art collector. Now his town house, his country house, his chambers in Lima and even his chauffeur's cottage were crowded to discomfort with paintings and statues, with furniture and bibelots. A hundred paintings waited at the framer's with no walls left to hang them on. And still a day on which he found nothing worth adding to his collection seemed to him a day lost.

Many of his pieces had only the historical interest of their association with famous personages, and others were nothing more

than virtuoso works—intricate Chinese ivories, Victorian miniatures in the hollows of oyster shells. But in contrast with such
mere curiosities there were the naïve and powerful paintings of
the school of Cuzco. I have already talked of our admiration of the
Cuzco painters. But nowhere had we seen so many of the best
examples of their work gathered in one place, and as I looked at
them glowing in all the purity of their colours from the mirror-
studded frames on the crowded walls, it struck me that they
represented not so much an imitation of European art as the real
flowering of the artistic talent of the Quechua.

Surrounded by his treasures, explaining them and pointing out
their merits with an enthusiasm that at times grew lyrical, Señor
Alzamora struck me as the happiest rich man I had met, an example of the truth that the only possessions worth having are those
that possess us by opening the sleeping gates of the imagination.

Our days in Lima drew to an end, and at last the hotel porter
unloaded our bags and wished us 'Angenehme Reise!' as he shook
hands at the Limatambo Airport. We said good-bye to Donald
Sanderson, who was supervising the departure of the plane, and
then, as we waited for the call to go on board, a reporter from one
of the Lima newspapers came up and asked me for an interview.
My mind was half on other things; I was wondering particularly
whether the customs officers would make difficulties about our
taking out the huacos we had bought in Chimbote. So I answered
him with the obvious remarks about the grandeur of the Andes,
the beauty of the jungle; I put in a plea for Chan Chan, and remarked that more should be done to preserve the ancient monuments of Peru. But there were other things I did not say, and if I
had now to answer my interviewer, I think I would speak mostly
of two things. I would describe my sense of the social tragedy that
at present hangs over this harsh and divided land. And I would
express a hope that, when the processes of history bring more
abundance, more freedom and more equality to their lives, the
Peruvians may still retain those virtues of a leisured age which
made us feel that we had never travelled among a people more
friendly or more likeable.

Index